Critical Muslim 39

World Order

Editor: Ziauddin Sardar

Deputy Editors: Samia Rahman, C Scott Jordan, Ebrahim Moosa

Senior Editors: Aamer Hussein, Hassan Mahamdallie, Ehsan Masood

Publisher: Michael Dwyer

Managing Editor (Hurst Publishers): Daisy Leitch

Cover Design: Rob Pinney based on an original design by Fatima Jamadar

Associate Editors: Tahir Abbas, Alev Adil, Abdelwahab El-Affendi, Naomi Foyle, Marilyn Hacker, Nader Hashemi, Jeremy Henzell-Thomas, Leyla Jagiella, Vinay Lal, Iftikhar H Malik, Peter Mandaville, Shanon Shah, Boyd Tonkin, Medina Tenour Whiteman

International Advisory Board: Karen Armstrong, Christopher de Bellaigue, William Dalrymple, Syed Nomanul Haq, Anwar Ibrahim, Robert Irwin, Bruce Lawrence, Ashis Nandy, Ruth Padel, Bhikhu Parekh, Barnaby Rogerson, Malise Ruthven

Critical Muslim is published quarterly by C. Hurst & Co. (Publishers) Ltd. on behalf of and in conjunction with Critical Muslim Ltd. and the Muslim Institute, London.

All editorial correspondence to Muslim Institute, CAN Mezzanine, 49–51 East Road, London N1 6AH, United Kingdom.
E-mail: editorial@criticalmuslim.com

The editors do not necessarily agree with the opinions expressed by the contributors. We reserve the right to make such editorial changes as may be necessary to make submissions to *Critical Muslim* suitable for publication.

C. Hurst & Co (Publishers) Ltd., 83 Torbay Road, London, NW6 7DT

ISBN: 978-1-7873-8551-1 ISSN: 2048-8475

To subscribe or place an order by credit/debit card or cheque (pounds sterling only) please contact Kathleen May at the Hurst address above or e-mail kathleen@hurstpub.co.uk

Tel: 020 7255 2201

A one-year subscription, inclusive of postage (four issues), costs £50 (UK), £65 (Europe) and £75 (rest of the world), this includes full access to the *Critical Muslim* series and archive online. Digital only subscription is £3.30 per month.

A Cataloguing-in-Publication data record for this book is available from the British Library

Critical Muslim

Subscribe to Critical Muslim

Now in its tenth year in print, *Critical Muslim* is also available online. Users can access the site for just £3.30 per month – or for those with a print subscription it is included as part of the package. In return, you'll get access to everything in the series (including our entire archive), and a clean, accessible reading experience for desktop computers and handheld devices — entirely free of advertising.

Full subscription

The print edition of *Critical Muslim* is published quarterly in January, April, July and October. As a subscriber to the print edition, you'll receive new issues directly to your door, as well as full access to our digital archive.

United Kingdom £50/year
Europe £65/year
Rest of the World £75/year

Digital Only

Immediate online access to *Critical Muslim*

Browse the full *Critical Muslim* archive

Cancel any time

£3.30 per month

www.criticalmuslim.io

CM39

SUMMER 2021

CONTENTS

WORLD ORDER

ARTS AND LETTERS

REVIEWS

ET CETERA

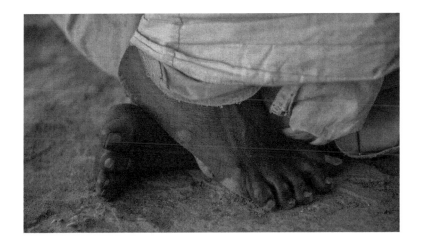

WORLD ORDER

INTRODUCTION:
SAME OLD TROPES

C Scott Jordan

I want to let you in on a little secret. So you know what to expect when you are watching a film or reading a novel and suddenly the protagonist comes across an organisation or club or grouping of individuals – usually all wearing matching uniforms – that wants to employ his or her assistance. You know, they tend to walk in step with one another, like to repeat a lyrical motto, and justify their philosophy and actions in the name of preserving, establishing, or re-establishing some sort of stated Order? Well, there is a good chance these folks are actually antagonists. This trope, presently bordering on being a cliché, is being employed with an alarming frequency amongst 'creative' writers. Traditionally, this trope was applied to some allegory for Nazis or Commies, and because these entities were fairly universally seen as bad, there was no need to labour the point. More recently, writers have been attempting to apply this trope as a trick, a bait-and-switch. Certain writers think they can pull a fast one, introducing this group as the 'good guys' only to pull the rug out from under you with a mid-second-act reveal that they are, in fact, fascists and they have been using our protagonist to unwillingly see out some seriously evil stuff. I see this, over and over, and think what is going on? This is not a twist, is it not obvious? Sure, they tone it down a bit, cutting out comical salutes, blue-eyes with blonde-hairdos combos, and the wearing of arm cuffs, but Hitler in sheep's skin is still Hitler, right? The unoriginality alone boggles my mind. I mean, it is a bit ridiculous. There has been a wholly unoriginal obsession with using this trope (I assume because it is an easy way to make your film *meta*) with some form of 'time police', fanatically bent on maintaining 'the timeline'. This is used in three ongoing series I can think of, right off the top of my head, *Rick and Morty, The Umbrella Academy*, and *Loki*, and I am sure there are plenty more. The one remotely clever thing they will do to make this trope a twist is to make the protagonist morally dubious. But we have known for decades that the days of perfect superheroes are long gone. How could these writers break a key principle: do not insult the intelligence of your audience?

But slowly I begin to think that what I see as a literary *faux pas*, actually reveals a much darker reality.

Despite human beings' preternatural ability to pick up on patterns and perceive the uncanny valley, something about our contemporary world has made us eerily colour-blind, at least blissfully ignorant, to fascism. Perhaps it is all fatigue. An over-application of Godwin's Law, which states that, regardless of topic or context, the longer an online conversation thread extends, the more probable it is that an analogy to Hitler and the Nazis will present itself. Today, it is such a cliché to compare someone's actions to the Nazis, that we fear what the public might think of us if we were to do something so remarkably unoriginal. Forget if it looks like, quacks like, and probably is a duck. This is indeed, a piece of the puzzle, but I pin a bulk of the responsibility for the state of things on a silly little lie, hidden in an iconic image.

In 1941, the 1 March issue of Marvel Comic's *Captain America #1,* hit racks emblazed with a cover depicting the titular hero punching out the still-sitting Führer of Germany, Adolf Hitler. This image immortalised and registered the idea, the lie: fascism is dead, we beat it. And an image with that kind of power is hard to break. Given life by this depiction, the lie lived on to become a key pillar of American politics. If it were to be revealed that they had not, in fact, defeated the Nazis, and the Nazis were within, what an existential crisis the US would have on their hands! Nazis in the twenty-first century equates to dividing by zero. Error. Undefined. Does not compute. So, when 2016 began with a group of right-wing gun nuts — interestingly uniformly dressed in camouflage — occupying a wildlife preserve in Oregon... well, we cannot just start slinging around labels, now can we? And when the 2017 fall semester at the University of Virginia began with a group of foaming-at-the-mouth white nationalists — too young to grow the emblematic beards of their Oregonian brethren — these human approximations of fragile masculinity took tiki torches, polo shirts, and boat shoes as their uniform — marching through Charlottesville... well, you know, 'boys will be boys'. And, despite how much the far-too-many pro-Trump rallies held over the last four years looked, sounded, and felt (likely smelt, but I was not there to confirm) like it, remember, Captain America had defeated Hitler and the Nazis. And even after 2021 was rung in by the sound of the idiotic incoherent wails of a tripartite coalition of neo-fascist militant groups, the Oathkeepers, the Proud Boys, and the Three Percenters – while not necessarily uniform, they dressed themselves in various uniforms ranging from colonial revolutionary soldier garb to the disgusting appropriation of Native American traditional dress, topped with the revered Confederate flag – that mental hurdle could not be easily climbed over. And they say the greatest trick the Devil ever pulled was convincing the world he did not exist. But he really has to up his game when he plays in the same league as the United States of America.

What I think writers are attempting to do with the reimagining of the trope is actually eloquently demonstrated by the British philosophers Mick Jagger and Keith Richards, of The Rolling Stones fame, in their 1968 hit song, 'Sympathy for the Devil'. The song is essentially a long first-person introduction with a fun take on the Rumpelstiltskinian game of 'won't you guess my name'. On the surface, this appears to just be a song about the Devil singing us his storied career of evil deeds. But if this was, as the drinkers of the Satanic Panic Kool-Aid would have us believe, then why would they give away the culprit in the title (and based on interviews, the title was carefully considered by the band). You see, the Devil is a trickster, and when he repeatedly asks us what his name is throughout the tune it is a jest, mockery. The twist, rather a reveal, comes halfway through the third verse when they ask who it was that killed the Kennedys, with the answer that, of course, it was us all along. And suddenly, a silly tune about the Devil points the finger. We are implicit. The point of the song is that it has always been easy to pass the buck. And so, when something truly horrible takes place, fear not, this was the work of evil, some supernatural entity. So long as we remain good, blah blah blah, at least now we can sleep at night. The writers using this trope fail because they overcompensate with morally grey antiheroes, another overused cliché, and often to no good effect. Shock and awe, now please see yourself out. Yet, the Rolling Stones, through 'Sympathy for the Devil', ask a question that I feel has become an essential milestone of maturity for all those of us growing up in America today: Are we sure we are the good guys?

Now, having suffered over thirty years of paradigmatic revolutionary constipation, the need to ask this question takes discussion of world order to a new level. When you really think about it, this is a scary, sobering question. The sort of question that makes it so that you can see your own breath when such doubt-filled words mix with the atmosphere. The reverberations of such an utterance shatters any rose-tinted glasses. It is also uncomfortably familiar. Why didn't more 'Good Germans' speak up and prevent the rise of the Third Reich? How did the granting of an independent Jewish state to the Israeli people, an international gesture largely motivated by a needed response to one of the most horrific episodes of human rights violation in the twentieth century, lead to one of the twenty-first century's most grotesque displays, complete with notes of conquest, erasure, and apartheid – things we thought we put to rest, definitively, in the previous century? Where do all those fascists sitting in the Parliament of the European Union come from? How come the so-called biggest democracy in the world is ruled by an ever so popular neo-fascist party? Ditto Brazil, Hungary, Poland. And what can we say about Orwellian China and a Russia ruled by nationalist thugs? These questions are complex and each time we repeat them they grow in complexity. Yet they are too often examined through simple lenses. The resultant simple solutions refract against the complex questions making things a whole lot worse. Instead, we must vivisect the web of lies that brought about the current world order to maintain contextualisation and navigate a path forward.

From the start we should keep in mind that webs of lies can be quite deceptive. This may seem obvious, but such profoundly simple affirmations keep us on course in travelling the trails of complexity. Through the combined efforts of lies, propaganda, uncertainty, and language-games, the web conceals two concepts that, if I am unable to convince you they are facts (heaven help us in these post-truth times), their consideration will be useful in moving through this issue. First, World Order is a very new concept only going back about as far as the beginning of globalisation. To clarify, colonialism for me is not globalisation, there is a great difference between resource extraction and giving enough of a damn about the world beyond your doorstep to recognise the existence of a wider world and the other people in it. Second, the World Order, as we know it, was created by the Americans for the purposes of peace, driven by war or the threat of it. Having said that, I caution against giving Americans too much credit (you know how we Americans are with our egos). World Order is a simple compound bastardisation, arrived at through a long evolution, thrust upon a complex world. The hubris is well stated in the words of the late, great American comedian, George Carlin, when he said 'evolution is slow, smallpox travels fast'.

These words ring prescient in a world seemingly ordered by a virus, as explored by Kanchana Mahadevan in her review of Vinay Lal's *The Fury of COVID-19*. But to label our current times by such a catchy banner is a bit ominous. Viruses exist in paradox and so an order by virus would see us in a much more chaotic place than even the current turbulent world. The existence of a virus is dependent upon the destruction of its host and then the seeking out of yet another host until, well, extinction. The virus has given some a clearer perspective on the messy state of our affairs which may well lead to extinction and given others an opportunity to grab yet more power.

This brings us to the first lie: that world order is a historic entity. First, it is folly to assume that if something is historic, any attempt to unpack it leads one down the rabbit hole into the abyss of the past, therefore to hell with history. Our present, and even our future, is always comprised of a significant configuration of the past and that is often taken for granted. I am reminded of Bill Clinton's 1992 campaign slogan 'It's the Economy, Stupid'. 'It's continuity, stupid'. So, when examining this lie, it is not to dispatch with history, but to dispatch with the colonial power of taking the past for granted. Certainly, there is an organisational element to time and progress that extends well before those creatures called humans crawled upon the Earth's surface. We have even evidenced the ordering power of nature, but this phenomenon has been somewhat co-opted and appropriated by the West's greatest Frankensteinian creation – Modernity.

Modernity showed how truly powerful the granting of empowerment and agency, even if only to a select few, can be. So much so that postmodernism has failed to usurp its domineering hangtime. Postmodernism, like many critiques of modernity, cannot exist outside the parameters set by modernity. Postmodernism had the success rate equal to an individual wishing to challenge the reality of gravity by jumping off of the Empire State Building, only supplied with two extended middle fingers and a 'I reject your reality and substitute my own' mentality. The power wielded by modernity comes through its adeptness to colonise thought and the scientific advancements that could provide theoretical justification. But these are not perfect, especially when the ability to colonise thought is also to colonise the epistemology of your science.

This particular spectre haunts the science behind the notion of race and how, as Yuri Prasad points out, it has become 'intricately woven into the world order'. Prior to the contemporary notion of world order, the West was obsessed with the order of nature, or at least where nature lacked order, it demanded the organising or taming by a higher being. Enter humans and natural law. But categorisation has proven itself to be quite the Pandora's box, rather everything must be put in its own box, each box subdivided into another box and so it goes, *ad infinitum*. And whether or not scientific justification was demanded by the Enlightenment, Science, revved up to make great strides, saw no problem putting itself to the job of normalising racism. And while great work has been done to debunk the pseudoscience of race, the idea germinated popular parlance and public opinion. Since Science could walk away from the race controversy, for now at least, a more solid laying bare of cracks in the foundation would be necessary to call it into question.

The Soviet agronomist Troflam Lysenko, as mentioned by Jerry Ravetz, would demonstrate the fatal flaw of science as unquestioned wisdom in terms of policy influence. Lysenko saw the brand of science practiced in the West as corrupted by the idea that the world was ordered by competition and capitalism, knowing the true way of the world was communism. This idea drove him to recommend an agricultural philosophy where crop seeds were to be planted close together as they would cooperate in proletarian brotherhood to share resources and grow together. And while I like to think that the top one percent of Western crops do not fund the endemic structures that keep other crops from flourishing, the science does not hold out for commi crops. Lysenko's influence would lead to catastrophic famine not only throughout the USSR, but also in the People's Republic of China after Mao saw to the adoption of Lysenkoism. But Ravetz points to a dire crisis in science that goes beyond the turbulence of pseudoscience and populist sentiments.

Instead of waiting around for a superman to bring about a new world order, Ravetz has been feverishly writing on the postnormal predicament in science. Things need to change, but keying in on subtext from former US president Eisenhower's farewell address, Ravetz notes an ossification where 'enlisting of the symbol of science in policy debates leads inevitably to the politicisation of science itself, and then to the confusion and hence corruption of its norms. Simplistic policy crusades invoking Science, demonising all who withhold uncritical support, threaten the integrity of science as no overt attack ever could.' Ravetz's first proposed solution was to extend the 'peer community', but in light of how complex the problem has become, a greater rethink is in order which not only brings even more voices to the decision-making table, but incorporates new innovations forged in a cross cultural and transdisciplinary jazz of thought.

Cross-cultural enrichment is also the message of Anwar Ibrahim's report on the state of the ummah. Ibrahim begins with a debunking of the concept of the Muslim World as some sort of monolithic entity. After all, Islam was born into a world of difference, not only seeing itself as an intrinsic piece of the global mosaic, but the ultimate navigation forward. To think it would be without a little diversity is unrealistic. Ummah, Ibrahim argues, is an ought category. It has plural meanings, especially throughout its many uses in the Qur'an, their significance depending on each context. Ibrahim takes this to the next level explaining that ummah stands not for the reality of a civilisation, but an ideal that civilisation ought to strive for, 'that despite the diversity of the Muslim world, differences and contradictions, polities and politics of past and present, the dissensions and discords of history and contemporary times, there ought to be some semblance of unity amongst Muslims.' This lies at the heart of Ibrahim's calls for *La Convivencia* – a return to a transcendent multiculturalism modelled after the Al-Andalus of Umayyad yesteryear.

Yet, before we can see where we ought to be going, it becomes necessary to examine the reality of where we are. Abdelwahab El-Affendi questions the vicious cycle of violence the Middle East appears to be in by asking the question: 'how did the region's brightest moment, the Arab Spring protests of the 2010s, turn so suddenly and unexpectedly into the whole world's darkest moment?'. Tragically the answer is by design, but in the details lies the path to farce. The design is cast in the spirit of peace. A confluence of contradictions has condemned the Middle East. 'In the good old days, savages who stormed our region from the uncivilised wilderness ended up being civilised by the experience. More recent hordes are not so lucky,' El-Affendi writes. Instead, the so called civilised become barbarians and the tables are turned, all in the name of the New World Order, conceived in the ashes of World War II.

In the blood-soaked years of the early twentieth century, if the concept of World Order was not created, then it was at least made professional. The Europeans had failed at crafting a world order. This was one of the key hypotheses that has not only formed the United States of America but formed the vision of the world they would seek to build. It was a slow evolution. And the US really had the world thinking they would bring about a new world as the first post-colonial state. But an internal contradiction would only be fitting for a nation that would craft such a fragile world order. With each expanse, a swift return to hermitage. A historical pendulum keeps the cadence of American history. First, a fight for self determination of the Thirteen Colonies, but then a turn inward when France sought to do the same. Then the Monroe Doctrine breaking the new world from the old followed by a civil war. Then Manifest Destiny, followed by the age of isolationism. Then the American Empire, the World Wars, the Truman Doctrine – which truly cut the world in twine – and the Bush Doctrine that tried to modify the Truman Doctrine for a world of us vs. them, where them was transitioned from communists to terrorists. The pendulum pushes the US into the pit of despair as four years under Donald Trump both sought to continue the War on Terror while also making NATO pick up the slack, and having the country look inward to make America Great, again! As the American business writer, Tom Peters, once put it, 'if you're not confused then you're not paying attention'.

World Order began with US President Woodrow Wilson. The Great War was largely a European war. Indeed, battles took place elsewhere, especially in Asia, but those that were not the proxy conflicts of their European colonisers would have occurred irrespective of whether or not the rest of the world was into the trend. But Wilson saw his Fourteen

Points as the first proposal of a true *world* order. The war may have been European, but the peace would be global and a 'peace to end all peace' while we are at it. This peace was embodied in the doomed League of Nations. The subsequent US President Franklin Roosevelt dreamed of a vast improvement in a second iteration. His successor Harry S Truman would see to its baptism in two nuclear bombings. A lasting peace, motivated by both the refreshing air of peacetime and the terror of its antonym. A conference in San Francisco in April of 1945 would create the United Nations as the embodiment of the world order as successor to the ineffective League. And then suddenly the evolutionary process of global dialogue stopped. A second iteration was apparently enough. The world now had a platform to come together on so that they would not actually have to talk to each other. And so, the superpowers would not. Instead, they would spend around four decades exchanging cold looks and occasionally hand down announcements. Palestine is to be cleaved; Israel gets a state. The US is allowed into Korea, but appeasement then means that Korea also gets cleaved. Suez goes to Egypt; troops to Cyprus. The People's Republic of China is in; the Republic of China (Taiwan) is out. Piece by piece the board is staged. The world is carefully bifurcated.

Then came 9 November 1989. A gaff during a routine civil service press conference resulted in a rhetorical bomb that prematurely opened up travel between East and West Germany. Within hours, men, women, and children were hard at work tearing down the Berlin Wall and the countdown to doomsday for the USSR had been set in motion. And for the last time, a world order hinged on us vs. them would have something resembling a clear demarcation for such labels. Many asked, how would the world order be constructed now? Yet no international dialogue took place. While the Cold War hosted four decades with no shortage of events that should have provoked such a dialogue, no talking was to be had. Logically, no talking was to be had after the Cold War either. While everyone assumed a new world order was afoot, some were too afraid to give it a name, while I think others assumed it was time to rest on the laurels of progress. The mountain top had been attained, right? The good guys had won the day!

There is a vast discussion of the Cold War and what came next throughout this issue. The fall of the Berlin Wall is a focal point because it was the last time all agreed that what must come next was a New World Order, but what that order would be was very uncertain. It all happened so fast, even those who saw the writing on the wall were fully unprepared for what was fundamentally a world at peace. For the American political scientist, Francis Fukuyama, it was the end of history. History seen narrowly as this naïve duelling of the fates without a worthy challenger was to then, forevermore, be the age of Western supremacy. Others looked to the next upcoming contenders. The UK and Europe could not take for granted their status as superpowers, as this club did not necessarily offer lifetime membership, annual dues needed their paying. Even the US understood this.

However, when a nation spent two centuries fighting, uncertain if it would ever 'win', it does not know how to live beyond the fight. This sort of anxiety brought in a need to make sure no other could challenge such a supremacy. The Republican Party that claimed to have won the Cold War, needed only to take power, hold onto it and declare a New World Order. Thus, President George H.W. Bush, spoke of the New World Order. In fact, between the summer of 1990 and March 1991, President Bush used the phrase 'new world order' at least forty-two times. But was that enough repetitions to make a lie become the truth? Even Bush understood that for a new world order to be sustainable, it needed to be tried and tested. Then came Operation Desert Storm and the First Gulf War. A couple years without the world on the brink demanded that the American warboys stretch their legs. But to what avail? Kuwait was defended, very few casualties were suffered, but a lot of oil was destroyed and Saddam Hussein remained the leader of Iraq. It was hailed a victory, but can that be unequivocally said to be so? Did the conflict really end? Hardly. The Second Gulf War followed. Iraq was destroyed. The War on Terror destroyed Afghanistan and unhinged Pakistan. Had the Cold War actually ended? Hardly. Russia was never completely upgraded from its status as supervillain. And if America was to be the world police, what of their own indiscretions? From Native Americans to non-white racial minorities a lot of unanswered questions remained. The CIA, geopolitical terraformers *par excellence*, as evident in their handy work in Central and South America, seemed to be defying the new world order regularly. Could all this be justified in the name of the world order?

The fundamental problem is that the new world order was new in how the post-Covid new normal is new. That is to say there is nothing new, neo, nouveau, nova, or nu about it. Its disgustingly familiar. The world order remains as it has always been: the vision of American exceptionalism. Democracy, except where undemocratic means can justify free market neo-liberalism. Peace, except where war can bring about greater peace. Neoliberal economics, except for when the wrong monopoly gets too powerful or on the occasion that the bankers need a hand with cleaning up a global financial mess they made. In the worst of cases, it's the perpetual extension of the present, in perpetuity, that is, until those most benefited by such a system have their eyes opened up and ask 'Am I on the right side of history?' Yet the bar is set. English is the *lingua franca*, the US dollar is the new standard of wealth, and a move made without the express permission of the US Executive or its military had best prepare to face the consequences for such insubordination.

Aided by ignorance and an absence of imagination, this looks to be the state of things for some time to come. Ravetz suggests we are moving from postnormal science to postnormal times. In fact, the move is complete; and postnormal times comes in to provide an interesting framing for the discussion of world order. Postnormal times allows us to see the compounding of endemic contradictions that chink away at the foundations of our present world order, allowing for chaos and complexity to tear it all down. Yet postnormal times also allows for loops of ignorance to keep the ultimately broken machine running until nothing is left. So, in a way, our world order, which is the American world order, which is a world order of ignorance, is not declining, but evolving. And here is where I place my second act twist.

The West, a monster made in the US of A and Europe, has pulled the great trick of convincing you that it is in decline, or as some have frankly put it, dead. The West has gone beyond death. The West is now immortal. And until we can imagine our way out, we are trapped in its game. And even if the day may come when the US goes the way of Rome or all the nations of Europe sink into the sea, the West will remain, an ouroboros in constant consumption and constant hunger. We wait for the next global alignment, the new, new world order. Shall it be China or India who are the next global superpowers, marinated in hubris and nationalistic juices.

Will the Asian Century ever come, or has it come, maybe it is just running a little late? Or even if the monolithic world order succumbs to a decentralised, democratised world of cities and people. We have to ask, has anything actually changed in these scenarios. Or must we take the first step, and when our number is called, we all rise and say 'I am Spartacus', 'I am America'.

The blurring of the lines now warps reality. The US and the USSR differed in approach but sought the same ends. Who is the good guy and who is the bad guy? Its as arbitrary as the difference between terrorist and freedom fighter. Or more appropriately the difference between today's China and the US, blood-soaked hands with too many internal inconsistencies to be guardians of any international order. Manifest Destiny? Belt and Road Initiative? *Quelle est la différence?*

James Brooks spells out this absurdity in his analysis of the new doctrine from one of today's most perplexing international anomalies, France's President Emmanuel Macron. His Paris Consensus is almost completely indistinguishable from the tired old Washington Consensus and he does not even appear to have the visual acuity to comprehend this. Not surprising of course when we consider Monsieur Le President's inability to see Muslims outside of an Islamophobic lens. Riding the international acclaim of having said something about our climate crisis – which embarrassingly is all it takes to be a hero of the green cause – Brooks points out Macron's attempts to usurp the new world order with the new world order, but this time French. And of course, France isn't the only one playing this game. Such undertones reek of Vote Leave. And the feral nationalism required to build up the arrogance to try to take on the world order, by feeding into the world order, has terrifying consequences. Jasmin Mujanovic exposes how a new wave of Serbian supremacy threatens to awaken old ghosts in the Balkans all in the name of some artificial need to demonstrate a world order. In this instance a *Srpski svet*, Serbian World.

In attempting to imagine our way out of this labyrinth, it will take more than putting on a new name or speaking words in different languages. Otherwise, any resistance merely feeds into the consumption loop of America's 'new' world order. As I said, this was the failure of postmodernism. And it threatens other fringe thoughts. Key among them are feminist alternatives, LGBT+ alternatives, black alternatives (especially promising, yet equally vulnerable are the new waves of Afrofuturism), indigenous alternatives, and environmental and sustainable alternative strains of thought. Samia Rahman explores one artificial pit hole that threatens to sink any effort at alternative progress: culture wars. Majorities under threat appropriate minority identities to crush any challengers. Rahman puts it beautifully when she said 'polarisation and ratcheting up extremism is creating false grievances, which cynically exploit people's fears and their need to locate the enemy that resides in the darkest recesses of their imagination.' Even the new, new, world of a promised egalitarian utopia that the cybersphere was sold as has fallen to the corruption of the immortal world order. Andrew Brown traces public stoning, a community building exercise that also instils a social order, to its contemporary descendant, the mucky social media arena of trolls, haters, and shamers. In this, perhaps not final, frontier what could have been the ideal of democratic political discourse instead is an open space for screaming, where anonymity erases all responsibility and ideology and identity blur further. Here bully and bullied are indistinguishable and that ultimate contradiction, coming together to be pushed apart, is a well-oiled perpetual motion device. It may appear the only way out, at the moment, is one of the Manifestos of the End as argued by Christopher Jones. And while those manifestos discussed in his article explore new ways in which the world ought to be ordered, perhaps the best solution is the undoing of the very notion of world order itself.

And while this issue has no shortage of anger and frustration, we are left with a modicum of hope. This comes in the form of a challenge and a metaphor. Colin Tudge challenges us to reconsider our aims in order to break from our monstrous world order. He does this by focusing on the economic order of our world, which he shows informs and flows through other orders that structure our complex world. Where, usually, we look to economics to deliver wealth, perhaps even value (note the subjective nature of both concepts), Tudge nudges us to consider a more universal and clear goal. Our mindset should move from capital accumulation to the construction of a sustainable world of compassion and cooperation. His approach is to have us consider our role as humans in an ecological network. He proposes a renaissance of thought driven by a respect for a oneness with nature and planetary harmonic order. Tudge's proposition partners well with a metaphor put forward by Naomi Foyle.

In a thought-provoking essay, Foyle considers humanity's relationship with technology and nature as well as mythology and story as we continue navigating through the Covid-19 pandemic. As Zoom and other screen fatigue sets in, and we all long for the freedom to go out into the world, perhaps such metaphors as man as machine, cogs in the system of ongoing capital accumulation brought to you with care by neoliberal economic regurgitation, is really not accurate. Foyle proposes the symbol of the tree. Trees feature prominently throughout various cultural mythologies and the human has a lot more in common with a tree, a fellow living thing, than a computer. And all the more so with recent dendrological research revealing highly social behaviour amongst trees and within their ecosystem, the forest.

Foyle explores the World Tree of Norse mythology, Yggdrasil. This tree is the backbone of the universe and during Ragnarök it is said to convulse, causing earthquakes and floods. Ultimately, Yggdrasil will burn as the universe collapses and the world ends. Many an eschatological story is less about the ending, but more a way to cope with change. These myths are often allegories for seasonal weather changes or even the cycle of life and death. In their cyclical nature lies patterns and repetitions, but I do not think this is to give us comfort in transition, but to ease the shock to the system and prepare us for radical change. After Ragnarök, a handful of second and third generation gods are said to survive along with at least two humans to repopulate. And much as the ashes of vegetation all around the world replenish the soil with nutrients for new life, so too do the ashes of Yggdrasil give way to a regreening of the planet. The story sort of dribbles out at this point, but must we assume that another universe spanning monolithic Yggdrasil will grow in its place? Why not a wisdom forest of many Yggdrasils?

The World order discourse has always been about the next war. Just like 'disarmament talks', as an American humourist who used the *nom de plume* Beachcomber once said, are 'a series of informal chats about the next war'. We may be heading towards yet another world order involving conflict with China. After subjugating Hong Kong, China is ready to make its move on Taiwan. And anyone who stands in its way, as President Xi

Jinping announced during the celebrations marking the centenary of the ruling Chinese Communist Party, 'would have their heads bashed bloody'.

There is strong temptation for us to take to the forest, axe in hand, while hearing Jagger repeatedly asking us what his name is, in search of that one monolithic tree that is the World Order. But there is hope in the appreciation of disorder, moving from what is to what ought to be, in a dream of *La Covivencia*, and the power of renewed imagination. By taking to it with an axe in hopes of destroying it, we play into the all-too-familiar Western game of a never-ending cycle of violence and war. Instead of perpetuating the cycle, we need to direct our thought on navigating our way out of it; there's little point in attempting to kill what has become immortal. As an alternative, why not take away its power, live with it as another element of the ecosystem, and ignore it for its inability to keep up with the brighter, plural, and open order provided in a planetary garden unhindered by unity in disorder. As Odin and the Norns never really died, similarly new scientific theorems push old ones into obscurity. And as we go about cultivating new gardens and forests, we will be able to imagine a world beyond the good guys and the bad guys. Should a grouping of uniformed and overly regimented chaps happen upon our path, hoping to enlist our skills in the name of one Order or another, we won't fall for the same old tropes.

UNHOLY DESERTS OF EVIL

Abdelwahab El-Affendi

In May 2021, Israel prepared to celebrate seventy-three years of its formal existence by dispossessing yet more Palestinians (for the second time since it emerged on the world scene). To add a flavour to this, it also decided to tear-gas worshippers in Islam's third holiest site, on the holiest night, in the holiest month in the Muslim calendar. This provoked protests all over Palestine, and rocket volleys from Gaza. In eleven days of devastating retaliatory bombing, the Israeli military killed 242 civilians, made 72,000 homeless and deprived Gaza of what little fragile infrastructure it has for sustaining lives, in particular in health, electricity, and education. Israeli security forces also murdered scores of peaceful protestors in the West Bank and within the so-called Green Line, arrested thousands, and injured hundreds. (No response to 'terrorism' pretexts here, especially since 'terrorist' Jewish settler extremists, under police protection, were often leading the attacks on unarmed Palestinians.)

But all this is not news. Israel has been piling misery on the Palestinians with impunity for over seven decades. The UN arbitrarily divided Palestine between its Arab inhabitants and a flux of Jewish refugees in 1947, giving the latter 56 per cent of Palestine, even though they represented less than a third of the inhabitants, owning merely 7 per cent of the land. Since then, the Israeli governments have been systematically displacing and dispossessing more Palestinians, grabbing more and more land and other resources, especially water. Today Israel controls over 93 per cent of all land and is fast eroding the 7 per cent that the five million plus Palestinians should at least enjoy unmolested.

What was remarkable, the *real news*, was the official international reaction. The US led a chorus of voices championing 'Israel's right to defend itself'. A political entity that is less of a state than a robbery in progress has a right to defend its crimes, while the victims should not even complain! No less remarkable was the siding of a number of Arab states with Israeli aggression, mostly tacitly in the face of the popular Muslim outrage at the assault on the Al-Aqsa Mosque in Jerusalem and other televised atrocities. Over the last year, four new Arab countries (UAE, Bahrain, Morocco and Sudan) have publicly recognised Israel and established diplomatic relations with it. Saudi Arabia all but joined.

At a time when Israel was ruled by the most chauvinist and intransigent regime in its history, morally bankrupt Arab regimes decided it is time to legitimise Netanyahu's mendacity and land grabs. While Anwar Sadat, King Hussein of Jordan and the PLO pretended their so-called 'peace' deals were steps to restore Palestinian rights, this new crop of quislings offered no such pretexts. They could not even persuade Netanyahu to stop embarrassing them by boasting of their unconditional surrender, even though none had fought any war with Israel anyway. In fact, their 'peace' might be their first war, since it has directly embroiled them in Netanyahu's interminable wars and pogroms.

This immorality is not an isolated phenomenon. All over the region, major political actors have created an ethics-free zone, a Machiavellian moral desert where only power matters. This ominous turn asserted itself, ironically, after the very promising reclamation of ethical high ground by the Arab masses during the 2011 revolutions. In that moment of rare unanimity, the peoples made clear their utter disgust with regimes whose depravity touched rock bottom, proclaiming a new dawn of liberty and moral regeneration. But, alas, the experience was fleeting and ephemeral.

The forces of darkness soon made a triumphant return. Some, as in Syria and a couple of Gulf regimes, never abandoned their fortifications, doubling down and fighting with unprecedented ruthlessness. Russia and Iran collaborated to save the Assad regime in Syria by levelling most of the country to the ground, sending half the population into exile. Iran's nemesis, Saudi Arabia, helped neighbouring Bahrain beat the uprising. The Saudis and their UAE allies then created a fiercely anti-democratic coalition to push back against popular aspirations for freedom. This time, the anti-democratic forces did not mince their words or take prisoners, often literally. After Bahrain, it was the turn of Egypt, where the coalition incited and then funded a military coup in July 2013, aiding and abetting a huge massacre against peaceful protesters in August 2013. Libya was their next stop, where rogue militias were armed, funded and encouraged to mount a (largely unsuccessful) coup in May 2014. All over the region from the (Arabian) Gulf to the (Atlantic) Ocean, a huge dark cloud hung, letting no light through.

Interestingly, Israel cheered the Egyptian coup, having expressed scepticism from the beginning towards the Arab democratic uprisings, describing them as Iranian-style 'Islamic revolutions'. That led to a bizarre coalition between Israel and four Arab countries (Egypt, Saudi Arabia, UAE and Bahrain), that later linked up with Donald Trump and his family in an ambitious scheme to shape the region into an alliance of pro-Israeli oligarchies. To remove obstacles to this pipe dream, they waged a war on Yemen in 2015, followed by a blockade on neighbouring Qatar in 2017 to intimidate it into submission. The feisty emirate was seen as responsible for fanning the flames of Arab revolutions through its influential Al Jazeera TV network, and backing assorted dissident groups, in particular Islamists.

All these adventures ended up disastrously. The Yemen war became a quagmire, Qatar refused to buckle under the siege, and in fact gained in stature, prosperity and resilience. While the Trump-Netanyahu alliance appeared at first to boast remarkable achievements, including the so-called Abrahamic Project of new Arab-Israeli 'peace deals', it is fast losing momentum.

However, what has happened and is happening in the region is shaping the whole world.

After Hypocrisy

The post-United Nations phase of modernity declared a break with the Machiavellian ethos of naked power that characterised colonial politics of Western ascendancy, vowing instead to put an end to atrocities and the law of the gun. Practice did not immediately oblige: colonialism lingered into the 1970s (1990s in South Africa and Central Asia) and is still going strong in Palestine and other places. Civil rights in many 'democracies' had to wait for the 1960s revolutions to pretend to catch up. However, a rhetorical commitment to virtue, or something like it, continued to dominate. Everyone continued to praise democracy and human rights, and declare their undying commitment to justice and liberty.

Not anymore. Nowadays, no one is bothering with hypocrisy any longer. Even before the naturalisation of evil and deception as official policy by outgoing American President Donald Trump, most major 'democracies' were happy to ignore genocide and other evil deeds when perpetrated by subservient regimes, or even by 'hostile' ones such as Assad's Syria, if the victims were not worth bothering about. The trend did not die with Trump's departure. As mentioned above, the proclamation in unison by most Western countries of Israel's 'right to defend itself' was a mark of the time, even when combined with timid admissions that what Israel has been doing to the Palestinians was indefensible. At least one country, France, admitted that Israel was conducting what could be described as apartheid. However, defending the indefensible was perfectly acceptable, again if the victims were of the right kind - that is, not human enough to deserve 'human rights'.

One device used to legitimate this wilful moral blindness was to re-tell the story differently. A recent policy brief by the European Council on Foreign Relations depicted the conflict in the region as one of rivalry between 'Islamist' Turkey on the one side, and a 'moderate' United Arab Emirates on the other. Each was fighting to increase its influence and safeguard its regime, while the West was being sucked into this rivalry. According to this narrative, Turkey supported the Arab revolutions because they empowered 'Islamists', while the UAE opposed them because it favoured 'moderation'. Rival coalitions emerged, with Turkey and Qatar on one side, favouring Islamists, and the UAE on the other, favouring 'moderation' and 'tolerance', and allying itself with the West.

This is not how most of us remember developments, which have been, luckily for our sanity, meticulously documented. We have watched it all on live TV, and it has been recorded in great detail through social media and all sorts of other tools. It is true that the Gulf monarchies have been extremely unsettled by the suddenness and swiftness with which allied dictators have been swept away from the scene. Having survived the threat of Arab radicalism of the 1960s, and the Iranian menace of the 1980s, and benefited from the oil boom from the 1970s, the Gulf monarchies had begun to feel secure, even adventurous. The Arab Spring revolutions were thus a big jolt. In particular, they felt threatened (and deeply dismayed) by what they saw as American 'betrayal' in refusing to stand by close allies such as Egypt's Hosni Mubarak, who had done everything he had been asked. The expectation was that he, and them, should have been protected, no matter how vile were the misdeeds. This was the rule during the Cold War. So, regimes suddenly felt deeply insecure, given the fragility of Western support on which they have relied so much.

However, the other side of the story was that Gulf countries also initially benefited significantly from the uprisings. Apart from Bahrain, where the Saudis intervened decisively and very early to help quash the protests, the Gulf Cooperation Council (GCC), played a proactive role in the revolutions, mainly under the influence of Qatar. Under GCC leadership, the Arab League supported the NATO intervention in Libya. (The Saudi King had a grudge against Gaddafi, accused of an assassination plot against him). The UAE even took a token part in the bombing of Libya. The GCC-led Arab League also sent the first monitoring mission to Syria, and later supported replacing it by a UN mission. It also expelled Syria from its membership, thus withdrawing recognition from the Assad regime. The GCC, on its own this time, brokered a transition deal in Yemen, where President Ali Abdallah Salih was persuaded to cede power to a transitional government headed by his deputy.

The narrative of Turkey supporting the revolutions because of their 'Islamist' colour, and the UAE opposing them for the same reason is problematic for other reasons. The whole world, including the majority of Arab states, supported the revolutions. That included a flurry of UN Security Council resolutions, acts of UN or other military intervention, massive support (including military support), for the opposition in Syria. The latter also benefited from strong EU and US political support (as shown by the 'Friends of Syria' group, formed in early 2012, with membership reaching 114 countries at a conference in Morocco in December 2012).

What happened was that opportunities later presented themselves for the forces hostile to democracy in the region, mainly a core of key Gulf states, plus Israel, Iran, and Russia. Though not formal allies, even enemies at times, this indirect coalition cooperated to undermine democracies. The start was in Egypt, where the Saudis and Emirates funded and encouraged protests hostile to Egypt's first democratically elected President, Mohamed Morsi. The protests were then used by the military as a pretext to mount a coup in July 2013. The two countries, in addition to Kuwait, made available $30 billion dollars to shore up the new military regime, and provided it with full diplomatic, media and PR support. From 2012, the beleaguered Assad regime began to receive support from Iran and many of its Iraqi and Afghan militias, with the Lebanese Hezbollah playing a vital role. Then in late 2015 as the regime teetered on the edge of collapse, Russia decided to intervene militarily, with devastating consequences.

As the rest of the world, except for Turkey, played dead, the Syrian people did not have a chance. Whole cities, such as Homs and Aleppo, practically disappeared from the map. Whole suburbs of Damascus were similarly obliterated. Chemical weapons, and every other weapon imagined, were used. The war was unprecedented in its ferocity, disregard for any moral or operational restraint. The indifference of the so-called international community amounted to active complicity. The US and all major Western powers had troops on the ground and active aerial operations over Syria and neighbouring Iraq. It was impossible for the Iranian militias, or for Syrian air power to operate without coordinating with these actors. No one pretended to obstruct them, even when they bombed hospitals and used chemical weapons. This was a modern instance when pure evil reigned, unopposed, unconstrained and unmitigated, in plain sight. A sign of our times, with almost universal complicity.

In Libya, things deteriorated fast due to the difficulty in agreeing on a constitution, integrating the militias in the military, maintaining security, or conducting effective governance. International and regional support remained minimal, in particular after extremists torched the US Embassy in September 2012, causing the death of the Ambassador. Following the failure of the attempted coup backed by the UAE and Egypt in the shape of a militia calling itself the Libyan National Army, a deal between rival factions was agreed in Morocco in 2015, whereby a power-sharing government was instituted. However, the UAE, Saudi Arabia, and Egypt continued to support the renegade general, who obstructed the political process and blocked attempts to organise a referendum on the agreed constitution. France decided to back this renegade coalition, and the militia was then encouraged to attack the Western region outside its control, including the capital Tripoli. Air support was provided by France,

UAE, and Egypt, and Russian and Sudanese mercenaries were enlisted and paid for by these powers. Tripoli was only saved by a timely Turkish military intervention, which routed the renegade forces, and finally forced an UN-sponsored political agreement in February 2021.

Barbaric Civilising Missions

The developments of the last decade raise a key question: how did the region's brightest moment, the Arab Spring protests of 2010s, turn so suddenly and unexpectedly into the whole world's darkest moment? Why had a period of rare unanimity around a desire for freedom and peaceful political cooperation to build a bright future for all, been greeted with such an unprecedented amount of cruelty and violence?

An inkling of an answer can be found in a recent article by Jacob Mundy of Colgate University, New York. Mundy dismisses as irrelevant questions about why the Middle East continues to be such an arena of sustained violence. The issue is linked, he argues, to the question: 'What is the Middle East?', which in turn refers us back to 'the intensively violent arrangements, practices and processes' involved in the region's conceptualisation and constitution as a region. The violence originated in imperialist 'cartographic practices' and the bureaucracies associated with them, and proceeded through 'externally driven processes of militarisation, conflict exacerbation, and peace deferment'. The objective was to incorporate the region 'into larger global processes aimed at restructuring the political and economic dominance of the North Atlantic powers'. This involved the creation, maintenance and reproduction of states of 'permanent war and irresolvable conflicts', a goal accomplished through 'processes of epistemically violent realisation'.

We know how these processes proceeded: the spilling over of European rivalries and burgeoning nationalisms into the management of the Ottoman state as 'the Sick Man of Europe', and later the dismantling of the Ottoman state, followed by French and British incursions, then full-scale colonial intrusion, culminating in the creation of the state of Israel. More interventions to sustain this state, defend oil supplies, respond to Cold War imperatives, 'contain' regional threats (Iran, then Iraq, etc.), and finally the 'war on terror'. Insecuritisation was introduced as a technique, then as a pretext for massive military interventions (in the Gulf in 1990, Afghanistan in 2001, Iraq in 2003), leading to entanglements in local wars and provocative presence all round.

Ironically, this intrusive presence has never been there when really needed, such as for saving Syrian victims of ongoing genocide, defending Palestinians from decades of persistent humiliating dispossession, or ending the conflict in Yemen. Interventions are usually targeted to support the strong against the weak and perpetrators of injustice against their victims. The resulting instability is then blamed on those troublesome victims who refuse to die quietly, or suffer slavery 'in peace'. They *deserve* to be governed by the Assads, Sisis or Netanyahus of this world. We should all be grateful for these helpful guys, who gas and bury protesters, bomb Gaza into oblivion and torture civil rights activists to death. That is how 'civilisation' could be safeguarded, according to the Macrons of our time. French presidents have a history of telling Arab human rights activists to 'eat up and shut up', as one key Tunisian activist summarised the advice provided by the then president Jacques Chirac to human rights groups complaining of Ben Ali's abuses. For Monsieur Chirac 'the first human right is the right to eat'. Well, the inmates of the Stalinist Gulag were also offered some food.

More recently, the right-wing columnist Guillaume Bigot sparked a storm of protests when he remarked on CNews TV (the French equivalent of Fox News) that Algerians should be told: 'We, the French, are proud to have been colonised by Rome. You, Algerians, should be proud to have been colonised by France'. Ironically, not all Arabs regard such suggestions as outrageous (although many French citizens did, as one commentator reminded Bigot that as a person of Viking heritage, he did not embrace Rome). At the end of the last millennium, official Egypt outraged most of its citizens by deciding to commemorate the bi-centenary of Napoleon's 1798 invasion of Egypt as '*l'annee franco-egyptienne*', where a series of joint cultural events and celebrations were planned. No mention of the atrocities perpetrated by the French emperor and his troops.

This leads us to the crux of the matter. Regardless of how a situation has been created, it tends to be 'indigenised'. During Algeria's so-called 'dark decade' in the 1990s, the brutal counterinsurgency was conducted by a coalition dubbed the 'Party of France.' It was made up of francophone politicians and intellectuals, and led mainly by some of the Algerian officers who fought on the French side during the Algerian war of independence, defecting to the nationalist side only in the twenty-fifth hour. This constituency did not hide its disdain for Arab/Islamic culture, and strived to 're-francophonise' the country. In Egypt, a significant anti-democratic constituency has been created by the long period of Hosni Mubarak's rule, made up of a small fraction of 'liberal' and left-wing intellectuals, religious minority factions, business interests, the overpopulated security forces and the sprawling bureaucracy, plus many other interest groups. This constituency was revived and unified by huge funding, propaganda, intelligence operations during the brief semi-democratic interval of 2011-2013 by the Saudi-UAE coalition, with backing from Israel and tacit (and not so tacit, as in France) Western backing to offer a 'popular' façade to the July 2013 military coup. Similar tactics were used in Libya, Mauritania, and Sudan.

The strategy was to leverage anti-Islamism as a key rallying cry, claiming to fight against the Islamist threat, and to champion liberalism, secularism, and tolerance. The coalitions serving this strategy in Egypt, Yemen, Libya, Bahrain, included hard-line Salafis loyal to Saudi Arabia. The religious establishment is usually fully mobilised in support of the anti-democratic agenda. For countries like the UAE, even non-Muslim extremists could be enlisted. Following the recent Israeli assault on Gaza (in which UAE-backed media did not hide its sympathy for the Israeli side), the UAE ambassador in Israel, Mohamed Al Khaja, paid a visit to Rabbi Shalom Cohen, the spiritual leader of the ultra-Orthodox Shas party, where he solicited and received a 'benediction'. He also expressed the need for the rabbi's 'wisdom' to tackle the 'crazy, crazy' things happening in the region. The ambassador blamed the Muslim Brotherhood and Qatar for stoking this 'craziness'. (It is to be recalled that Shas is an extremist *religious* party, whose founder had often called for the extermination of Arabs as vermin).

It would look that the 'threat' is not one of religious extremism, but democratic moderation. The anti-democracy coalition sees democracy as a threat to allied interests: local despots, Israel, external interests, and aspiring regional hegemons. In the past, these entities used to have divergent/conflicting agendas and interests. For example, Western powers were concerned with three main objectives: Israeli security, cheap oil, and Cold War alignment. These objectives were not always easy to align. Conservative Arab regimes (usually controlling the oil as well) were keen to secure Western support against local radicals, and were ready to cooperate in oil supplies. However, they were not ready to go along with flagrant Western partiality to Israel, and for this reason, were not as enthusiastic Cold Warriors as the West would have liked. In the 1970s, hostility to Israel became a source of profit for the conservative oil producing regimes, and their new wealth gave them some level of autonomy that some of them were happy to relish.

However, a number of related developments, including Egypt's flawed peace accords with Israel, the Islamic revolution in Iran, and Israel's incursions into Lebanon, brought great turmoil and instability to the region. This combination also made Israel more recalcitrant, increasingly dominated by extremist 'religious' bigots, making any genuine peace a remote possibility. The situation was made worse by the inordinate influence enjoyed in the United States by pro-Israeli lobbies, minimising US leverage over Israel. The reverse was in fact happening, with Israel enjoying more clout in Washington than any US administration has in its own capital, let alone in Tel Aviv. This was graphically demonstrated by Netanyahu's March 2015 defiant visit to Washington, against the then President Obama's will. The way Congress genuflected to that little local rogue actor, with multiple standing ovations at every turn, made a mockery of that supposedly democratic institution. However, it cemented Israel's insistence that any future 'peace' with the Palestinians will entail total Arab submission: no right of return, no ceasing of settlements, no viable Palestinian state, a one-sided recognition of Israel as a Jewish state, but none of Palestinian statehood. In short, a total marginalisation of the Palestinians as a people, to be left with, at best, something resembling the 'reservations' of native Americans.

To achieve this, the whole Arab region and its Islamic depth would also have to be subdued. During the Trump era, practical steps were taken to bring this fantasy into a reality. A coalition of renegade Arab states willing to go all the way into Israel's arms was assembled. Saudi Arabia under its new ambitious Crown Prince, Mohamed bin Salman (MBS) and, even more enthusiastically, the UAE under its de facto ruler, Mohamed bin

Zaid (MBZ), led the pack. They were hoping to have a broader coalition, but it did not work as planned.

The Road to Darkness

Like highways to hell, the road to the current abyss had been lined with a few good intentions, lots of wishful thinking and quite a lot of misguided 'short-cuts'. The first landmark was the oil shock, itself a direct result of the escalation of the Arab-Israeli conflict. To avenge the humiliating defeat of June 1967, and restore the credibility of the Eastern Bloc, Egypt and Syria launched the Ramadan-October war of 1973, surprising Israel, inflicting an initial painful major setback on Israel's allegedly invincible military. The Arab oil producers decided to back Egypt and Syria with an oil embargo. The outcome was a seismic economic 'coup' in the world economy in favour of Third World raw material producers, with a first and significant reverse flow of wealth to less developed nations.

However, the political outcome was disastrous for most of the initial 'winners', in particular for the Eastern Bloc. Instead of the war showcasing Soviet military hardware and shoring up local allies, the reverse happened. With Soviet timidity in backing its allies, lacklustre performance of East Bloc arms and a dismal mismanagement of both the military and diplomatic efforts by Egypt, the bolder American intervention, combined with diplomatic and military prowess, made Egypt the actual loser. It also damaged the Syrian-Egyptian alliance irreparably. The Arab oil producers, (and Iran), all sided with the US, changing the international balance of power in the region. When Egypt made 'peace' with Israel in 1977, the whole scene changed.

It could be said that the Cold War was won there and then. When Sadat broke off his alliance with Russia in the mid-1970s, the Soviets had already suffered one of their first major setbacks in the region. Sudan, for a brief while a major new Soviet ally, defected to the West in 1972. Somalia followed suit in 1977, by which time both Libya and Syria became lukewarm towards the East. From then on, it was all downhill for the Soviet Empire, with its disastrous invasion of Afghanistan in 1979 sealing its fate. As oil-rich Arabs joined powerful Western actors to back the

Afghan 'Jihad', Russia was brought to its knees, and its Soviet empire disintegrated.

However, instead of exploiting the opportunity provided by the end of the Cold War to make a new beginning, helping to restore a modicum of sanity and some fairness to the region, the major Western actors chose opportunism instead. When Saddam's Iraq invaded Kuwait, the main actors jettisoned the option of a diplomatic solution that would have restored stability to the region, pursuing instead the illusion of unchallenged dominance. The insanity of this road to ruin became apparent too late for those who dismissed the warning at the beginning, and became smug following the initial 'victory'. Still, denial continued.

Even though the centrality of the Palestinian issue was apparently discerned during that misguided adventure, with the Madrid Conference organised immediately after the war in Kuwait, two moves voided this apparent correct turn. First, the debilitating sanctions imposed on Iraq created another 'Palestine on the Tigris', while the genuflection to Israeli dictates on the so-called peace process ensured that things would get much worse on that front. This trio of sins: Foreign presence on 'holy' Saudi soil, the trap of unavoidable but unstainable sanctions on Iraq, and the cowardness in the face of Israel's intransigence, paved the road for all subsequent disasters, from 9/11 to the current quagmires in Iraq, Afghanistan, and Egypt.

A lot of this was easily predictable. In a chapter published in a 2003 edited volume *American Power in the 21st Century,* I pointed to the obvious: George W Bush's problematic 2003 invasion of Iraq would turn out to be Bush's own 'Islamic revolution', or a series of them. In one fell swoop, the American tanks and bombers removed the Islamic revolution's archenemies in Afghanistan and Iraq, and handed Iraq on a plate to the mullahs in Tehran, adding as a bonus, the destabilisation of Khomeini's other nemesis, the Wahhabi Kingdom of Saudi Arabia. The Lord's ways are mysterious indeed!

Stupidity, rather than celestial miracles, may be the better explanation, but that is another issue. However, the post-Arab spring debacle may be ascribed more to evil than stupidity, or evil stupidity, to be more precise. It is ironic that Bush and his allies have sold Iraq's rape as the virtuous act of spreading democracy, an objective the 'Bush doctrine' had earlier sold as an antidote to the scourge of terrorism. However, when democracy appeared on the Arab scene unchaperoned, genuinely miraculous and pristine, its vocal evangelists preferred to embrace the most genocidal regimes modernity has produced.

Here there was not a shred of pretence of virtue, not a single fig-leaf of hypocrisy to feign hiding the espousal of unapologetic Machiavellianism of the crudest kind: sacrificing any partiality to virtue for the sake of short-term ends. It started with opportunism, trying to use Saddam's stupidity to dominate the region, but painting oneself into a corner where the choice is either to sustain criminally inhuman sanctions, or risk unleashing Saddam once again on the region. Ethical norms kept sinking lower and lower, where despots like Hafez Assad looked like statesmen, and Israel graduated from accepting designated terrorists like Menachem Begin as leaders to choosing Ariel Sharon as its 'hero'. The combined crimes of Sharon, and the atrocities of the sanctions would have redeemed Saddam as a 'hero' as well!

The only solution left was to champion an 'Islamic revolution' in Iraq. Things did not stop there. For even the supposedly 'saintly' Obama decided to extend this revolution to Syria! As one would have thought it impossible for the region, after Sharon, Netanyahu, Saddam, Gaddafi and the Assads, to sink lower in moral depravity, the Obama-Putin-Khamenei trio told us otherwise. But while Bush might cite the pretext of having sleepwalked into handing Iraq over to the mullahs on a gold plate, the Obamas of this world took the role of Qasem Soleimani's unpaid air force with eyes wide open. The undisguised evils of the Assad regime in Syria, and those of its Iranian and Russian champions, were not state secrets. They were televised daily, live, for even the most uninitiated observer to see what was going on. So were the evils of Egypt's post-2013 junta, and misdeeds of the war in Yemen. With not a fig leaf anywhere, the whole world had chosen to espouse genocide, the greatest evil ever, as a 'lesser evil'. In order to win an election here, or appease populism there, pure evil became the 'norm'.

Nothing like this has ever been witnessed before, no era could ever be darker, no comparable universe of pure evil has ever been even imagined. No condition could ever be less sustainable. We live in a world where a worldwide, perpetual plague may be its only salvation.

Conclusion

The 'Middle East' is an invention that involved plenty of violence to produce and sustain, since it is in essence a denial of reality that must perpetually change to fit external interests. Its internal politics had been, from the dawn of modernity, distorted by the model of the capitulations, 'treaties' that gave the rights of foreign-backed minorities priority over the rights of local majorities. The abominable practice of colonialism was introduced to the region in its twilight, with the added anomaly of armed 'asylum seekers', who decided to enslave and then seek to replace the indigenous population, rather than accept its hospitality. The twin claims of 'divine right' and 'civilising mission' were invoked to allow atheists to claim religious mandates, and commend the virtues of barbarians to the cradle of civilisation.

To achieve their objectives, the invaders decided to turn the region into an ethical black hole, a moral 'desert of the real', where anything goes. Colonialism has always depended on the anomaly of an ethically grounded suspension of ethics. In the British philosopher, J Stuart Mill's justification of imperialism, the necessity of tyranny was proclaimed as the only way to rule 'savages' or morally immature people, so as to guide and eventually prepare them for self-government. These outdated norms are being reclaimed today, with colonialism (and its worst kind, settler colonialism and its adjunct, apartheid), alive and well. The dominant wisdom had become that the peoples of this region do not deserve self-government. Tyranny is what is best for them, the crueller the better. All the major crimes against humanity: torture, ethnic cleansing, genocide, you name it, are permissible to achieve this noble 'civilising mission.' If it takes forever, that is also fine.

There are two drawbacks to this strategy: barbarism can never be civilising. Victims of cruelty tend to rebel, using tactics of savagery matching those of their tormentors. And they usually win. The US was ejected from Saudi Arabia, and then from Iraq and Afghanistan. More to the point, a blowback of the barbaric tactics used in Palestine, Iraq, Syria, and Egypt, has come to haunt its perpetrators. Not just as terror by Al Qaeda and ISIS, but as home-grown barbarism. Washington now resembles Baghdad and Kabul, with religiously inspired militias seeking to overturn the election and overrun the Congress. A clone of Gaddafi spent four years in the White House. Similar ones now run major European countries, or aspire to do so soon.

In the good old days, savages who stormed our region from the uncivilised wilderness (Mongols, Crusaders) ended up being civilised by the experience. More recent hordes are not so lucky. They have exhausted the reservoir of civility that sustained this region for millennia. So much so that they tend to become even more barbaric during their sojourn, and then take their enhanced barbarism back home. It is Abu Ghraib, then Guantanamo, and finally the Capitol.

WHERE IS THE UMMAH

Anwar Ibrahim

The unprecedented and unpredicted changes in global, political, and economic arrangements have altered the realities of the present. After the crumbling of the Berlin Wall in 1989, and the unravelling of the Soviet empire, the Austrian management and business innovator, Peter Drucker, suggested that the world had changed and the new *gestalt* must be viewed as 'configurations' that embrace several aspects of our lives. A year later, American political scientist, Francis Fukuyama saw the collapse of the Cold War dualistic vision as the harbinger of the triumph of the Western model of liberal democracy, and declared

> What we may be witnessing is not just the end of the cold war, or the passing of a particular period of the post-war history, but the end of history as such: that is, the end point of mankind's ideological evolution and the universalisation of western liberal democracy as the final form of human government.

That unparalleled hubris now lies in ruin. The last decade has seen economic, political, and cultural power shift from the West to the East; and liberal democracy, given the recent events in the US, India, Brazil, Hungary, Poland, and elsewhere, appears to be in an intensive care unit. Indeed, the world has become more contradictory, complex, and chaotic; and we now face the new reality of postnormal times, where uncertainties in social, economic, cultural, and political life have become the new order of things. Worse, the new reality, for want of a better term, is not constant but ever changing, configuring and reconfiguring the world.

The postnormal reality that confronts us includes the climate emergency, the incorporation of different varieties of ignorance with knowledge production, the emergence of surveillance capitalism, the problems and challenges of digital economies, the social pathology of social media, the Covid-19 pandemic, as well as the old issues of justice and equality. These are interconnected issues that urgently need a sense of complexity that is neither a flirtation with nostalgia nor romanticism. Complexity in our thinking and approach to problems and issues is something we desperately need to learn to comprehend because it is pre-eminently the condition in which we live. It is impossible for any of us to attain a sustainable lifestyle that embraces complexity without also embracing a plural vision of human futures. For this reason, there can be no end to history, but there must be a relearning of the history that has made the world today. This is why Muslim scholars from the Arab historian, Ibn Khaldun to the Algerian philosopher, Malik Bennabi have emphasised the cyclical nature of history.

To be sure, cyclical theories are not exclusive to Muslim scholars. There is a long history going back to the classical Greek philosophers – Aristotle's cycle of regime change and Polybius's theory of anacyclosis – as well as the Chinese historian, Sima Qian's dynastic cycle theory, of intriguing comparative schemas of apparently divergent civilisations. But to reach its apogee as a systematic, empirically based study, cyclical theories had to wait for Ibn Khaldun with his fourteenth century social and philosophical expositions on the rise and fall of sovereign powers, including civilisations, based on the twin doctrines of *'umran* and *asabiyya*. His magnum opus *Al-Muqaddimah* (Introduction to History) could well be regarded as the culmination of the efforts of his predecessors in historiography and social studies such as the philosopher Al-Farabi, Persian philosopher Ibn Miskawayh, and Persian polymath Nasir al-Din al-Tusi.

Following Ibn Khaldun, Malik Bennabi suggests that 'each cycle is defined by certain psycho-temporal conditions proper to a social group: it is a civilisation in these conditions. Then the civilisation migrates, shifts its abode, transfers its values in another area. It thus perpetuates itself in an indefinite exodus, through successive metamorphoses: each metamorphosis being a particular synthesis of man, soil and time'. There is merit in Bennabi's ascription of the transitory nature of civilisation 'which allows one to discuss not only the conditions of progressive development but also the factors of regression and decadence: the force of inertia of a civilisation'. And it is in this vein of decline that we appreciate the elan of Bennabi's assertion that until Muslim societies free themselves from the 600 years of 'civilisational bankruptcy' and move towards *islah* and *tajdid* (reform and renewal) predicated on the true Islamic tradition, 'the equilibrium necessary for a new synthesis of its history' will remain elusive.

So, how are we to deal with new metamorphosis – the postnormal transformation that is shaping current and emerging realities? Where does the ummah fit in all this? And what is the relationship – if any – between the ummah and the 'Muslim world'?

Let us begin with the Muslim world. During the period of the Cold War, the world was supposedly ordered in two great but hostile *blocs*. The First World, also known as the Free World (North America, Western Europe, Japan and Australasia), which in being free naturally embodied all that was democratic, just, and free. The Second World, or the Communist Block of the Soviet Union, Eastern Europe, and China, which was allegedly the anti-thesis of the Free World. Depending on one's perspective, these blocs were either oppressive, totalitarian, and severely restrictive, or capitalistic, reactionary, and imperialistic. The countries in between, argued Frantz Fanon, the French West Indian cultural critic and philosopher, constituted a third power bloc – the Third World. The Muslim World, that is the aggregate of newly independent Muslim countries, was said to be part of the Third World. There were other categories of division – developed countries, developing countries, and underdeveloped countries; and, sometime later, less developed countries.

Of course, the three-world format is redundant in postnormal times but the core problems afflicting the countries placed in the Third World category – poverty, hunger, illiteracy, disease, pollution, the debt problem, and global militarisation – far from being resolved have become worse. What the sophistication of modern technology and material abundance can achieve for some is even further removed from the life of the poorest than it was at the start of the 'development' decades. But it is important to realise, that the three worlds arrangement was, in fact, an attempt at economic management within one civilisation, that of the West, that embraced and affected all the rest. It made perpetual accumulation of economics and material resources the major objective of human ingenuity, at the cost of too many other necessities without which material advance loses its meaning and, on the evidence, may be rendered unattainable.

During my university days in the 1970's, the term Muslim World was synonymous with the Third World; we were part of the Third World, the 'too little' countries in the words of Fanon. But the term was also used in the geographical sense. Conventionally, the Muslim World was the global middle belt stretching from Morocco to Indonesia, and south to north, as far down as Zanzibar to Kazakhstan in central Asia. To this traditional geographical representation, we added large Muslim communities in the West and other parts of the world. We considered India, which has more Muslims than Pakistan, as part of the Muslim world. The Organisation of the Islamic Conference (OIC), as it was then called, introduced the notion of Muslim-majority countries and Muslim minorities. There were long discussions on whether India should be included in the OIC. When we talked of the Muslim world, we meant the general Muslim population of the world.

However, recently the notion of 'the Muslim world' has been questioned by the Turkish American historian, Cemil Aydin. In his controversial study, *The Idea of the Muslim World*, Aydin argues that the term is little more than a product of Western colonialism, designed to sow racial divisions within Muslim subjects of Empire and colonies. Moreover, Pan-Islamic Muslim thinkers, from Mohammed Abduh, the Egyptian scholar and theologian, to Mohammad Iqbal, the great South Asian poet–philosopher, contributed to the racial connotation of the term. By the time we enter the twenty-first century, Aydin suggests, the illusion of the Muslim World is deeply entrenched, reinforced by successions of Islamist and Islamophobic eruptions.

If the Muslim world is a modern concept, then we should not be surprised to note that it is embedded with all the intrinsic ambiguities of modernity – not least imperialism and racism. Most of Aydin's arguments are based on the 'illusion of unity' – that the Muslim World has never been united, which, given recent history, is almost a truism. However, if the idea of the Muslim world is a modern idea, it cannot be stretched back to pre-modern times of the early Ottoman Empire and even further back to the formative period of Islam. To suggest that the very notion of a collective Muslim identity is little more than an invention of the colonial powers is not only a grossly sweeping generalisation, but it also denies any agency to Muslims and labels and consigns Muslim thinkers to the province of racism.

However, we cannot deny that the term has been used by colonial powers to serve their ends, or indeed that certain Muslim politicians or religious authorities have sometimes used it to further their own ends. But this does not mean that it loses its geographical significance. The introduction to Ziauddin Sardar's 1977 book, *Science, Technology and Development in the Muslim World*, has the title: 'what *forms* the Muslim world?'. Sardar is interested in the topographical shape of the Muslim world; and proceeds to examine the science policies of states and communities, with different national and ethnic identities, all claiming to be Muslim. Despite their disunity, which Sardar emphasises, he discovers a worldwide Muslim consciousness. In contrast, the introduction to Aydin's book is entitled: 'what *is* the Muslim world' — an entirely different ontological question, which Aydin proceeds to answer with some astute scholarship. But the question 'what is' the reality of the Muslim world does not invalidate 'what forms' that reality, what geographical shape it takes, and what consciousness gives it that form – even though the reality itself may be in a complete and utter mess!

The idea of the Muslim world, I would argue, is intrinsically linked to the idea of the world: what kind of world we wish to make, what kind of world we ought to leave for future generations, and what kind of world would invite the Grace of God. How Muslims see the world is how they come to see their own location and responsibility in it. Of course, the idea of the world is based on how we *think* the world actually works; and that itself depends on our ontological and metaphysical outlook. Which brings us to the notion of the *ummah*.

Indeed, 'the term 'Muslim world', as Aydin notes, 'does not derive from ummah, a concept as old as Islam'. But what is the ummah? Where is it located? Is it simply a single, united community of believers? No doubt, the concept of the ummah was problematic for Muslims right from the inception of Islam. When the Muslim community was small, it was easy to see it as a single unit of believers. But the divisions emerged almost immediately after the death of the Prophet – not least with the emergence of the Shi'ites and the Kharijites. The first four Caliphs were seen as religious rulers; and they were non-hereditary rulers who were, by all accounts, selected on the basis of an electoral process. But three of the four Caliphs were murdered, and despite the intricacy of the selection process, it could not stem a civil war. Divisions only multiplied as the territory expanded. What followed, in the shape of the Umayyads and the Abbasid dynasties, was more like empires of antiquity, waxing and waning autocratic tendencies, rather than the system of governance introduced by the Prophet in Medina.

The Abbasids professed to acknowledge the Shariah as the rule of life which formed the basis for the Muslim community, the Muslim ummah. The problem was that the Abbasids professed different things at different times. So, when the Caliph leaned towards the philosophy of the Mu'tazalites, he outlawed the theological school of the Ashari – and vice versa. And the Sufis were frequently declared as heretics. So different groups were in and out of the ummah from time to time.

The situation was made worse by certain classical scholars with a tendency to denounce deviation from orthodoxy, established by the Abbasids, as heresy. And the heretics, of course, could not be included in the ummah. Although Al-Ghazali in his *The Incoherence of the Philosophers* roundly denounced the works of Muslim philosophers, it would be an exaggeration to say that he declared all of them as heretics. But just to stretch the argument further, it would be to no avail to say that Ibn Rushd, renowned in the Latin West as Averroes, had valiantly come to the rescue of the condemned philosophers because he himself, having gained the accolade of 'Father of Rationalism', has never been regarded as the ideal referent for orthodoxy. Nevertheless, as American historian Sarah Stroumsa shows in her book, *Freethinkers of Medieval Islam*, such great freethinkers as Ibn al-Rawandi, al-Kindi and Abu Bakr al-Razi were categorised as heretics – and outside the ummah. Thus, looking at Islamic history for the meaning of the ummah is not particularly fruitful.

It may well be a category mistake if we seek to define the ummah in terms of what is, or indeed what was. The ummah is not an *is* but an *ought* category; and, as an ought category, the ummah cannot simply be based on what is. As a meta concept, it is above the messy, and often unpleasant, reality of the Muslim world – then and now. Moreover, ummah is not about political unity, or a giant polity that unframes the entire Muslim population. Or, the demand that all Muslims must express exactly the same confession of faith. As Chandler Barton notes in his review of Aydin's book, 'we must naturally be hesitant to give credence to such a "No True

Musliman" theory because it is not only unrealistic, but also untenable. After all, never in human history has such a hegemonic unity ever existed that the totality of individuals identifying with one particular religion (or any other identifier for that matter) acted or thought in complete solidarity, especially when we are talking about millions or even billions—1.8 to be exact in modern figures—of individuals claiming to be Muslim'. Indeed, a single political entity for all Muslims would soon degenerate into authoritarianism and conformity. No. This is not, and cannot be, the goal of the ummah.

As an ought category, the ummah is a metaphysical concept. It is concerned not so much as what the world is, or what political or structural *forms* it takes, but with what it *ought* to be. As a metaphysical concept, its meaning cannot be rigidly defined but constantly sought. This, I believe, is what the Qur'an teaches us.

Ummah is a frequently used term in the Qur'an, occurring in sixty-two verses. But the term does not have a single meaning, which changes according to context as we proceed in the chronology of the revelation. To begin with it could simply mean people in general; or more specifically a community. But, a more important point to realise is that there is not one but many ummahs. There have been many ummahs in history; and 'God has sent each ummah a messenger' (6:42, 13;30, 16: 34, 64). Prophet Abraham represented an ummah himself: 'Abraham was an ummah obedient to Allah, and true to faith' (16:120). The People of the Book, *the ahl-e-kitab*, are an ummah, or at least those who are righteous amongst them: 'if they had observed the Torah and the Gospel and that which was revealed to them from their Lord, they would surely have been nourished from above them and from beneath their feet. Among them are ummahs who are moderate…' (5:66). The ummah can also be a tribe, just like the twelve tribes of Israel: 'there is a group among the people of Moses who guided by truth, and who act justly according to it. We divided them into twelve ummahs' (7:159-160). Then, there is the ummah of the Jinn ((7:38), as well as 'all creatures that crawl on the earth and those that fly with their wings are ummah like yourselves' (6:38). But all this diversity of ummahs is not by accident: 'mankind was a single ummah, then God sent prophets to bring good news and warning, and with them he sent the Scripture with the truth, to judge between people in their disagreement'

(2:213). The ummah, we learn from the Qur'an, is a dynamic, pluralistic concept with different significance in different contexts.

Moreover, the Qur'an says: 'we have assigned a law and path to each of you. If God had so willed, He would have made you one community (*ummatan wasatan*)' (5:48). It is clear that this verse is addressed not to just one community but to 'each and every' community, dispelling the notion that divine law here (*shir'ah*) refers only to the *Shari'ah* of the Muslim ummah. This is indicative of God having ordained different ritual and legal formulations for the different religious communities, and each religious community is independent of the laws of other such communities, even if the essential truths and principles are the same.

As such, the ummah does not simply apply to a community of all those who profess to be Muslims. As the righteous among the people of the book are also ummah (3:115, 5:66, 7:159, 7:168), at the very least the concept suggests that Muslims actively collaborate with Christians and Jews in good deeds and works. The single most important implication of ummah is that it is a moral concept of how Muslims should *become* a network of communities in relation to each other, other communities, and the natural world. It is manifesting in thought, action and openness a distinctive moral vision that is the *raison d'être* of the ummah. It is an enduring commitment to the dynamism of a constant set of moral concepts and precepts that creates the contours and ultimate configuration of the ummah.

But between the 'ought' and the 'is', the ideal and reality, lies the slippery slope, where we should be reminded of the poetic refrain of 'what might have been and what has been'. And nowhere is the gap between the ideal and the reality demonstrated more profoundly than in Muhammad Iqbal's aspiration, through his poetry, for the universality of the ummah, composed in body and soul of a belief in the unity (*tawhid*) of God, bonded in brotherhood (*ukhwah*) by the message of Prophet Muhammad. The purpose of Iqbal's poetry was to provide a common platform for Muslims – living far and wide, and across geographical, ethnic, and cultural boundaries – to come together as an ummah. Indeed, as the late Shahab Ahmed, the noted scholar and author of the monumental *What is Islam?* points out, we cannot 'overemphasise the meaningfulness of the experience of the idea of the universal community of Islam, or of Islam as universal community, in Muslims' conceptualisation of Islam'. It is well and good to proclaim that the ummah is not circumscribed by geographical constructs or that it belongs neither to East nor West nor anywhere in between, because it transcends race, colour, or nationality, but ultimately the reality bites hard. I say this less with cynicism than with a deep sense of humility. Thus, when we talk about the ummah, we are not describing the reality of the Muslim world but rather expressing an ideal: that despite the diversity of the Muslim world, differences and contradictions, polities and politics of past and present, the dissensions and discords of history and contemporary times, there ought to be some semblance of unity amongst Muslims.

This desire to be an ummah stems from a deep-rooted metaphysical and religious concern that binds Muslims, but it does not bind them into a single polity, or even a single community. The ummah is not a cultural entity patterned on the norms of any one dominant group nor is it the product of cultural contingency. It does not embrace cultural relativism but exists within and is expressed through diverse cultural groups. What binds the ummah, indeed all ummahs, is an ethical consciousness, an awareness that God 'forbids disgraceful deeds – whether they be open or hidden' (7:33)'. The unifying force of the concept of the ummah is a shared ethical consciousness – whatever the specific beliefs of different individuals who constitute a particular community, or the different polities and politics of different communities, within an international ummah. Moreover, the ummah is not an end point; rather, it is a goal to strive for constantly and continuously.

Even though Muslims have hardly been united, in history or in the present, the notion of the ummah has existed as an integral part of Muslim consciousness, seen as trans-geographical in history and as trans-nation-state in modern times. It is a manifestation of the saying of the Prophet that 'Muslims are like a human body, if one part hurts the whole-body suffers'. Ibn Battuta, the fourteenth century jurist and globe trotter had a strong sense of ummah consciousness, and global solidarity with Muslim communities. This is in fact what enabled him to move from community to community with some ease and without internal angst. Much can be said of other classical travellers such as, the ninth century geographer, Abu al-Hasan al-Masudi, the tenth century Turkish intellectual, Muhammad ibn Hawqal, and the twelfth century Qur'an scholar from Valancia, ibn Jubair.

In recent times, the concept of the ummah has periodically played an important part in bringing Muslims together. For example, after the debacle of the 1967 Arab–Israeli war, King Faisal bin Abdulaziz Al Saud invoked the idea of ummah to bring Muslim states closer together. Despite its shortcomings, the OIC has consistently generated enthusiasm through its discourses on the malaise of the ummah and common determination and commitment to surmount contemporary problems. The notion of the ummah is also constantly invoked by global Muslim charities such as the Red Crescent, Islamic Relief, and Muslim Aid to galvanise Muslims after disasters to raise money for humanitarian work.

What is wrong with institutions like the OIC is what is wrong with Muslim societies themselves; and it is traditionalism. Our tradition has become ossified in history; and has been transformed into traditionalism, un-thought through, incompatible amalgams of incompatible elements that lack the coherence of a consistently applied dynamic frame of reference. The limitations of our traditionalism are part of the reason for many of our contemporary problems and must be resolved if we are to realise our capability to change things to make a more appropriate and better future. What we have to recover is dynamism, our ability to utilise our tradition as a code for changing things. We need to begin by changing our perception of our own tradition.

That change, I suggest, begins with appreciating that the ummah is not a being but a form of becoming. We need to debate what refines our perception of the ummah and make it more than an abstraction, and transform it into a goal that we constantly seek.

The extrinsic challenges to the Muslim world of today are real, as are the intrinsic weaknesses of the Muslim communities; together they frame the agenda for change. The quality of life in Muslim countries leaves much to be desired. They have one of the highest rates of illiteracy in the world, most notably among women. They are seats of violent social and political upheavals. They present us with the greatest disparity between rich and poor. The dignity of humanity gets mutilated and consistently abused through political repression and rampant corruption. The loss of self-identity is nowhere more apparent than in the Muslim world – hypocritical abhorrence of Western tradition and culture in their exhortations, while at the same time an aping of its morally decadent facets and the trivialities of the West in the crudest possible manner. This superficiality was evident even in the Muslim revivalist movements, lending credence to the argument by French political scientist, Bertrand Badie, that

> the revivalist formula consisted in reinterpreting and remodelling the borrowed elements on the basis of a legitimacy derived from Islam. Irrespective of whether the concern was with the right to revolt, equality, the fight against despotism or the shaping of a modern society based on scientific progress, the 'patchwork' was affected with reference to the revivalist premise of the existence of a modernity *peculiar* to Islam.

Today, Muslim societies, which so superficially absorb and are so deeply affected by the dominant world order, have in several respects become insular, full of contradictions and dichotomies. Conscious of its identity, only to find itself aggrieved, the Muslim world has bred a sense of exclusivity that denies the openness that is an authentic meaning of ummah. It is only through recapturing the dynamic of becoming an ummah that we can open up, liberate ourselves from the stultifying hold of our persecution complex. In seeking to become an ummah, in the genuine meaning of the term, we must see our social structure as an interactive model, a means of relating pluralism within the confines of the diverse professions of a common faith. Ummah consciousness delivers us with a universalist outlook that provides the means for existing within a genuinely pluralistic world. It regards intellectual pluralism as consonant with the spirit of the Islamic tradition.

Postnormal times has produced a whole array of challenges for Muslim communities, well-illustrated in *Muslim Societies in Postnormal Times: Foresight for Trends, Emerging Issues and Scenarios*. These include problems associated with the climate emergency such as degrading environment and its impact on liveability, temperature rises, rising sea levels, and fresh water shortages – all of which could lead to a massive increase in Muslim refugees. There are also issues with new and emerging technologies such as social media and artificial intelligence, cyberattacks and cyber wars, and genetic engineering. These problems cannot be solved in isolation by Muslim states but require a joint, coordinated effort to tackle and overcome. Ummah consciousness provides us with a tool both to grasp the truly global nature of these tribulations and navigate our way out to more desirable, sustainable futures. Ummah consciousness is the one and only real thing that can bring Muslim communities together to work collectively on complex, interconnected problems and issues. The conceptual shift to ummah is also a tool of reason, a source of critical awareness. It calls on us to think differently about our environment because we see it as a value, and through this paradigm of thought to devise new ways of operating that are morally and ethically defensible and sustainable. We have too little debate on global interdependence in the face of climate crisis and environmental problems. The ummah as a network of communities is required to acknowledge moral and practical responsibility for the Earth as a trust and its members are trustees answerable for the condition of the Earth. This makes ecological concerns a vital element in our thinking and action, a prime arena where we must actively engage in changing things in rapidly changing times.

Equity and justice are prerequisites and imperatives of ummah consciousness. This means putting the eradication of poverty at the top of the Muslim agenda and finding means to enable the poor and powerless to work with adequate economic support and dignity. The major challenge is making resources available to assist the poor to attain self-sufficiency, rather than for them to remain in continual dependence. Set against our experience of the failure of the 'development' decades, the applicability of this approach is demonstrable. The ummah is a vehicle for making us active along these lines and a mouthpiece for the kind of sanity the world needs in the sphere of international assistance if the scourge of hunger, famine, want, neglect, and all its horrors are to be abolished.

Ummah consciousness also makes the eradication of illiteracy a first priority, a moral crusade. It is the development tool *par excellence,* the greatest practical means of enhancing future opportunities and the growth potential of any country. Our concern must then become quality education for life for the new future that we envisage. Appropriate education through appropriate institutions, organisations, and curricula, will demand and facilitate internationalising and synthesising the heritage and fruits of a pluralistic world so that it can be handed on to the next generation as a liveable reality. Only with access to appropriate education can ummah consciousness take root and make possible the ummah of tomorrow as a personification of the moral principles of Islam endowed with creative, constructive, critical thought.

To promote 'ummah consciousness' there are two important consequences of our recent acquaintance with 'Islamic fundamentalism' that must be overcome. But we shouldn't fall into the Weberian trap of pigeonholing Islam into stereotypical configurations. Terms such as 'fundamentalist' or 'Islamic fundamentalism' are amenable to a variety of interpretations and no hard and fast rule prevails. While it may encompass a wide spectrum of organisations and movements generally intolerant and exclusivist, it may yet point to some that are manifestly pluralistic and inclusivist or to some that are purely devotional movements. Yet others may be primarily political, some authoritarian, and some violent. Yet another view links it to Salafi reformism traceable to Wahhabism and its notorious intolerance of credal differences. Nonetheless, the prevalence of the term 'Islamic fundamentalism' shows, once again, the triumph of reductive labels as a prop of ignorance and a barrier to mutual understanding. Among Muslims, it encourages a confusion that enables redundant and moribund traditionalism to flourish. It enables obscurantism to go unchallenged because it claims a legitimacy that we have not yet learnt to debate, let alone deconstruct and think our way beyond. What has come to be seen as Islamic fundamentalism sets a false agenda of peripheral issues as the only topics that get serious and sustained attention. In its conventional understanding, Islamic fundamentalism causes division and engenders unnecessary conflict.

How Islamic fundamentalism has developed among Muslims gives credence to the hysteria of non-Muslim reaction and rejection. The non-Muslim world ignores or misconstrues the genuine concerns of Muslims to all our detriments. It uncritically accepts all its own stereotypes as well as ignorance of Islam as a vehicle of understanding to the detriment of all. In an increasingly interdependent world, we need a new agenda for what we need to know, if we are to make peace a reality that is attainable and sustainable, rather than being dragged by our mutual ignorance into crisis after crisis.

Certainly, Islamic fundamentalism that is founded on an exclusivist outlook, violates the necessary moral meaning of the concept of Ummah. It enables some expressions to become Muslim imperialism writ large or writ small. This runs counter to the model of the Medina state under the leadership of the Blessed Prophet Muhammad. Recapturing the contemporary meaning of that model would necessitate that Muslims engage with other people, nations, worldviews, religions, and ideologies to work for a set of moral objectives that we all agree on and that we respect the ummah of other people. It is a concept that first had communal existence in the multicultural and multireligious community of the Medina state whose written constitution guaranteed the right of continued self-expression and development through their own institutions to its non-Muslim citizens. Islamic history does provide exemplary models of multiracial, multicultural, multireligious, pluralist societies. If ever we had need of recovering such an imperative, it is now.

The reductionist nature of our view of the world, the dominant neo-liberal mode of thought for the past half a century, was a means of perpetuating injustice and the intolerable in the name of laudable objectives. We need to construct a future devoid of one-dimensional reductionism, a plural future where all peoples can flourish and collaborate with fewer false restraints and constraints, fewer misguided impediments. We need to think about the world and ourselves differently to enable positive change to come into being. We need to create the freedom and tolerance for people to think about themselves through their own identity as a moral, sustainable, expressible whole.

The term 'Muslim world' may have been tainted with racist connotations. But the ummah retains its authenticity and power. It does not matter what is the 'Muslim world', or what form it takes, the ummah is ever present: it is the universal consciousness of Islam, and, as such, an integral part of the very being of all Muslims – whatever their sect, ethnicity, nation or other identity. In these postnormal times, ummah consciousness is an essential requirement for Muslim communities to navigate the great challenges we face.

The Muslim communities of the world have never been more disunited, more fragmented, and more brimming with contradictions. We are definitely not an ummah. But we ought to be.

THE EDICT OF RACE

Yuri Prasad

Race is so intricately woven into the world order – indeed, the very fabric of life – that few people can see beyond it to a time when the world was not organised and controlled this way. As notions of superiority and inferiority among groups of people seem ever present and almost unchanging, many commentators are happy to report that race, racism, and the desire of the strong to dominate, are features of human nature itself. The beauty of this approach is that it requires no intellectual effort, no analysis, and no history.

For today's elites, this theory of a timeless racism is convenient precisely because it ignores the way that imperialism threw backwards some of the most advanced societies of the age. It means they need not discuss the way that ruthless robbery and exploitation of the 'New World' provided the seed money for the development of capitalism and the industrial techniques that allowed the new European empires to dominate the world. It also means they can largely ignore, or at the very least downplay, the capture and transportation of millions of African people as slaves because the bloody trade was little more than an expression of human nature. And by providing an excuse for the past, the idea of a world naturally divided into a hierarchy of races also provides excuses for the present – and the widely accepted notion that some human lives are simply more valuable than others by virtue of the culture they inhabit.

But a look back to the early contacts between civilisations of what became Europe, and those that became Africa and Asia reveals a far more complex picture. It was one where British, Dutch, Portuguese, and Spanish travellers and traders often met societies at least as advanced as their own. In 1510, Leo Africanus, an exiled Moor from Granada, travelled to Timbuktu (in modern Mali) and wrote: 'here are many shops and merchants, especially such as weave linen and cotton cloth. Corn, cattle, milk and butter this region yieldeth in great abundance. The rich king keeps a magnificent and well-furnished court. Here are great stores of doctors, judges, priests and other learned men.' And in 1600, a Dutch trader entering the city of Benin in West Africa wrote: 'The city looks very big when you go into it. The houses in the town stand in good order as our Dutch houses are. These people are in no way inferior to the Dutch in cleanliness. They wash and scrub their houses so well that these are as polished as a looking glass.'

When the ships of the British East India Company arrived on India's west coast in 1601, they encountered a society in many ways more advanced than their own. The Mughal court was not too keen on Britain's woollen offerings and made them wait until they came up with gold and silver robbed from Spanish and Portuguese vessels returning from the Americas before trade could start. Only then could India's exotic spices, dyes and cotton be sold to the British ships moored off the coast in Goa, Chittagong, and Bombay. In 1700, Mughal emperor Aurangzeb's share of the world economy, according to the Indian historian, Shashi Tharoor, was around 27 per cent, larger than all of Europe put together. The idea of the innate superiority of the pale skinned man in these times would have seemed absurd. Across the world from China to India to Africa there were huge and prosperous empires populated by darker skinned people that proved almost the exact opposite. After all, it was not until Britain acquired Indian cotton that the British were able to claim that ultimate symbol of advanced culture – regular supply of clean underwear.

So, when and where did the racism that came to dominate the world emerge? Slavery, and in particular the transatlantic slave trade, was to be crucial in its formation. In the early days of the blood-soaked trade, African people sold into slavery were generally treated as indentured labour and exploited in ways which were similar to the debt-slaves transported from Europe to the colony plantations in the Caribbean and the Americas. But as it became clear that white indentured workers tended to die much younger than their African counterparts – mostly because of malaria – plantation owners shifted to solely African labour. And, during the process whatever limited rights those labourers had were removed and they became slaves – a commodity to be bought, sold, and otherwise traded in ways similar to other livestock.

The system of world trade that grew alongside slavery, and the vast wealth it created, gave rise to new Empires which from the start conspired against each other to divide up the world. What was new about imperialism was the way it brought together the economic, financial and military together and forged them into states that competed not merely for territory, but also for markets and raw materials. The aim of an imperialist empire was not only geographical reach, which had characterised the empires of the pre-capitalist era, but the pursuit of profit.

In a world increasingly dominated by new empires the supposed superiority of the pale skinned white plantation owner over his slaves was obvious to most Europeans. Nevertheless, the move to outright slavery was to create a moral and philosophical conundrum. The ideas of the Enlightenment that accompanied the rise of the mercantile class and the birth of capitalism talked of equality between human beings. The slogan of the French Revolution, Liberty, Egality, and Fraternity, so often evoked against the aristocracy now presented itself to the question of slavery. If all men were created equal, and therefore entitled to certain 'unalienable rights', how could it be that Africans were enslaved on the plantations?

The answer that came was that African were not really humans. Enlightenment philosopher David Hume wrote in 1753 that he was:

> Apt to suspect that Negroes, and in general all the other species of men (for there are four or five different kinds) to be naturally inferior to the whites. There never was a civilised nation of any complexion other than white, nor even any individual eminent either in action or speculation. No ingenious manufacture among them, no arts, no sciences.

At roughly the same time as Hume was pontificating, the British were marking their new found superiority in India. As the result of pressures both internal and external, the Moghul Empire began to crumble under the reign of Muhammad Shah, and into the void stepped the British East India Company. In a series of battles, local leaders were either crushed, as in Plassey in 1757, or brought to heel. The Company was then free to set about pillaging India, sucking wealth out of the country and transferring the loot to England. There were terrible consequences of this drain. In Bengal, which had a population roughly four times that of Britain, the

Company regime trebled the amount of taxes on people, and appropriated huge quantities of goods to be sold on the international market. The region was already economically devastated when famine hit 1770 and approximately one third of the population died.

The way in which the Company was able to dominate India both physically and economically required explanation, and what emerged were the legends of 'British genius' and 'Indian backwardness'. Here the Indians were said to be not so much a separate race, but of a more infantile version of humanity – a theme taken up enthusiastically more than a century later by the most famous novelist of empire, Rudyard Kipling, in his poem 'The White Man's Burden':

> Take up the White Man's burden—
>   Send forth the best ye breed—
> Go bind your sons to exile
>   To serve your captives' need;
> To wait in heavy harness
>   On fluttered folk and wild—
> Your new-caught, sullen peoples,
>   Half devil and half child.

The racism developed specifically to justify the slave trade was in the process of being transformed so that it could serve a similar purpose in the era of colonialism. Not only did theories of race explain why those with pale skin should naturally dominate those with dark skins, but it also served to create a new pecking order among the subordinate races. In the wake of the 1857 uprising against British rule in India, the Crown formed separate regiments for its native army based not only upon geography, but also upon ethnic and religious lines. 'I wish to have a different and rival spirit in different regiments, so that Sikh might fire into Hindoo, Goorkha into either, without any scruple in case of need,' said one British military figure. The Raj went much further down this route as pressure for self-rule grew, eventually creating even separate electorates for Hindus and Muslims in Bengal. 'Divide and Rule', the beloved phrase of the elite of the Roman Empire, now became a motto for the British, not only in India, but across the whole of the Empire. The consequences of this policy are still with us today as the divisions so carefully cultivated have often remained in place in the post-Empire world.

In the nineteenth and twentieth centuries, the age of technology, it was inevitable that there would come scientific reasoning that could explain how the world was divided into races, and why races needed to be understood as part of a hierarchy. In her book, *Superior: The Return of Race Science*, Angela Saini charts the way the British scientific establishment was only too keen to help anthropologists and geographers with the project of classification. They took for granted the idea that the races corresponded to intelligence, aptitude, and attitude. Saini notes the way British universities developed kits to measure exact skin pigmentations, eye colour and types of hair – and of course, instruments to measure the size of skulls. The pressing need was to justify the way that wealthy white Europeans had come to rule the world by framing the argument scientifically. The Europeans ruled because they were a superior race, with the others below them capable only of tasks appropriate to their place in the pecking order, or as Saini puts it:

> It's difficult to avoid concluding that the reason anyone pursued the scientific idea of race was not so much to understand the differences in our bodies, but to try to justify why we lead such different lives. Why Else? Why would something as superficial as skin colour, or body shape matter otherwise? What the scientists really wanted to know was why some people are enslaved and others free, why some prosper while others are poor, and why some civilisations have thrived while others haven't.

What did racism offer to the poor in Britain?

The cultivation in the nineteenth century of a more or less coherent set of racist ideas also had an effect in the British home of Empire where it gave many desperately poor people living in slums and working in factories and mills a comforting sense of belonging to something great... Great Britain. Scientists and philosophers were keen to bracket these working class people into a racial category somewhere far below themselves, nevertheless the idea of a commonality between the rulers and ruled could be extremely useful. This was especially true as trade unions and social movements of the poor challenged the existing order. Racism offered workers a mechanism for advancement other than struggle – an appeal on the basis of common 'whiteness'.

The construction of 'whiteness' had been a long time in the making. In his ground breaking book, *The Invention of the White Race*, Theodore Allen writes that when the first Africans arrived in Virginia in 1619, there were no 'white' people there. Nor, according to colonial records, would there be for another sixty years. The Africans who were shipped to the Virginia plantations were slaves, bought and sold by Europeans who went on to colonise all of the Americas. The Europeans did not describe themselves as 'white', instead identifying themselves with the land they had come from — England, Holland, Ireland, and so on. The idea of 'whiteness' had yet to be constructed. On the basis of whiteness, came a whole ideology of social division and control. And, in the centuries that followed, it would help generate a 'science' of racial difference.

In Victorian Britain, the claimed superiority of whiteness was well established, in part through the direct involvement of ordinary people in the Empire's wars of conquest, and in helping rule over the colonies as soldiers or administrators. Yet the maintenance of chauvinistic ideas among the less well-off required real effort because in their daily interactions, and especially in their workplaces, workers from across the world were forced together. A walk around the Museum of Brands, Packaging and Advertising, London, is a glimpse into the way even the most everyday items were loaded with symbols of empire, from Colonial Crackers to Frank Rippingille's cooking stoves, which were advertised by barely clothed black men complete with fat lips and animal tooth necklaces. The purpose of this relentless, yet mundane reinforcement was to continually remind all those deemed 'white' of their anointed place.

This offer of status with little in the way of material benefit – in 1840 some 57 per cent of working-class children in Manchester died before their fifth birthday – was something closely analysed by the black American sociologist and campaigner WEB DuBois. He had sought to explain why racism won out over inter-racial solidarity in the era that followed the American Civil War and outlined what he called a 'psychological wage' paid to white labourers alone:

> They were given public deference and titles of courtesy because they were white. They were admitted freely with all classes of white people to public functions, public parks, and the best schools. The police were drawn from

their ranks, and the courts, dependent upon their votes, treated them with such leniency as to encourage lawlessness.

Du Bois's crucial point was that it was the rich and powerful who paid psychological wages to divide workers. After all, who else could grant them the kind of 'privileges' that he talks about? The aim was to offer small concessions to poor whites in order to make them believe they were superior to non-whites, and therefore divide all of those who were exploited. As DuBois explained:

> The theory of race was supplemented by a carefully planned and slowly evolved method, which drove such a wedge between the white and black workers that there probably are not today in the world two groups of workers with practically identical interests who hate and fear each other so deeply and persistently and who are kept so far apart that neither sees anything of common interest.

In nineteenth century Britain, it was the split between the English and Irish poor, rather than between black and white people that was the central divide, with the Irish racialised as 'other'. But DuBois' insight is equally valid here, and Satnam Virdee describes almost exactly the same processes at work:

> Being able to lay claim to membership of the ruling race of the nation proved a powerful means by which to justify Irish exclusion from 'good jobs', as well as others who could not be imagined as an organic element of this island race. It gave the English working class another strategy for improving its economic and political standing—one no longer dependent on the manufacture of a broad class-based solidarity, nor a frontal confrontation with the state—by simply asserting their legitimate rights as members of the British nation.

The bond of racism was strong but not so strong that it could withstand the waves of struggle that engulfed Britain in the 1880s when new trades unions were born out of the most militant strikes yet seen in Britain. Hundreds of thousands of lower skilled workers joined up, including dockers, gas workers, match women, picklers, bottlers, laundry workers and tailors. And alongside whites, and for the first time, women workers, into these ranks poured the Irish, Jewish, and Huguenot poor. The combined struggle of these members of new trade unions was to break down many of the stereotypes that had dominated for years, and before long many of the most famous strike leaders were those who had been once said to belong to 'racially inferior' groups.

The importance of this episode is that it both points to the limits of the psychological wage and offers us a way out of the vicious cycle of imperialism and prejudice. If in times of great collective struggle people can break with long held ideas about the world and their place in it, is that not proof that in the right circumstances the hold of racist ideas can be broken?

The period after the Second World War was a traumatic one for the great Empires of Europe. Not only had the war precipitated a great shake-up of the imperial order and placed the United States firmly at the top, but there were now huge challenges to empire from within. Anti-colonial movements spread across Asia and Africa demanding self-rule and the end of colonial subjection. India, the 'Jewel in the Crown' of the British Empire was in 1947 among the first to secede but soon many others would follow. In itself this would have led to a crisis for the racist ideology that surrounded colonialism – how was it that these 'inferior types' could now govern themselves? Imperialism itself was to survive the ending of most formal empires, in fact the competition between rival powers to control the newly independent states was to be a central feature of the Cold War with competition between the West and the Eastern Block and China. And this inter-imperialist rivalry required all manner of racist demagoguery to justify conflicts from Kenya, Suez, Palestine, Korea, to Vietnam.

The constant refreshing of the racist imagination was aided by the start of mass migration of peoples from the remnants of empire into the 'mother country' to fill the roles in rebuilding the nations wrecked by years of global conflict. But here the precise nature of racism was forced by circumstance to undergo a dramatic change. No longer were black and brown people best understood as inferior branches of the human species – the revelations of Nazi eugenics in the death camps of Auschwitz and beyond had made open discussion of this nature difficult – but instead the notion of separate races was gradually replaced by ideas of separate 'cultures' that were more or less compatible with white society. Racism in Britain during these times were characterised by themes of whites being overrun by people from the Caribbean, India, and Africa with the smells of their cooking and the sound of their music driving the natives mad.

And, perhaps more than anything, there was the terrifying prospect of the mixing of the races and maternity wards filled by lots of 'half-caste' babies that were neither one thing nor the other.

So, the new racism rested on many of the same stereotypical assumptions about Commonwealth migration that stemmed from the era of Empire, but had undergone a subtle transformation when applied to people now making a life in Britain. It is tempting to characterise this form of racism as being solely driven by the competition for jobs and housing, and the downwards pressure on wages. But in the same way that chauvinistic ideas that many English workers held towards the Irish were based on far more racialised concepts than mere economic competition, so too was the new racism directed at black and Asian people. Behind both lay the belief in the superiority of whiteness, and exclusion of certain categories of people from it – a way of thinking whose bedrock was in the days when Britannia ruled the waves.

The post-war focus on 'culture' as a metaphor for race was to prove particularly useful in the recurring military conflicts in the Middle East. The region had been at the centre of imperial rivalry since the collapse of the Ottoman Empire in the wake of the First World War – and most crucially, the discovery of huge oil reserves at a time when military advance became dependent on the combustion engine. The racist stereotypes of Arabs perpetually eager for war were combined with older tropes that described the people of the region as duplicitous and generally untrustworthy. Decades later these myths would be added to as justification for the new waves of imperialism that followed the end of the Cold War in the 1990s. With much of the focus of military intervention being the strategically vital Middle East, and countries just beyond it, the specifically Muslim nature of 'the enemy' became part of the pro-war propaganda. But this time around the West's wars were cast as the route to liberation for the poor and oppressed under the Islamic yoke. Women in particular found their struggles constantly invoked by those arguing for 'humanitarian intervention' – though generally not mentioned when the West's bombs rained down on their heads.

For the most loyal philosophers of empire 'Islam vs the West' became the fight of the coming new century. Harvard's Samuel P Huntington gave academic gloss to the jingoistic posturing of George Bushand Tony Blair and their talk of a 'New World Order'. In his 1996 book *The Clash of Civilizations and the Remaking of World Order*, Huntington considered Washington's need for a new adversary after the passing of the Soviet Union. In later works, he wrote, 'The ideal enemy for America would be ideologically hostile, racially and culturally different, and militarily strong enough to pose a credible threat to American security.' Islam and Muslims clearly fitted the bill.

Arun Kundnani unpacked the core components of this new Islamophobia that surrounded both Western military intervention in Afghanistan and Iraq, and the terrorist response that came soon after.

> Islamophobia is sometimes seen as a virus of hatred recurring in Western culture since the Crusades. Others view it as a spontaneous reaction to terrorism that will pass away as the effects of 9/11 recede into history. Many believe it does not exist. My emphasis is on Islamophobia as a form of structural racism directed at Muslims and the ways in which it is sustained through a symbiotic relationship with the official thinking and practices of the war on terror. Its significance does not lie primarily in the individual prejudices it generates but in its wider political consequences – its enabling of systemic violations of the rights of Muslims and its demonisation of actions taken to remedy those violations.

This demonisation required the construction of a racist picture of the 'enemy abroad', a ruthless warlord who lived in caves, feared the modern world and kept his wife and daughters in servitude. But the metaphor was soon extended to cover the 'enemy at home'. Here the common religion of Muslims in Britain and Muslims fighting in Afghanistan, Iraq and beyond was enough to declare joint enterprise. Of course, it was aided in being fixed in the public's view by the terrorist attacks that followed the wars in the Middle East, but the 'othering' of Muslims in Britain was happening long before that reaction.

In this the state became the key driver of Islamophobia, and the charge of 'systemic racism' chimes with that so clearly raised by the Black Lives Matter movement in the months following the police murder of George Floyd in 2020. The systemic approach rests heavily on the idea that racism exists to perform a specific 'function' within a capitalist society, that of creating and maintaining division – rather than merely reflecting the individual prejudices of people with biases. So the government's Prevent

Programme, for example, which is aimed at identifying and countering political and religious 'radicalisation' among individuals, acts as both a source of racism, and its ideological reinforcement. The programme, by singling out Muslims for special attention, acts as a specific racist threat to Muslims because of their perceived beliefs. And because of the way it places a duty upon all public sector bodies, and the personnel within them, to report behaviour which could be deemed indicative of extremism, it acts as a populariser of racist attitudes. That is to say it drives new waves of racism into the popular imagination. This interaction of state and individual was to manifest itself on the streets in the early 2010s: first in the form of the far right English Defence League, and then later under the guise of the Football Lads Alliance. Both were on occasion able to mobilise in their thousands against 'terrorism' – a euphemism for Muslims. And, this reaction is far from limited to Britain.

In Germany from 2015, a movement calling itself Pegida grew rapidly with a series of weekly demonstrations based mainly in the towns of the economically abandoned east. Its programme was specifically anti-Islam and far-right. In Hungary, Prime Minister Viktor Orban could claim to be defending 'European culture' from the Muslim hoard as his government persecuted refugees from Syria and beyond. But it is France where the logic of the Islamophobic state is being taken to new extremes. There the language of Islamophobia, once confined only to the large but somewhat isolated far right, has now became the norm, infecting mainstream discourse. The demand for the banning of the Muslim headscarves came after the successful 2011 campaign to ban the full-face veil in public places. But anyone who thought that the new polite society racism would only be directed at Muslims was wrong. It was in such a climate that President Macron, a poster boy for European liberals, could say, in 2017, 'Africa has a civilisational problem'.

Perhaps the most alarming recycling of empire racism has come not from its European heartlands but from within countries that were themselves colonised. The new India, announced to the world by Nehru in 1947, was supposed to be a state where all followers of all the nation's religions would be free to practice – it would be truly secular, despite the communal carnage that came with its birth. Today, under Narendra Modi and his hard right BJP party henchmen, the state has effectively declared war on Muslims and other religious and political minorities, while constantly seeking to ratchet up tensions with neighbouring Pakistan, particularly over the disputed status of Kashmir. New citizenship laws threaten to make millions of 'illegal migrants' stateless – even those who have lived on their land for thousands of years. Religious faith is now being made a condition of citizenship. In Assam in north India two million residents have been left off a citizen's register that requires proof of residency before 1971 when Bangladesh became an independent country. The actions of the Indian political elite have been followed up by attacks on Muslims by gangs of Hindu chauvinist thugs, often with the backing of the police. These were to culminate in anti-Muslim riots in New Delhi in 2020. Just as the British used divide and conquer as a means of controlling the Raj, today's ruling elite in India resort to the same techniques.

It is as though the tactics of the main powers, developed over hundreds of years of colonial oppression, have been distilled down by imperialism's junior partners now to be used against those it deems to be an 'enemy within'. This is done in the certain knowledge that they will not be contradicted by leaders of the 'free world' who have chosen similar targets for similar reasons.

It's no wonder that statues and monuments to Britain's faded imperial glory become targets of Black Lives Matter campaigners in the summer of 2020. The rage on the streets of Bristol, where the statue of slave trader Edward Coulson was toppled and then rolled into the river, was not aimed at erasing or washing away the memory of the empire, slavery and colonialism. Instead, it demanded that we consider how our present is connected to our past. One of the movement's many achievements was to show that what is 'remembered' about imperialism, and what is conveniently 'forgotten', are not accidents of a historical process. When the UK Secretary of State for Education insists that black history will not be on the national history curriculum, but insists that Britain's 'proud' past will, that is a political decision. The choice concerns how Britain today sees itself as a nation, and what place now exists for those of us descended from people who were enslaved or colonised. And this is not limited to Britain; it is a choice facing the US, Europe, and Australia.

And, while mass anti-racism has galvanised those against oppression, it has sown fear in the ranks of our rulers. They are terrified that their carefully cultivated myths of white superiority and the inimitable 'greatness' of Great Britain are now at best tainted, and at worst, trashed. What future can there be for Britain when the young continually demand 'decolonisation', they ask. Post-Brexit Britain has revealed the country to be something of a third rate power, with its component parts in Scotland and Northern Ireland straining to break away. Meanwhile the Oxbridge and Eton-educated elite, whose wealth and privileges tend to date back to the days of slavery, desperately attempt to continue the charade. For millions of people in Britain even the purchasing power of 'psychological wage' that DuBois detailed has declined to the point that black British scholar Paul Gilroy could write, 'there's a poverty of imagination compounded by anxiety and depression. Let's face it, whiteness isn't worth what it used to be worth. Its value is falling globally.'

One of Black Lives Matter's greatest political strengths has been the way it asked us to understand racism as 'structural' – that is to say, deeply entwined with capitalism as an economic and political system. Rather than seeing racial prejudice in terms of 'individual injury' and focusing on attempts at personal liberation, the movement looked towards the collective. The impact of the Covid-19 pandemic upon the Global South, and the disproportionate way it hit black and Asian people in Britain, has reinforced the idea that there is something systemic about racism. One of the beauties of this approach is the way that it opens the door to solidarity between people who experience an array of different forms of oppression, so it was not accident to find that many young people who joined their first ever demonstrations during the summer of Black Lives Matter had by this spring moved on and were now on the streets in protest at the Israeli bombing of Gaza. For many it was a common sense connection to see the hand of the system behind both racism and the oppression of the Palestinian people. No wonder then that a mural of George Floyd painted on Israel's separation wall in the West Bank became an emblem of global struggle, and that protesters in East Jerusalem held placards that declared, 'From USA to Palestine, Racism is a Crime'.

Herein lies the hope for a better tomorrow. If those who continue to suffer from oppressions rooted in imperialism can find common cause with others exploited by the same system, then the divides intended to keep us subordinate can truly be broken.

CULTURE WARS

Samia Rahman

In March 2021, the market town of Batley in West Yorkshire found itself splashed across UK national news headlines. A teacher at the secondary grammar school had, as part of a lesson on free speech, allegedly shown his class a cartoon of the Prophet Mohammad. The image was taken from the controversial French satirical newspaper *Charlie Hebdo* and depicted the Prophet wearing a turban that was hiding a bomb. A Muslim parent complained and the teacher was immediately suspended pending an inquiry. What should have been a matter for the school to investigate and resolve sensitively, became a stage upon which actors of the so-called culture wars of our times played out their drama. Proponents of freedom of expression were in uproar, while hysterical media reporting led to burgeoning anti-blasphemy protests outside the school gate seemingly led by those with no direct connection to the incident. The teacher, warmly described by right-wing tabloids as a 'rugby-loving, burly, Yorkshire lad' was said to fear for his life after receiving death threats. With a chill, thoughts turned to the horrific murder of teacher Samuel Paty in France, beheaded after a similar accusation of having shown *Charlie Hebdo* images to his school pupils. The number of protestors, mostly young Muslim men from outside the area, began to swell. Commentators of all stripes and persuasions derided the group and swiftly conflated them with anyone expressing concern at the teacher's actions. This 'mob' and its tacit cheerleaders were dismissed as ignorant, reactionary, an affront to British values of free speech and tolerance. Hand-wringing at what must be done to counter the likes of such fanatics and their ilk rebounded. After all, weren't they letting the side down and feeding anti-Muslim sentiment with their emotive and irrational response?

Elsewhere, former chairwoman of the Conservative Party, Baroness Warsi, was tweeting her own response to the blasphemy furore. Having spoken to those involved, she indicated that objection to the use of the cartoons arose because it created 'a hostile atmosphere and led to Islamophobic discourse and language'. Pupils had been left upset. 'Islamic bullying in the playground is well-documented and taunts such as "terrorist" are regularly used, leading to issues around mental health and poor educational outcomes'. This resonated. I remember, as a youngster at my predominantly white, grammar school in leafy, middle-class Surrey, sitting through a lesson on immigration. The ugly and unmediated views that were unexpectedly unleashed by classmates I hitherto considered to be my friends left myself and the only other non-white girl in the class in tears. The teacher was unwilling or unable to challenge the racist rhetoric and bigoted attitudes being bandied around, having given little thought to how, after introducing the topic, it should evolve into a constructive discussion.

Warsi's attempt to contextualise the incident was an exception amidst the barrage of sensationalised column inches and hot takes. The saga was caricatured as yet another battle in the culture wars seemingly sinking holes in today's world order, as Warsi herself recognised: 'unfortunately this matter has been hijacked by extremists on both sides, to, kind of, create this culture war.' That she should evoke this trend whereby incidents are framed as symbolic of a deep cultural schism irrevocably dividing society, is telling. Certainly the media and various political stakeholders have decided that culture wars are an unquestionable plague ravaging the premised cohesion of our communities. Just as extremists are said to have jumped on the respective bandwagons in Batley's blasphemy quagmire, radicals are blamed for playing a dangerous and intractable game of cultural tug of war with issues and debates, which leave the apparently sensible middle ground floundering. But is it really all that it is made out to be?

To insist we are in the midst of a culture war would be to claim that all of what we are witnessing in the early twenty first century is a uniquely contemporary occurrence. But how did the criteria for what constitutes a front for the culture wars, no longer isolated events that are the culmination of their own specific pre-conditions, come to be solidified? The journey to this point has been a long one. The concept of culture wars can in fact be traced back to Otto van Bismarck's attempt to curtail the power and influence of the church after German reunification. One of his supporters, the German physician Rudolf Virchow, known as the 'father of modern pathology', described what he termed *kulturkampf* or 'culture struggle'. This would eventually come to define the morality-based sentiment of what we today regard as culture wars. Just as with the incident at Batley Grammar School, education was the field in which skirmishes, in this case between warring Protestant and Catholic factions, saw intellectual swords drawn.

It wasn't until the 1990s, however, that sociologist and author James Davison Hunter introduced the term and its ideas into the mainstream. This came at a time when postmodern theory dominated critical thought. Some years earlier, in the mid 1980s, Fredric Jameson unpacked the postmodern notion of fragmentation and its relationship with post-industrial characteristics of capitalism in his book, *Postmodernism, or the Cultural Logic of Late Capitalism*. He identified the impact of this new way of working upon the human psyche, and the feelings of meaninglessness it spawned: 'In psychological terms we may say that as a service economy we are henceforth so far removed from the realities of production and work that we inhabit a dream world of artificial stimuli and televised experience.'

The cumulative effect of this social and economic shift lead to what postmodernists positively identified as the 'fragmentation' that gripped communities in the West, and across Europe. This was initially celebrated as having the effect of liberating individuals from the conformities of absolute and rigid identities, but eventually it became clear that without the existence of reality, a person's capacity to articulate the systemic injustices visited upon them may be derailed. The late economic anthropologist, David Graeber, wrote extensively over the past couple of decades on this fragmentation and how it could be addressed by re-introducing the notion of working for the common good, which had previously been a source of fulfilment and meaning in people's lives. However, neoliberalism marched on, the tech revolution pummelled and while postmodernism soon became unfashionable, fragmentation was now ingrained. Liquid modernity, described by the late British sociologist, Zygmunt Bauman, emerged and the seeds of today's perceived culture wars were sown. Societies all but abandoned the search for meaning and instead became tourists, hurtling from one transient social experience to another, constantly on the look-out for the next thrill to tick off the bucket list of mindless experiences.

For Hunter, the response of society to late capitalism's perfect storm of liquid modernity, and its psychological impact, was an indelible fault-line dividing orthodox and progressive worldviews. Nowhere was this more pronounced than in the US. As a newly fractured society devoid of a collective sense of purpose, the culture wars became a fight 'over the meaning of America, who we have been in the past, who we are now, and perhaps more important, who we, as a nation, will aspire to become'. Divided nations and societies are nothing new, there are endless examples of civil war, coups, revolution and sectarian or communal conflict throughout history, each with their own specific cauldron of conditions that brought them to the boil. What is specific to today's antipathy is that division permeates significantly deeper than mere disagreement. Who hasn't heard the old adage that in polite society religion and politics are unacceptable topics of conversation at dinner parties. What Hunter identified since the 1980s was an abandonment of that unspoken rule. At the same time, a demarcation along the lines of distinct world views burrowed deep into societal consciousness. Each side remained passionately and vehemently convinced that they are right and the other is wrong. What's more, it was argued that two clear doctrines had emerged, separating people who subscribed to an interconnected set of value-laden views. A position taken on any one particular controversial issue, would very likely indicate where a person stands on a range of other topics.

As Hunter's work on culture wars gained prominence, his ideas were becoming popularised in a different field altogether, one which would seize upon the theory in a way that would come to alter the world order as we know it. In 1992, one year after Hunter had published *Culture Wars: The Struggle to Define America*, Pat Buchanan, American conservative politician and broadcaster, stood in front of a rapturous audience at the 1992 Republican National Convention, and, with the oratory and zeal of an evangelical preacher spelled out a warning: 'There is a religious war going on in this country. It is a cultural war, as critical to the kind of nation we shall be as the Cold War itself.' This call to arms had a profound cumulative impact on US voters over the coming decades. By tapping into hardly distant memories of the cold war, an ideological war that the US was widely considered to have won, Buchanan was grasping for a new enemy to distract conservative voters in their search for meaning in their lives. Just as British documentary filmmaker Adam Curtis had hypothesised in his documentary *The Power of Nightmares,* the politics of fear – whether it takes the form of perpetuating the fear of Islamism in the Arab world, in the absence of communism, to feed the growth of US neoconservatism – proved, in time, to be an impeccably effective tool to unite societies and rouse them in support of populist right-wing movements that would come to form the shadowy umbrella alt-right movement. It's agenda propelled Donald Trump to the US presidency and is thought to have fuelled the hate that motivated the Christchurch attack and other acts of anti-Muslim violence. Finding an enemy against which one can define one-self, is crucial to strengthening identity. It is when the enemy is not exclusively the 'other' but is a set of values that already resides within spaces in which you exist and seemingly seeks to assert itself upon your vision of the future and the past, taking your institutions and laws and social norms in a direction to which you are vehemently opposed, that the perceived war gets truly ugly.

In his speech, Buchanan nakedly exploited this move away from individuals seeing themselves as workers, and regarding themselves instead as cultural consumers. He presented to voters a populist vision of traditional culture as the moral foundation upon which global politics is based. Only the realisation of this vision could offer meaning to the lives of citizens and provide a truly positive framework for living for them to aspire to. As Hunter opines, the enmity is no longer between different groups as it was in the past, whether they be religiously or geographically separate, but instead within groups, divided loosely according to either traditional or progressive worldviews. Buchanan, freshly frustrated in his attempt to secure the Republican presidential nomination which was won by George Bush Senior, turned his ire on Democratic nominee Bill Clinton. His message was clear – by electing Clinton there would be a capitulation in moral values. He took a series of relatively fringe yet incendiary issues of the time that he said Clinton stood for – feminism, LGBT rights, environmentalism and education, and packaged them as a front in a war for the soul of the nation. Each 'side' can be assured collective views will orient on values-based topics, and so individuals can clearly choose whether they are with the 'progressives' or 'traditionalists'.

This is a persuasive and neat vision, but in Batley, the lines blurred. The anti-blasphemy protestors would most likely regard themselves as the upholders of 'traditional' values, such as demanding respect for religious sensibilities – a view that could align with Buchanan and his supporters. Those defending free speech no doubt fervently regard themselves to be protecting traditional British values of freedom of expression and the right to blaspheme. Would they therefore be allied with the progressives? As we can see there are many inconsistencies in the culture wars we are supposedly fighting.

The inconsistencies become even more glaring if we take a closer look at the various issues that have become vicious tenets of contestation. The fear of traditionalists is that progressives are seeking to dismantle systems and 'the order of things' that have been part of the social fabric for decades, centuries even. In 2020, protests took place across the world calling for statues of prominent slave-owners to be taken down. Accusations that this was an attempt to erase history or distort the past to suit twenty-first century discernment erupted among traditionalists and the reactionary right-wing media. Yet, as Rahul Rao of SOAS at the University of London, who is writing a book on the politics of controversial statues, explains, the building of slave-owner statues was often an assertion of white supremacy during periods of anti-racist struggle. The majority of confederate statues were built during two specific periods: either in the first two decades of the 1900s when Jim Crow laws were being introduced by southern US states to segregate public spaces or in the 1950s and 1960s when the civil rights movement was fighting for desegregation. The statue in Bristol of the Atlantic slave-owner Edward Colston was erected almost 150 years after his death, in 1895, at the height of the colonial project. Rao states: 'controversies about statues aren't mainly about the past. They are almost always about the present.' The idea that statues are neutral markers of the past is a fallacy. Any notion that the removal of statues threatens the preservation of a nation's history is absurd. Commemoration is not the same as education. If statues are intended to celebrate a moment in a community's history, they should not be an affront to members of that same community, however marginalised or part of a minority they may be. This is not censure or erasure, but a recognition of the decontextualised nature of statues of people. British journalist and academic, Gary Younge, wrote recently that he considers all statues, regardless of how derided or eulogised the person, to be distortions of the history they claim to represent. This is because moments in history are never really about one person – but about the structures that enabled them to elevate their legacy beyond others.

One man who was determined to preside in monumental form was Cecil Rhodes, considered by many to be one of the architects of apartheid. Campaigners in South Africa fought for his statues to be pulled down. They did this to reclaim the space he held and from which they felt excluded. Rao argues that by doing the same, the US can begin 'to re-imagine American identity in non-racist ways', particularly because, as Hunter theorises, culture is how we now have come to define purpose and identity as societies. Emma Dabiri, Irish-Nigerian author and academic, has explained that the culture wars discourse tied to statues and identity politics and race hugely simplifies the white/black binary that was invented in 1661 by the colonial British in the Caribbean, to justify the enslavement of Africans which the economies of Europe were becoming increasingly dependent upon. This was done by associating inferior characteristics to the black race and superior characteristics to their 'masters', the white race. Immediately prior to this categorisation, indentured Irish labourers as well as enslaved Africans had been embroiled in revolts against English and Scottish landlords, who they jointly perceived as their common enemy. The introduction of the idea of 'white superiority' explains Dabiri, was a device used by the governing classes to undermine the solidarity that had bound those active in Irish and African uprisings against shared experiences of oppression.

If the culture wars of our times are merely a series of flashpoints that societies are navigating in an effort to re-imagine identity in non-racist ways, then surely that can only be a good thing. But for some who have always reaped the benefits of 'the order of things', anti-racism is interpreted as oppression when they feel the loss of that privilege. Whether this is a tangible loss is open to question, however, despite all the talk of 'woke' armies leaving everyone terrified of 'saying the wrong thing'. Discussion of injustice and the capitalist system that upholds structures of oppression therefore become hijacked by superficial debates on the policing of language and behaviour. When the world rose up in fury at the murder of African-American George Floyd, by a white policeman, performative acts of anti-racist allyship belied any tangible change as the roll call of deaths of African-Americans at the hands of white police officers persists. The commodification of culture compelled brands and celebrities to make statements, pledges, stands, for fear that by not doing so they would damage the optics of where they stand in this particular culture war, which could cause profit margins to falter. Instagram posts were littered with decontextualised quotes from iconic figures such as Audre Lorde, James Baldwin, bell hooks and Malcolm X, reducing complex ideas and nuance to bite-size digestible blurbs of meaninglessness that is served up as an apparently irreproachable embodiment of cultural values. After all, who doesn't want to be seen to be on the side of Black Lives Matter, however superficially? Everyone apparently, but only as long as it doesn't make them uncomfortable.

In November 2020, Tory MP Ben Bradley lamented to the House of Commons that the UK Equality Act should explicitly protect the rights of straight white men and claimed it failed to do so. His mourning of the death of blokey banter, and calls for a Minister for Men, were met with derision. However, his sense of grievance garnered sympathy among those who feel their power diminished by demands for equity, and who are becoming convinced that they are the aggrieved party in the so-called culture wars. Claims to victimhood can be traced to the aftermath of a very real war, as Joseph Darda details in *How White Men Won the Culture Wars*. Just as Pat Buchanan compared the culture war with the fight to overcome communism, Darda considers the trajectory from the permissive 1960s cultural revolution and the social unrest to which US soldiers returned in 1975 after their defeat in Vietnam. What his research found was that Vietnam veterans co-opted the discourse and approach of the protest movement to illustrate their unease at the transformed society they encountered when returning from the war. Interestingly, despite the fact that US soldiers serving in Vietnam were predominantly working-class men of colour, narratives of trauma and marginalisation were created to depict dispossessed white, middle-class men cast aside by the new politics they had stepped back to. The poster boy for such grievance was Alan Bakke, a former Marine who had served in Vietnam. In 1978 he took the

University of California to court after twice having his medical school application rejected, claiming that he was a victim of reverse discrimination. He alleged that the newly introduced quota system discriminated against him, a white and well-qualified applicant. The Supreme Court found in his favour and the verdict set a precedent that quotas could not be used and affirmative action programmes could only be pursued with the aim of ensuring diversity within the student body. The historic systematic and deliberate exclusion of African-Americans from university admissions was therefore not acknowledged or addressed and racial justice became re-engineered through the watered-down lens of diversity. By manufacturing the existence of a culture war and casting themselves as its victims, the dominant group is able to resist any attempt at redressing injustice. This is, according to Darda, how white men have won the culture war, and why it is in their interests to perpetuate the myth of its malignancy.

Whether it is moral panic about statues, hysteria at critical race theory or frenzied talk of so-called 'cancel culture' and 'no-platforming', those who draw another line in the so-called culture wars do so by decontextualising events to preserve victimless victimhood. What started with populist right-wing appeals targeting the aching chasm of emptiness felt by blue-collar workers in the US, has proliferated across the ocean to permeate Europe and elsewhere. It is not the case that we are importing US culture wars to the UK and the rest of Europe, what is occurring is the deliberate stoking of a perception that we are in the midst of a culture war anywhere; to distract and demonise those fighting injustice; to maintain the status quo that social and racial justice movements are attempting to disrupt. The protestors at Batley Grammar School were dismissed and reviled by the same elements in the right-wing British press and political arena that claim Muslims are exceptionalised and protected from any and every critique.

Nowhere has this belief caught hold more ferociously than in France. Just as the anti-blasphemy protestors in Batley stubbornly refused to fit into the neatly parcelled culture wars of our nightmares, perceived polarisation in France has also mutated from the meticulously choreographed progressive vs conservative melee to a blurred fusion of ideologies causing right-wing politicians to spout their incredulity via the platforms provided by right-wing media outlets. This was the scenario when French Minister for Higher Education and Research, Frédérique Vidal, told populist CNews that 'Islamo-leftism is plaguing the entire society'. Her alarmist statement referred to a conspiracy theory that alleges so-called 'Islamo-left' views are beginning to dominate French academic culture, due to imported US 'campus wars'. France's aversion to religion is rooted in its revolution, and the notion of *laïcité*, which is conventionally defined in universalist terms to mean that French identity transcends any cultural, social or individual sense of belonging. This is in direct contrast with multiculturalism, which is growing in popularity among younger generations who are drawn to its validation and recognition of the cultural diversity of their lived realities. Just as with the incident at Batley Grammar School and Otto van Bismarck's *kulturkampf*, education is once again the battle ground.

In 1882, French schools and universities introduced the notion of republicanism so that French education would effectively create the ideal French citizen. In 1946, *laïcité* first appeared within a legal framework to reinforce the theory of universalism, or the commitment to remaining blind, or neutral, to expressions of identity that did not conform to specific French ideals. Such assimilation is an unsustainable model, however, in a culturally fluid society. The rigidity of identity that was once upon a time radical and emancipatory has become oppressive, and the non-negotiable notion of what it means to be a model French citizen is now being disrupted by the left and minority communities. This solidarity among marginalised groups has panicked the French establishment who have responded to the dissolving of ideological demarcations by creating the myth of a culture war. The supposition is that an ideological alliance has been forged between the brutal and frightening external enemy in the form of Islamist networks infiltrating France and parts of Europe, and leftist academics and intellectuals who are, essentially, the puppet masters, an elite internal enemy who have formed a front to push a Marxist agenda and undermine the capitalist world order. It is by powering this paranoia that any clamour for change, for example the anti-racist renaissance brought about by the world-wide convulsion at the murder of George Floyd in 2020, may be delegitimised. This is also illustrated by responses to the horrific terrorist attacks in

France in recent years. These attacks have elicited emotional invective aimed at French Muslim communities. At times of crisis civil liberties should be reinforced, yet the opposite is occurring. Attempts, particularly in higher education institutions to talk about identity and radicalisation with nuance has led to wild accusations of siding with terrorists by anti-Muslim sections of the right-wing media and political establishment. Trying to highlight racial and social injustice or any attempt to understand and contextualise events is branded as trying to excuse Islamist extremism.

In the UK, those sections of the media and political establishment that flirt with the alt-right, are obsessed with cultural symbols as a bellwether of tradition, with Tory MPs and even members of the opposition endorsing the flying of flags at schools as a crude show of loyalty to the nation, or police sent to protect statues from so-called 'woke militants'. In France, meanwhile, it is 'La République' which must have its sanctity preserved. Both are presented as needing constant defending from imagined enemies, which cannot always be imagined, so with an enemy that is impossible to locate, one must be constructed, and the most effective way to do that is to apply that violence to actual bodies. Outrage over faux distortions of history is simply a consequence of the narcissism of post-imperial countries who negate the horror of that history and, significantly, their imagined relationships with that past. Brexit is perhaps one of the most insidious manifestations of this in recent years. In France it translates into a defensiveness of discourse around colonialism with France's implicated role in such horrors barely acknowledged. Instead, jaw-droppingly offensive commemorative landmarks are protected, such as the naming of an avenue in Paris after Marshal Thomas Robert Bugeaud, Governor-General of Algeria in the nineteenth century, whose barbaric military strategy included inventing gas chambers to orchestrate the mass murder of thousands of Algerians. The role of France in the holocaust, meanwhile also remains censored, with any mention of France's Nazi past provoking a clamour of 'offended' voices across the political spectrum. The ideas that the 'woke' left is cancelling anyone who disagrees with a progressive position is not borne out by the reality. Rather, fear of the past goes beyond anti-Semitism and Islamophobia in the UK and France, both of which are widely prevalent, although it could be argued that Islamophobia has more political capital, and also has spun a money-making model of its own where anti-Muslim sentiment can prove lucrative and career-enhancing, as former extremist and author, Ed Hussain's recently published factually compromised book *Among the Mosques* proves. The concerns of Muslims, such as the parents at Batley Grammar, are dismissed as hyper-sensitive and reactionary, while any attempt to contextualise the atrocities of a nation's war-mongering past is deemed a grave insult.

Manufacturing culture wars serves to uphold a neoliberal, conservative, capitalist and anti-environmental agenda that centres financial growth and continued levels of consumption, allowing little possibility for alternative futures. Governments compete with populist far-right factions, fanned by sensationalist media reporting, by mainstreaming the rhetoric of extreme right-wing discourse. In France it has served the Macron government's interests to perpetuate the menace of Islamo-leftism while in the US, and the UK, 'critical race theory' is the new harbinger of social disintegration. The ease with which such smears have become mainstreamed has been possible due to the incendiary combination of social media, which seems to operate within its own ecosystem of faux outrage, and the calling out and cancelling of people, that rarely permeates lived realities. In more extreme cases someone may lose their job after a social media pile-on, but being cancelled is always only ever temporary and the right-wing media will give acres of air time and column inches to someone who without a twinge of irony will not keep quiet about being silenced! Twitter seems to reward outrage and fan the flames of hysteria while Facebook is a mine of misinformation and confirmation bias. On top of this the concept of 'fake news' routinely trips off the tongue of those who wish to cast doubt on anything that is contrary to their world view. People are quick to insist something they refuse to believe is fake news, declaring it to be fake news merely because they said it is, rather than engage with the issue in any way, shape or form. Refusing to engage with an argument, and instead focusing on semantics or delivery in order to achieve a 'win', has been particularly problematic when looking at the impact of identity politics on culture war discourse.

This reductive component has been utilised by both sides, but has inflicted the most damage on progressive arguments in the culture war construct. Terms that were initially used to denote awareness of the power of language to oppress, and an attentiveness to injustice, whatever form it takes, have been co-opted, stripped of all historical context and meaning, before being weaponised by the right and used as a term of derision against those who once wore the badge with pride. The alt-right has encouraged the idea that labels such as 'woke' are used by cultural elites against the masses who wish to express themselves without having to consider the impact of their words. Once again, just as with the case of Alan Bakke, we witness the claim of victimless victimhood by those who already benefit from existing power structures and are uncomfortable with being confronted with consequences for harmful speech or behaviour.

This is not to deny that the often dogmatic and intolerant policing of language that occurs in the goldfish bowl that is social media can be alienating, alongside providing ammunition for those who seek to cast traditionalists as the victims of a curtailing of freedom of expression, which may as well translate as the right to be racist, sexist, homophobic, transphobic, offensive, and so on. Shaming, and calling out as a means of achieving political, social, and cultural change, can be counter-productive. Dismantling structural racism and responding to institutional racism does not start with hollow mantras that lack the rudimentary understanding of the way in which race, or specifically whiteness, was constructed. Instead of organising and activism, digital spats around language create the impression of the imposition of a racial binary onto every issue at the expense of the very real and continued struggle at the lack of political traction. All the while the focus of the media is on the simplified ascribing of power to white people and powerlessness to people of colour and micromanaging behaviour and obsession with language that leads to victimless victimhood. The reaction to discourse around white privilege has been furious among white people, particularly middle-class men who erroneously feel they are now without any of the advantages they have been accustomed to, and are in fact actively discriminated against.

Listening to populist politicians and right wing media, you would be forgiven for despairing that culture wars are wreaking havoc and inflicting chaos and division. However, this cultural cleansing campaign is more a manufactured moral panic than a tornado ripping through the heart of the world order. A 2021 report by King's College London revealed how irrelevant to people's lives such discourse around culture wars actually is and the media's and populist government's deliberate inflaming of the issue. In 2020, 534 articles on culture wars featured in UK media compared with just twenty-one in 2015. Despite this, the study found that half the UK population has little clue what the term 'woke' means, with the other half evenly split between those who consider being called 'woke' a compliment and those who consider it an insult. In addition, most people asked about which issues they thought of in relation to the term 'culture wars' could not come up with any at all.

Division and dissent are organic facets of any functioning society and while social media has intensified the fault lines of disunity today, the culture wars phenomenon is more an exercise in distraction than rooted in real life. By claiming to be free speech martyrs, those perpetuating a moral panic around culture wars are obscuring what is little more than an electoral strategy procured by the alt-right to undermine and delegitimise social and racial justice initiatives that challenge their domination of the world order. Polarisation and ratcheting up extremism is creating false grievances, which cynically exploit people's fears and their need to locate the enemy that resides in the darkest recesses of their imagination. In our self-absorbed world that is uncomfortable with restorative collective action, conflating identity with meaning, and meaning with cultural values, and cultural values with our singular, narrow and dogmatic world view, erodes social cohesion and trust. The toxic political and media landscape that has concocted this war to maintain its hegemony will continue to turn disparate local issues, such as a school safeguarding issue in the Yorkshire town of Batley, into a battle in the concocted culture wars, where points-scoring and commodified outrage dehumanise us all.

AN ECONOMY FIT FOR PURPOSE

Colin Tudge

If we want the world order to change for the better, a world that is fit for humanity and our fellow creatures to live in, or indeed one where it is possible to live in, then everything we do and think has to be conducive to that end. We need to spell out our goal in life very clearly: know what we are trying to achieve; we have to develop the right technologies and the right practices – farming, building, and the rest; and we have to have the right mindset, and in particular cultivate an attitude of kindness, cooperativeness, and compassion, as opposed to the ruthless competitiveness that now prevails and is apparently supposed to be both necessary and virtuous.

But right in the middle of all our thinking and action is the infrastructure: the way we organise our affairs: the nature of governance – top down or bottom up; the law; and, holding everything together, the economy. The economy in practice is played out as a game of money, or as a whole complex of interacting games of money, and since money is the universal currency, the instantly understandable symbol of material worth and the most convenient medium of trade, that is perhaps inevitable. In truth, though, the economy is much more than that. It is the mechanism, the means, by which we, humanity, seek to translate our aspirations into practice and hence into reality. In practice then, *the economy is the matrix, the context, of our lives* – and indeed, since human beings are such an influential species, it is the context of all life on Earth. We have to get it right: to ensure that we have the right aspirations in the first place, that we are trying to do good and appropriate things; and that the economy is structured to enable good and appropriate things to come about.

In practice, very few societies have ever managed to install an economy that works as well as it should and surely could – for the benefit of all humankind and the biosphere (where 'biosphere' means 'the living world'). The system that now prevails worldwide – the variant of capitalism known as neoliberalism – is a disaster, even though its principal architect, Milton Friedman of Chicago (1912–2006), was awarded a Nobel Prize for his efforts; and so too was Friedrich Hayek (1899–1992) who first inspired Friedman. (Has the idea of the Nobel Prize past its sell-by date? How can we predict the long-term effects of innovations, however ingenious or well-intentioned?). Coupled with uncritical technophilia, the conviction that high-tech can solve all our problems and that nothing else can, the neoliberal mindset is threatening to kill us all.

To put things right we first need to ask what's gone wrong, and why. In truth the problem lies not simply with the present economy, or indeed with any particular economic system, but with the entire discipline of economics.

What's wrong with economics?

The greatest economists, like the greatest scientists, are able as many are not to put their own subject into perspective. They acknowledge that for all the brilliance of and importance of its insights, their chosen discipline is limited in its scope and vision and cannot answer all of life's problems. As one of the greatest of all economists, John Maynard Keynes (1883–1946) put the matter, in an ideal future:

> the economic problem will take the back seat where it belongs … and the arena of heart and head will be occupied where it belongs, or reoccupied by our real problems, the problems of life and human relations, of creation, and of behaviour and religion.

Keynes also commented, apparently in conversation: 'If economists could manage to get themselves thought of as humble, competent people on a level with dentists, that would be splendid.'

In short, economists are indeed vital for the smooth running of complex societies but in the end, like dentists, they are technicians. They carry out essential tasks and must train long and hard to become expert at what they do and so should be respected and well rewarded. Like everyone else in a democratic society, they should be free to think and be able to contribute to the general flow of life. But economists *qua* economists are not prophets, or gurus, or even philosophers. We should not rely on them to shape our lives or indeed, as in practice is the case, to determine who should thrive and who should go to the wall, or to decide the fates of other creatures and the fabric of the Earth.

One fundamental mistake has been to suppose that economics is a *bona fide* science – and to compound this mistake by assuming that science really is the royal road to truth and indeed to wisdom. As the Cambridge economist Joan Robinson (1903–1983) observed:

> All along [economics] has been striving to escape from sentiment and to win for itself the status of a science ... [but] ... lacking the experimental method, economists are not strictly enough compelled to reduce metaphysical concepts to falsifiable terms and cannot compel each other to agree as to what has been falsified. So, economics limps along with one foot in untested hypotheses and the other in untestable slogans.

To be sure, economics can be made to look like a *bona fide* science not least because its textbooks are festooned with mathematical symbols and formulae – but, said Joan Robinson: 'I never learned mathematics, so I had to think'. Then again, even if the ideas in the economics textbooks were *bona fide* science, and the blizzard of maths really did encapsulate testable ideas that had been rigorously tested, that still would not mean that they are cast-iron and all-embracing. The insights even of the best-established science are always provisional. In fact, if we really want to get to grips with economics and so sort out the wheat from the chaff, it may be better not to try to learn about it formally *via* its standard texts. As the English economist Kate Raworth comments in *Doughnut Economics*: 'Every now and again, being untutored can be an intellectual asset—and this is one of those moments.'

Certainly, the present well-nigh disastrous state of the world on all fronts suggests that the discipline of economics for all its mathematical pretensions and the eminence of some of its practitioners falls far short of what humanity and our fellow creatures really need. In this as in all things, we need to start again from first principles – with the innocence of the untutored. So here is my own untutored take on things, starting with the questions: what are we trying to achieve – and what, if any, are the basic principles?

Our Goals

Oddly – and fatally! – governments rarely ask this question, and still less do they provide a satisfactory answer. Most governments, including the most influential, are content with vacuous though pernicious slogans. The Americans under Donald Trump were invited to 'Make America great again!', where 'great' was evidently equated with global dominance. In Britain the politicians and business leaders who backed Brexit exhorted us to 'Take back control!', which in practice means, 'Cede what is left of control to the global "free" market and to the transnational corporates who in practice preside over it!'

In contrast, in my latest book, *The Great Re-Think*, I suggest that all humanity should be trying to create 'convivial societies, with personal fulfilment, within a flourishing biosphere'. 'Biosphere' is a far better term than the more usual 'environment', which simply means 'surroundings' and is commonly equated with real estate, and given a cash value. My own slogan is only a suggestion (I do not aspire to be a prophet, authorised from on high to tell humanity how to live) but I have invited a great many people from all walks of life to try to improve on this suggestion and nobody has, so far, and until they do, I will stick with it. I further suggest, albeit simplistically, that all actions and ideas that contribute to the cause of conviviality, personal fulfilment, and the wellbeing of the natural world can reasonably be considered to be 'good', and all that detract from it are 'bad'. The neoliberal economic system that now prevails seems, by this criterion, to be the precise opposite of what's needed. It exacerbates social inequality and injustice, and the discontent that results, and it is wrecking the natural world.

In all our attempts to frame a better world we need to ask three basic questions:

1: What is it good to do?
2: What is it necessary to do? And
3: What is possible?

So long as what's possible exceeds what is necessary, we are in with a chance. When what is necessary exceeds what is possible, we are in trouble. Right now, it's touch and go. 'Life as we know it', as they say in *Star Trek*, hangs by a thread.

Question 1 is approached via moral philosophy and questions 2 and 3 are best approached through science, and in particular via the somewhat neglected science of ecology. Thus, I suggest, all *human action should be guided by the principles of morality and ecology*. Those principles can reasonably be considered 'bedrock'. Indeed, these are the only principles that truly deserve to be called 'principles'. Political principles are mere ideologies, which is not the same thing at all; and economic 'principles' in the end are just wheezes. Both morality and ecology – indeed all science – in the end are rooted in metaphysics: premises that are of supreme importance which we can and should think about but are beyond exhaustive analysis. Of course, it is fashionable to argue that 'morality' is too vague a concept; that different individuals and different societies have different conceptions of it, and that what is good in one society is bad in another, so that morality in the end is just a matter of opinion. But people who argue this (including some who are considered to be 'intellectuals') for the most part simply confuse moral principles with manners – which obviously do vary from time to time and from place to place. For in practice the moral codes of all people everywhere are primarily defined by the underlying religion – for even the most 'secular' countries, like Britain, have a religious past. And for all their differences in doctrine and ritual, all *bona fide* religions (as opposed to cults) emphasise the moral principles of *compassion, humility*, and *an attitude of reverence towards the natural world*. Notice that all but one of the chapters of the Qur'an begin by praising 'the compassionate one'. Christians tend to speak of 'love'. Cynics are wont to suggest that human beings are 'naturally' selfish and incapable of sustained compassion but modern biology and common observation suggest that this just isn't so. The most effective survival tactic is to cooperate, and cooperativeness is best underpinned by a true concern for the welfare of others – which is compassion. Compassion, in short, far from being an invention of 'civilisation', is a Darwinian prediction.

Economies, I suggest, have very rarely – in fact never – been consciously founded in the bedrock principles of morality, compassion, and of ecology. Traditional economies as practiced by tribal people living in a state of nature may come close, since people living cheek-by-jowl in small communities must to some extent live harmoniously, at least with each other, or perish. Thus, in the 'gift economies' of Papua New Guinea people simply *give* each other things, without any sense of barter or trade – simply, it seems, in the cause of conviviality. People living close to nature must also take care not to exhaust the available resources – to drive their prey to extinction (although they often have).

But the economies and political systems of modern ('civilised') societies are rooted for the most part in a mindset which says that human beings should aspire to be happy and that happiness is increased by material wealth. Happiness is surely desirable although it is all too easily equated with hedonism, which quickly palls. Fulfilment is a better concept. But it's a huge mistake to suppose that wealth necessarily makes us happier, once we are comfortably above the breadline. This has been acknowledged since the dawn of civilisation. Hence the tale of King Midas in the ancient state of Phrygia, the land that is now Asian Turkey, who yearned to turn everything he touched to gold – and then discovered that the best things in life, like good food and indeed his own daughter, were best left in their original state.

But the idea that wealth leads to happiness and happiness is the ultimate good really took off formally in the eighteenth century with the birth of recognisably modern capitalism and with Jeremy Bentham's definition of ethical good as 'the greatest happiness of the greatest number'. Since capitalism was and is designed expressly to increase measurable wealth and since wealth makes us happy, it seems to follow that capitalism must be good. Doesn't it? From the outset it was clear that wealth could be increased most effectively through technology – especially the factory – and that technology advanced by leaps and bounds when rooted in science, to become 'high tech'; which, as it grew in power, seemed to promise of omnipotence. So, the modern *Zeitgeist* was born, the grisly alliance of capitalism and high tech, and the perpetual struggle between the superpowers and their cronies and hangers-on to maximise their own wealth and to dominate the rest, aided by ever-smarter and more powerful technologies, which now have brought the whole world to the brink of collapse.

So how can we devise an economy that really could lead us towards conviviality, and keep the natural world in good heart? In the end, for all its import and gravitas, economics *is,* inescapably, a game of money. So, what must be the rules of that game?

The Lessons of History

Capitalism grew out of old-fashioned mercantilism but is much more sophisticated. Old-style merchants, as portrayed in Shakespeare's *The Merchant of Venice* of 1605, simply bought 'goods' as cheaply as possible and then tried to sell them on for as much as possible. Then they stored the profit, if any, in the form of 'bullion', mostly gold and silver. This was their wealth, traditionally held in treasure chests.

Bona fide capitalists don't simply stash away their profits in chests or in holes in the ground but invest it in various ways in new enterprises. Neither do they seek simply to buy what they want, ready-made. They set up enterprises, businesses, specifically to produce whatever will generate more wealth. For this, three ingredients are needed: raw materials, labour, and (in traditional businesses) land. Broadly speaking, mercantilism was the economy of international exchange which worked well enough when the participants were evenly matched, but rapidly evolved into imperialism when one side out-gunned or out-manoeuvred the other. Thus, mercantilism was commonly associated with conquest and with exploration, to find new places to conquer and exploit. Capitalism emerged as the economy of the factory, which in turn required new and bigger technologies. The profit that came from producing goods that people wanted and selling them on was used to found bigger and better factories, and so the economy grew. This – the factories and the armies of men, women, and children who operated the machines, and the rising tide of wealth – was and is the Industrial Revolution.

From the outset it was clear that the new wealth and the ways of life that produced it could be brutal and foul – men, women, and children almost literally tied to horrendous machines for fourteen hours a day, working till they dropped, yet paid as little as possible and living in hovels; while the factory owners, 'bloated' capitalists, grew very rich indeed. It wasn't always like this of course but there were enough examples – including, in Britain, most of the industrial north – to convince many a social reformer that capitalism was and is foul. Among them were the young Karl Marx

(1818-1883) and Friedrich Engels (1820-1895) who wrote *The Communist Manifesto* of 1848; and Marx went on to outline his alternative vision of 'communism' in *Das Kapital*, of 1867. The evils of capitalism that were so evident in the nineteenth century are with us still in the wage-slave, the sweat-shop, and the unspeakable behaviour of some of the modern super-capitalists, the transnational corporates.

And yet: the economist who is commonly seen as 'the father of modern capitalism', Adam Smith, (1723-1790), was a pillar of the Scottish Enlightenment, and certainly was no brute. He was a moral philosopher before he was an economist, and evidently believed in the essential goodness of human nature – or at least in the human potential for goodness. His first book, published in 1759, was *The Theory of Moral Sentiments* in which he proposed that human beings in general are imbued with 'natural sympathy'. Specifically, he wrote:

> How selfish soever man may be supposed, there are evidently some principles in his nature, which interest him in the fortunes of others, and render their happiness necessary to him, though he derives nothing from it except the pleasure of seeing it.

Against this background he wrote his more famous book that is commonly taken as the urtext, the gospel, of modern capitalism: *The Wealth of Nations* of 1776, in which he spelled out his ideas on market economics. This was the same year, incidentally, in which America published its monumental Declaration of Independence. The US and capitalism grew up together.

In *The Wealth of Nations*, Smith wrote:

> ... by directing that industry in such a manner as its produce may be of the greatest value, [the trader] intends only his own gain, and he is in this, as in many other cases, led by *an invisible hand* to promote an end which was no part of his intention ... *By pursuing his own interest* he frequently promotes that of the society more effectually than when he really intends to promote it. I have never known much good done by those who affected to trade for the public good. (*My italics*).

In this brief paragraph – ninety words – Smith seems to be saying, or indeed is saying, that producers and traders need not be moralists. They should simply try to make money, in their own interests, without thinking about the greater good of humanity (and still less of the natural world).

Indeed, if they do waste time thinking about 'the big picture' then they will do nobody any favours. They will simply lose efficiency – make less money than they would if they had stayed more focused: and since society as a whole *needs* money, that does more harm than good. Of course, however, Smith was *not* suggesting that traders should be out-and-out crooks, pursuing their own interests with no holds barred. He envisaged that in the ideal market many different traders would compete for custom, and the customers would be discerning and have plenty of time to pick and choose and would talk to each other, so if any trader cheated or charged too much the word would soon get round, and the errant trader would have to mend his or her ways or else suffer the consequences. Besides, he evidently thought, human beings on the whole are *not* out-and-out crooks. We are as a species imbued with 'natural sympathy' and we don't normally seek to do each other down. Put the three things together – the competition between traders, the discernment of customers, and the underlying natural sympathy – and the 'invisible hand' will indeed keep things on an even keel, even if individual traders fall personally short of moral perfection, and even without oppressive legislation to keep everyone on track. In short, if the market is really 'free' – free to function as markets should – then no external control is necessary.

The neoliberals, however, taking their lead primarily from Milton Friedman, have adopted Smith's comments on the joys of the free market but in a quite different era and without Smith's moralist worldview. They still tend to claim Smith as their prophet although in the modern world the invisible hand can no longer operate as Smith envisaged, and his comments on the essential benignity of human nature have been put aside, if indeed the modern neoliberals are aware of them at all. Smith apparently envisaged markets roughly like modern street markets – dozens of small traders competing on a more or less level playing field. Most factories were still small in his day, by modern standards. Already there were some vast corporations – notably the East India Company – but Smith hated them because they pushed the smaller traders aside and so reduced the competition that he saw was essential if the invisible hand was to function.

The technologies that have arisen in the past 250 years, culminating in modern IT, have enabled the factories and markets to grow and coordinate, so that although small businesses far outnumber the big ones the world's production and trade are now dominated, overwhelmingly, by a steadily diminishing shortlist of giant corporates. As the corporates grow richer, they may become more powerful than most governments. They can and do override national laws, introduced by democratically elected governments at least ostensibly for the benefit of their citizens and, sometimes, of the natural world. Neither is the true neoliberal constrained by conscience. Their only *moral* obligation, so true neoliberals believe, is to maximise the profit of their shareholders – in effect by whatever means they can get away with. More generally, what are commonly called 'human values' disappear. Thus, when Britain's Boris Johnson pledged recently to put his weight behind the attempts to limit global warming, he also hastened to assure his putative supporters that he has not turned into a 'bunny-hugger' (his words). It's just that forest fires and desertification and climate refugees and all the rest are too expensive. In truth he may not believe that, but he evidently felt he needed to say it. For the true neoliberal – and neoliberals now dominate *all* governments, including those like Russia's that still claim anomalously to be socialist – measure all aspects of life in money, including the natural world which they perceive as 'natural capital', which provide 'ecosystem services'.

Overall, in the modern, neoliberal version of the free market, give or take a few cartels, all must compete for maximum profit and 'market share', as ruthlessly as they can get away with. Every now and again the odd executive or politician oversteps the mark and goes to jail but the law, on the whole, is seen to be negotiable. Lawsuits are just another (sometimes) unavoidable expense. Inexorably, the rich grow richer because they can command more space in the marketplace and pull more strings, and the smaller players are marginalised. Thus, inequality increases. The losers – the small farmers and businesspeople -- fall off the edge and end their days in some slum, or as refugees, or else rise up in righteous discontent. Inequality and injustice, real or perceived, are the prime cause of strife.

So, what's to be done? The answer surely lies in what is commonly called 'Green Economic Democracy': an economy designed *not* simply to maximise wealth in the vague hope that everything will turn out OK (or if it doesn't – too bad) but expressly to enhance the lives of human beings and of the natural world. Green Economic Democracy – GED – comes in many shapes and sizes. Here is my version of it.

Green Economic Democracy (GED)

Economists, inspired at least in part by the false idea that economics can be a *bona fide* science, and by the equally false idea that science deals in certainties and can be seen as the bedrock of wisdom, have commonly endeavoured over the years to encapsulate their ideas as formulae or indeed as algorithms; simple, sure-fire solutions to life's problems. Thus, Marx felt it was of key importance that the workers should own or control the means of production, while the neoliberals are content to leave the affairs of humanity and indeed the fate of the natural world to the market. In the neoliberal world, what people are prepared to buy is considered good, and what they will not buy is ipso facto bad. The market, not God or conscience, becomes the moral arbiter. It's odd that so many neoliberals claim to be devout, like the American Christian Right.

Behind this search for simplicity, I suggest, is the belief in 'Occam's razor'. William of Occam, or Ockham, was an English fourteenth century friar who famously declared: 'Entities are not to be multiplied beyond necessity'. This means that if you are trying to explain something, then don't invent ad hoc agents to explain what's going on. 'Occam's razor' is an extrapolation of this. It is taken to mean that all explanations of everything should be as simple as possible – and this is further taken most erroneously to imply that the simplest explanation is always the best and indeed represents the truth. Scientists commonly invoke Occam's razor in this extrapolated form – which is one reason why they like to reduce ideas to formulae. In truth, Occam's razor has served science well. Modern science is commendably free of extraneous, ad hoc suppositions. But it can be taken too far. As Albert Einstein warned – he one of the greatest scientists of all times: 'Explanations should be as simple as possible *but no simpler*'.

What applies to the ideas of science applies in spades to the altogether looser ideas of economics, which merely looks like a science (in certain respects). Don't try too hard to be too simple: too 'pure'. All this is a long-winded apologia for the inescapable fact that GED *cannot* be reduced to a simple adage, and neither should we attempt to do so. Instead, we can at best offer a shortlist of desirable and necessary features.

As I see things, GED can best be summarised as a heterogeneous shortlist of four basic premises, and six key mechanisms of a kind that have been shown to work.

The necessary premises are of a moral and commonsensical kind, including:

1: *No one should have less than is needed to live with dignity and to achieve fulfilment.*

2: *No one should have so much that their wealth interferes with others.*

That we should avoid harming other people is widely accepted by all except political or some religious zealots who evidently believe that other people can and should be swept aside to make way for their own favoured ideology. In many ways, the assertiveness of the very rich can make life hard for everyone else but as Pope Gregory I, aka St Gregory the Great (560-604), observed 1400 years ago:

> Those who make private property of the gift of God pretend in vain to be innocent, for in thus retaining the subsistence of the poor they are the murderers of those who die every day for the want of it.

3: *It isn't just absolute wealth that matters. Equality, or at least a sense of justice, matters at least as much.*

The inequalities in modern societies would be seriously compromising even if everyone had enough (which of course is far from the case).

4: *We must take care of the biosphere. More: we must feel that we are part of it.*

The idea that moral principles should be applied in our dealing with other species and with the fabric of the Earth again is ancient, though it seems largely to have been forgotten with the growth of 'civilisation'. It needs restoring. We need to rediscover our metaphysical sense of oneness and of the sacred (but that's another story).

As I see things, an economy that works best for all should partake of the following six ideas.

1: Social enterprise

All commercial enterprises of all kinds, whoever owns them or runs them, should be designed to serve the interests of their host society, of humanity at large, and of the natural world. Some existing enterprises surely do meet this requirement but it isn't clear that any corporate does. Some in effect are simply predatory. Those that do not meet the moral requirement should simply be illegal. The law is supposed to protect us (and the natural world) from what is harmful.

2: The tripartite mixed economy

Enthusiasts of the extreme Left would eliminate all private enterprise and private ownership. Zealots of the Right, including many US Republicans and British Tories, equate public ownership – ownership and control by national or local governments – with what they think is 'communism' and equate communism with despotism and therefore as the enemy of personal freedom, which they claim to see as the greatest good, even though in their own versions of the free society a great many people are anything but. In Britain, the Labour politician and former coalminer, Aneurin (Nye) Bevan (1897-1960), has often been portrayed as a 'loonie leftie' but in his personal manifesto of 1952, *In Place of Fear,* he wrote:

> A mixed economy is what most people of the West prefer. The victory of Socialism need not be universal to be decisive ... It is neither prudent, nor does it accord with our conception of the future, that all forms of private property should live under perpetual threat. In almost all types of human society different forms of property have lived side by side...

I like the idea of 'the tripartite mixed economy'; the economy comprised of private ownership, public ownership, and community ownership. Chief of these I suggest should be community ownership – the strand that has received least attention. Communities can often achieve what individual citizens cannot – including, crucially, owning and running local farms and markets. *All* land should be community owned – or rather should be deemed to belong to no-one and everyone. Different individuals and groups should merely be licensed to use parcels of land for the general good but should never be given *carte blanche,* as commonly is now the case; *and there should be no market at all in land* – which at present there is, to the detriment of everyone except bankers and financiers who can manipulate the machinery of finance.

3: Positive investment

I suggest that neoliberalism – the extrapolated modern version of capitalism, with the social conscience ripped out of it – is both foul and dangerous. But capitalism as first envisaged by Adam Smith should not be written off *a priori*. Many of the mechanisms that have grown up under the capitalist umbrella are potentially of value, including the sale and purchase of shares in companies (which or course people did even in pre-capitalist days, as in the mercantilist economy portrayed in Shakespeare's *Merchant of Venice* in 1605). What matters is what people invest in – social enterprises that are designed to do good, or whatever brings most short-term profit. 'Ethical' investors avoid putting money into enterprises they don't like, like arms and tobacco. Positive investors go one step further, and put their money only into enterprises that they feel are truly worthwhile, like small and serious publishing companies or local farmers' markets.

4: Universal Basic Income (UBI)

UBI directly addresses the key idea that no-one should have too little to live on with dignity – irrespective of whether they work or not. It is often suggested that if people can live without working, they will slump into idleness and mischief but when UBI or its variants have been tried it tends to transpire that the opposite is the case. People freed from the drudgery of obligatory labour often do more, and more that is of social value. We need, like Adam Smith, to have more faith in human nature, and to devise systems that bring out the best in ourselves.

All of the above ingredients are human-orientated, at least potentially able to further the causes of conviviality and personal fulfilment. Truly to be 'green', to adjust our lives to the needs and realities of the biosphere, we need to cultivate the sense of oneness, with an attitude that is at least equally biocentric (or ecocentric, or indeed gaiacentric -- acknowledging Jim Lovelock's key concept of Gaia). The economy must be correspondingly:

5: Minimalist *and* 6: Circular

Minimalist implies that we should not, as economists and politicians apparently perceive is their duty and *raison d'etre*, be seeking to maximise production and consumption, but the complete opposite: asking how *little* we really need to meet the human need for fulfilment and conviviality. By the same token, fisheries experts seek to achieve 'maximum sustainable yield'. Instead, as in many ancient, indigenous cultures, we should take from nature only what is absolutely necessary.

Circular entails re-cycling of course but it also implies that all machines should be made so that they can be dismantled so the parts that are more robust can be re-used in new machines. After all, some bits of some machines may last for decades, even centuries, but as things are they tend to be scrapped along with all the more ephemeral components. Obviously, all inputs should as far as possible be endlessly renewable – not coal and oil but wind and tide, ultimately powered by solar energy and by lunar gravity.

How do we get from where are to where we need to be?

The key lies with the concept of *Renaissance*. Reform is vital and can achieve a great deal but is not sufficient. It is too slow for present purposes and new governments tend to reverse the good reforms introduced by their predecessors. Revolution is too uncertain and rarely achieves what its perpetrators intended. Renaissance implies that we should use whatever democratic latitude is still left to us to build the kind of enterprises we feel we need – including community owned farms and markets – *despite* the status quo. We need first to create islands of sanity the world over and encourage them to expand and coalesce to form a genuine alternative. As Mahatma Gandhi is alleged to have said, 'be the world you want to see'.

Overall, a completely new mindset is needed, based on the ideal of compassion and oneness with the natural world, and the economy must be designed in accord with those values. In the present world we attempt to do things the other way around: install an economic doctrine, encapsulated in a few economic formulae, and then shape our lives, and the biosphere, and indeed our conception of right and wrong, accordingly. No wonder the world is in a mess.

MANIFESTOS OF THE END

Christopher B Jones

World order? Absolutely! By all means! At least that is how it seemed to me during my formative years, young adulthood, and well into my professional life. I visited the United Nations New York Headquarters at age ten, spent most of my teen years in Latin America, and came of age in a time of hope and optimism for the UN system, as a legacy of two world wars and the hope of a generation that there would be no more global conflicts. It certainly seemed true through my first decade as a political science professor, where I was responsible for teaching international relations and comparative government. I was active in the local World Affairs Council, participated in regional Model United Nations conferences, and ran a mid-1990s spring workshop at Novosibirsk State University in central Russia. The two working groups in the Russia workshop were each comprised of a dozen international students and the brief given to each group was to develop a timeline leading to the 'future fact' of the creation of a global government by 2050. By using ten-year increments on a timeline leading from 1995 to 2050, they were asked to examine the events and trends that could lead to world government 2050.

Perhaps not surprisingly, both groups independently used the UN as a vehicle to 1) establish global government and 2) limit nation-state sovereignty. Both groups used public health and education and the UN Millennium Development Goals, and the UN Universal Declaration of Human Rights as starting points, and global health care needs as the driving forces that brought nation states together. Both groups had similar ideas about an eventual World Parliament being constituted by 2050; also not surprising was that world government, for one group, emerged due to a global pandemic crisis. This fitted the model of global progress in my head and in my teaching in the 1990s—one of greater regional consolidation and integration, like the European Union (EU) that was then coming into being. My mental model was one of an increasingly interdependent world that was evolving towards a central government, in the same way that the thirteen colonies became the United States of America. As a naïve young American, it makes perfect sense that I had this idea that the world should look more like the USA. Eventually, I came to realise that the processes that created the US were not the same as those that created the EU or the UN. My belief in a natural progression and centralisation of power did not jibe with the realities emerging in the post-Cold War world in which I lived. If my assumptions about U.S. exceptionalism were naïve, my optimistic assumptions about growth and then about sustainable development were ignorant. How the world order has changed during the last couple of decades!

One can no longer engage in a discourse about world order without challenging the basic assumptions about the trajectory and end state of global 'order,' and particularly, pose the question: are we moving towards global disorder; or indeed, the collapse of all order? That is precisely the message of the *Uncivilisation, the Dark Mountain Manifesto* written by poet and author Paul Kingsnorth and author and social entrepreneur Dougald Hine, and their Dark Mountain Project. The manifesto is a small pamphlet first published in 2009, but *Dark Mountain* is a larger literary and artistic statement about the dysfunction of the current paradigm and a recognition of the deep damage and harm that humans have inflicted on other species and planetary systems. Now in its nineteenth edition, the *Dark Mountain* journal continues a tradition of manifestos—written social, cultural, and political demands for change in the current system.

Manifestos are mundane, as in parliamentary political platforms, but they have historically represented demands for big systemic changes. Political movements are often represented by manifestos, written as statements of principle or specific demands for change. Most of the manifestos that have had an impact on society make such demands, but *Uncivilisation* is not a call to action, but a *Manifesto of the End* - a statement that manifestos have run their course, and that the next manifesto will be what nature demands from us. In other words, world order has become a part of the runaway train called (western) civilisation, and we are on board for the end of the ride, however that may turn out. Our collective freedom of movement is limited in terms of what we can do about the forces we have set in motion.

My interest in manifestos began in my early adulthood. That was before I had a working definition or stake in the discourse. What is commonly considered to be a manifesto? My working assumption was that a manifesto challenges an existing global or professional order, paradigm, or worldview; it seeks to re-order or deconstruct fundamental assumptions or axioms. A review of recent literature illustrated the variety: hedonist, Nazareth, computer hacker, blockchain, magic mushroom, posthumanist, and many more manifestos. But it is not the history of manifestos or the variety, the scope and depth of them, that interest me. Rather, I was interested in the manifestos that point to civilisational level challenges, and seek to change the world order.

I came of age during the Vietnam war, experienced white privilege of the Jim Crow South, and lived half a decade in Latin America –experiences that opened my eyes to some of the deep structural shortcomings of my homeland and worldview. The embedded glass shards crowning the walls surrounding the missions that we lived in, our indigenous maids, the glaring economic inequality, and social movements back home and abroad subtly but incrementally shifted my own values and perspectives from suburban conservatism to a more radical view of change. My father was a New Testament Protestant theologian, so I saw that my own religious tradition was informed by Martin Luther and his Ninety-Five Theses. In the liberal university churches in the US at the time, Jesus of Nazareth was seen as a revolutionary for social justice. The four gospels, Mathew particularly, were argued to be a manifesto against Roman rule. I learned that our denomination, the Disciples of Christ, was born from a religious revival movement in the 1800s, a perhaps reactionary, yet nonetheless prophetic rejection of mainstream Christianity at the time in America. My journey within the church, in my late teens, lead to a public protest and large youth demonstration at our church's quadrennial national General Assembly that brought proceedings to a halt, after rejection by church members of a resolution in support of Reconciliation - Black reparations for slavery. Seven of us were hired by the church's Division of Homeland Ministries to help the domination better understand the disaffection and alienation of young people. We had no more success than did Martin Luther in changing the Catholic Church.

Within the next few years, I read the *Communist Manifesto*, the Port Huron statement of the Students for a Democratic Society (1962), writer and feminist Germaine Greer's *The Female Eunuch*, and saw that manifestos were not timid or bashful, but bold and demonstrative. They meant to re-order the world as we know it. Of course, it's unwise to be anthropomorphic, because there are people or individuals behind the words, but the manifestos do take on a life of their own. I also began to see that there were other things, other developments, other phenomena that had a parallel or similar force to that of a manifesto. Economist E. F. Schumacher's *Small Is Beautiful* did not present itself as a manifesto but was written and advocated for a more enlightened perspective than that of the dominant growth paradigm. Marine biologist and conservationist Rachel Carson's *Silent Spring* felt like a manifesto in 1962. She shone a light on DDT use in the US, and within a few years, it was banned. Maybe these were not actually manifestos, but they did contribute to a critical discourse challenging many assumptions that the dominant order took for granted or did not challenge.

But *Uncivilisation* is a different kind of Manifesto. Its roots are as deep and wide, as they are varied and bizarre. As a Manifesto of the End, it has a number of recent precursors – manifestos that address the rights of robots, clones, and digital avatars, as well as posthumanism and transhumanism. The rights discourse around robotics, artificial intelligence, and automation has generated manifestos on both sides of the human/machine equation. The rights of robots have been addressed in popular media, famously by the character Data in *Star Trek: The Next Generation* (the 'Measure of a Man' season 2, episode 9), and accelerates as developments proceed in artificial intelligence advances. Distinctions between algorithms and sentience becomes blurry as machine intelligence becomes more sophisticated. On the other side, the robotics community has also considered threats to humans from automation and robotics, particularly the loss of jobs and employment through job replacement and greater efficiencies. There are ongoing debates about whether, once super-intelligent machines achieve self-awareness, or sentience, there will be a place for humans. Perhaps as pets or curiosities? There are questions whether sentience and consciousness as we currently understand them are even possible in machines. That has not prevented advocacy for putative conscious machine intelligence or robots, reasoning that any entity with *free will* should have individual rights. In the movie *Blade Runner*, artificial humans have expiration dates and are used for slave labour. In a present when we can imagine such horrors, why would we not believe in rights for robots?

A similar discourse has emerged about the fate of potential human clones. At least since the cloning of the sheep named Dolly, questions have arisen about the potential for human cloning and whether clones would have the same or perhaps additional rights. This discourse has also included hybrid or chimera humans created through a mixture of human and nonhuman DNA. Feminist and scholar of science, technology, and consciousness, Donna Haraway, made a case for not only the rights of clones but celebration of them as key examples of 'the Other' in her much cited *A Cyborg Manifesto*. Haraway is a key figure in the posthumanist tradition. The subject of cloning humans, particularly, blurs the boundaries between posthumanists and transhumanists. Both movements are implicit and sometimes explicit manifestos for a new species or a transformed worldview. Cloning is seen by most transhumanists as inevitable, while most posthumanists would not be comfortable with the technologies that make cloning possible.

The rights of cyborgs discourse is not in the realm of science fiction, but is already an issue for humans who consider themselves cyborgs, or at the very least who have extensive technology body implants. For the emergent cyborg community, their enhancements are already a challenge in legal settings, for example, when passing through metal detectors. Given that some enhancements are associated with or covered in the US by the Americans with Disabilities Act (ADA), cyborg humans are concerned about discrimination. Furthermore, sensor sophistication and microminiaturisation, and direct neural connections, are revolutionising the ability of technology to mimic or substitute for the loss of many of the five human senses. Machine–brain research and innovation continue to advance the ability of machines to directly interface with the human body's nervous system and with the brain itself. What technology and innovation make possible also create the conditions and expectations for greater human power, agency, and therefore political and legal rights. On the other hand, 'normal' humans may feel threatened or discriminated against by enhanced humans setting up another postnormal dynamic of chaos and contradictions. Entwined with cyborg politics are the manifestos for avatars— representations of oneself in internet environments (or cyberspace).

The word avatar became popular after publication of science fiction author Neal Stephenson's *SnowCrash*. The concept has become closely associated with the notion of downloading ones' consciousness or personality to the internet, or into a clone or android body. There is still vigorous debate about whether such processes are even possible, but research and technology continue in this realm. Thorny questions arise with the possibility of downloading consciousness. If avatars are sentient, will they be able to inherit or transfer wealth and possessions of the original, deceased version? If there are duplicate copies – which is the true or real consciousness? Would deleting a sentient avatar be considered murder? Artist and author Gregory Little notes in his 'Manifesto for Avatars' that both cyborgs and avatars share numerous social constructions – like techno-optimism, progress, innovation, identity politics and individualism. Little sees similarities between avatars and zombies in that both ideas raise awareness of the problematic nature of binary choices and oppositions—life/death, human/nonhuman, and civilisation/nature. Virtual life after death would fundamentally change culture.

Posthumanism and transhumanism also contribute to the Manifestos of the End; they inform the conclusions and the call to consciousness about the great unravelling ahead. Posthumanism attempts to redefine our epistemology and ontology beyond the human, to the Other embodied in nature, in other species, in the atmosphere, the oceans, and especially other species and lifeforms on the planet—and the planet as-a-whole. Transhumanism is about the transformation of the human, biologically or technologically, to make a 'better' human, a transhuman. The transhumanists argue that the coming scientific and technological convergence, the acceleration of technological advancement, such as Moore's law of the doubling of transistors on a computer chip every eighteen months, will bring a Singularity, a quantum-jump in science and technology, but especially in genetic engineering, molecular engineering, quantum computing, and artificial intelligence (AI). At the point of

Singularity, man and machine will become one. This view sees a proliferation of human species as cyborgs infused with AI, particularly adaptable to outer space and other planets, moving into the solar system and beyond. Both movements implicitly and explicitly comprise manifestos for transformational change. Posthumanism calls for rejection of the idea that humans are separate from nature and argues for a more integral approach to coexistence and coevolution. Transhumanism calls for transcending the current human form by increasing longevity, genetic augmentation, and cybernetic synthesis with machines and cyberspace, and argues that the *Singularity is near,* as proclaimed by computer scientist and inventor Ray Kurzweil.

The discourses of trans and post humanism, as well as rights of cyborgs and avatars, is a manifestation of postnormal times. Postnormal times, which began shortly after the new millennium, is characterised, first and foremost, by the acceleration of change. The fundamental drivers of change, specifically speed, scale, scope, and simultaneity (the 4Ss), set in motion by technologies and social systems, as well as transformation in human and planetary systems – including the oceans, atmosphere, geochemical, and biological systems – generate feedback loops that range from hours to decades. As a result, human and planetary systems are now driven to states of chaos, complexity, and contradiction (the 3 Cs) – the characteristic factors of postnormal times produced by the underlying 4Ss. There is no evidence, despite a hugely disruptive global pandemic, that these dynamics of change will slow or decelerate. While postnormal times analysis and related futures work are not manifestos, they give us context for the Manifestos of the End. Postnormal times analysis helps explain the contradiction and chaos resulting from the explosion of cultural identities, aspirations, and frustrations with the dominant political and economic orders. There is a proliferation of options beyond the normal, and little likelihood that normality of the last century can be attained, and some suspicion that normal did not serve a good part of the global population, and certainly is not serving other species and the health of the planet. Posthumanism and transhumanism both clearly add to the confusion.

The proliferation of manifestos, characterised by a paroxysm of new memes and new narratives, appears to reflect the contradictions, complexity and chaos of postnormal times. One example of the new narrative is the growing popular acceptance of the concept of the Anthropocene, a new geological era, that posits that future geologists would clearly see evidence of human activity and transformation of the planetary surface in sediments and rocks. We have disrupted the global order at the geological level, on deep time scales of tens or hundreds of thousands of years. There are signs that our short-term view has obscured the reality of the long-term impacts of our species on our planet, and similarly we seem to be collectively blind to the emergence of postnormal times or existential dangers. As in the parable of the blind men feeling different parts of a large elephant, we only have a glimmering of the beginnings of the new era, because it is embedded in earlier paradigms and realities, modernism and postmodernism, for example, that linger and languish, as postnormal creep, tilt, and burst increasingly occupy our minds, bodies, and spirits. The 2020 global pandemic has further demonstrated the dynamics of postnormal behaviour across politics, economics, technological and global systems. Because manifestos are also generated by interest groups and single-issue politics, they often appear to be toothless dragons, hardly a clarion call for revolution but rather demands to be heard: 'pay attention to us!' Toothless manifestos distract us from seeing the elephant in the room: the consequences of pumping carbon dioxide into the atmosphere, peak oil and resource depletion, and the limits to complexity. These megatrends not only fuel the speed, scale, scope, and simultaneity of global change, but they will increasingly give credibility and credence to the realities that comprise the phenomena of the Manifestos of the End. In a sense, they 'pile on' to the claims of Dark Mountain that we are bombarded with the failures of civilisation to live up to its promise, that the harder we try to mend things, the faster things unravel.

The *Uncivilisation* Manifesto and the *Dark Mountain* journal are not anticipating the apocalypse but appear resigned to the fact that there is little that can be done to stop the runaway train of a civilisation heading to a chasm. In this view, progress turned out to be an evolutionary mistake. Historian and philosopher Ronald Wright catalogues the 'short' and troublesome record of progress over human history and notes that if civilisation is to survive, it would have to begin living on the interest, rather than the capital, of nature. There is little evidence humans are moving in that direction. *Dark Mountain* is a palliative care space, a hospice for civilisation, a coming-to-terms with our civilisational mortality. If we have learned anything from the Enlightenment, it is that evidence matters. *Uncivilisation* Manifesto is surely correct to point out that theories may differ, epistemologies and ontologies can be diverse, but evidence of human impact on the environment, tonnage of minerals extracted, the metric tonnage of oil and gas pumped from the Earth, the growing levels of carbon dioxide in the atmosphere, and the increase in global warming are facts. Human demographics are facts. Species' losses are facts. Oil companies and multinational corporations try to create new narratives or obscure facts, and the rise of right-wing nationalism and media take great efforts to muddy the waters, create conspiracy theories, or generate their own 'facts,' but ignoring the black elephants will only make matters worse for humans/civilisation in the long term.

Manifestos of the End have not materialised out of thin air. Neither are they one-off phenomenon. But they have a context, and a genealogy. Given postnormal conditions, it's doubtlessly idiosyncratic and personal for those who contribute to, and create material for, *Dark Mountain*. For my part, it was the manifestos of my youth, the Ninety-Five Theses of Martin Luther, the *Communist Manifesto*, the Students for a Democratic Society's Port Huron Statement and the social movements that they spawned. There were implicit manifestos in works of literature and in social science. I was particularly drawn to feminist science fiction, particularly Charlotte Perkins Gilman, Marge Piercy, and Ursula Le Guin whose images of the futures portrayed realities based on radically different epistemologies and ontologies. They notably challenged and transformed gender roles and questioned basic assumptions of the dominant paradigm, such as growth, materialism, and other aspects of modern or industrial society. The American Indian Movement, Hawaiian sovereignty, and other indigenous political movements had a big impact on my thinking during graduate school. These movements were also implicit manifestos for political recognition and social justice. First People's resistance to the Keystone XL pipeline - that would have carried 830,000 barrels per day of Canadian tar sand oil to the Gulf of Mexico - and protection of ancestorial lands, constitutes a fundamental conflict between the forces of planetary destruction and Earth stewards. The 2008 Bolivian Constitution asserted there are natural rights for the Earth. The legal inclusion of rivers and ecologies often advocated by indigenous people are a new kind of manifesto for the rights of nature.

A significant subgenre of science fiction, particularly the 'new wave' of the 1960s, produced critiques and implicit manifestos against growth, development, capitalism, and neoliberalism. Examples from science fiction included John Bruner's *Shockwave Rider* and Ernest Callenbach's *Ecotopia* that envisioned green solutions to perceived excesses of nationalism and development. This critical tradition has continued with a small renaissance in the subgenre of climate change fiction, so called 'cli-fi,' popularly illustrated by the success of author Kim Stanley Robinson who engages in explicit and implicit manifestos in a future Mars historical trilogy (Red Mars! No Green Mars! No Blue!). His Earth-based cli-fi novels have dealt with post-diluvian New York City in 2042 AD and describe a chaotic warming world ahead with massive social and physical dislocations. This body of work advocates for transformation if we are to survive as a species. His narratives are frequently a penetrating critique of postnormal change cross currents, the story of a civilisation hanging onto meaning and purpose in the face of extreme heat, coastal migrations, and chaos.

On the environmental front, paralleling the radicalisation of the green movement was the emergence of the green parties, particularly in European Parliaments. There were manifestos motivating the green movement, such as the Brundtland Commission report and the birth of organisations like Mankind at the Turning Point and the Club of Rome, indications that the global body politic were taking the *Limits to Growth's* environmental *global problematique* seriously. The movements (peace, antiwar, social justice and equity) supporting the emergence of the Manifestos of the End clearly include numerous initiatives within the UN system and related non-governmental organisations. The United Nations' Universal Declaration of Human Rights serves as a manifesto for human rights that are not universally recognised or adopted. Similarly, the Millennial Development Goals (2000-2015) and current Sustainable Development Goals (2015-2030) are clearly manifestos given how far apart the aspirations are from the realities on the ground. In the past decade, the environmental movement has continued to draw attention, the efforts of young people, such as Greta Thunberg—who scolded world leaders at the UN—the Sunrise Movement, and the Extinction Rebellion grab headlines periodically, even in the pandemic.

Thus, the roots of the Manifestos of the End are sociocultural, and informed by the cognitive dissonance, the contradictions, between the aspirations of global populations and the grim realities of neoliberalism and corporate capitalism, the capitalist world order as described by sociologist Emmanuel Wallerstein, historian Ferdinand Braudel, and others from the French Annales School. The postcolonial movement, recently reinvigorated by the Black Lives Matter protests in the US in the summer of 2020, is certainly a driving force in the deconstruction of Western cultural hegemony. The forces of globalisation, the COVID-19 pandemic, and global weirding are further eroding some of the basic principles of the modern state system, the legacy of the Treaty of Westphalia that established the primacy of territorial integrity and national sovereignty. The illusion is particularly dissonant in places such as central and West Africa, Asia, and the Middle East where colonial masters imposed artificial national boundaries across tribal, cultural, and bioregional geographies. Political and economic division was a way to conquer and subdue.

In the early days of the industrial era in Europe, the original Luddite movement, while not a written manifesto, was an implicit manifesto - a blowback against the new elites who forced changes in the mode of production. The revolutionary steam engine and incipient industrialisation provoked a serious backlash in response to the early industrial behaviour modification of individuals and communities. Implicit neo-Luddite manifestos and rage against the machine continue to this day. Even the word *sabotage* has roots in the rage against the capitalist machine embodied in the Wobblies (International Workers of the World) and the anarcho-syndicalist movement of the early 1900s. The anti-technology discourse is itself rich. In his much-cited 1964 book, *The Technological Society*, philosopher and Christian-anarchist Jacques Ellul critiqued the power and corruption of technology. Activist and eco-psychologist Chellis Glendinning published the germinal 'Neo-Luddite Manifesto' in 1990. It was not anti-technology per se; it embraced green technologies but not nuclear, industrial chemicals, engineering, electromagnetic technologies, or computer technologies. The neo-Luddite manifesto movement took a violent turn as well.

In the 1980s and 1990s, the 'Unabomber Manifesto' was a media phenomenon, a national obsession in the US, and tiptoed towards the Manifestos of the End. It began as a US Federal Bureau of Investigation (FBI) case investigating attacks on university researchers, high technology businesses, and airlines. The anonymous 'university' and 'airline' (thus Unabomber) attacker was able, with FBI encouragement, to publish his screed against high technology in the mass media, which lead to bomber Ted Kaczynski's eventual arrest (he was turned in by his brother). He was convicted to life in prison and has continued to modify and clarify the original manifesto. The essays published in the *Washington Post* and the *New York Times* were released as *Industrial Society and its Future*. The manifesto directly blamed technology for the destruction of traditional societies and argued that technology had become a threat to human liberty and freedom. He singled out the idea of progress itself and believed that violence and destruction of technology were justified. The bombings themselves were overshadowed by the sensationalism of the manifesto publication and the manifesto was widely republished. In my early days of teaching political science, I made it required reading. The vast majority of students agreed with much of his analysis of technology but were unsettled to find out he was the Unabomber. Students were even further perplexed to learn about Kaczynski's background as a mathematician and academic at the University of California at Berkeley, and his neo-Luddite transformation. There seems to be no middle ground about Ted Kaczynski's manifesto: it was generally seen as either genius or crazy nonsense.

Five years later, the legendary programmer and cofounder of Sun Microsystems, Bill Joy, produced his 2000 essay 'Why the Future Doesn't Need Us,' and continued the antitechnology manifesto thread. In many ways it seems like version 2.0 of Glendinning's 'Neo-Luddite Manifesto'. In his critique, Joy warned of the threats from emerging technologies: robotics, genetic engineering, and nanotechnology. Although he disavowed Kaczynski's violence and his Luddite behaviour, Joy acknowledged that Kaczynski has a point, that his 'dystopian vision describes unintended consequences, a well-known problem with the design and use of technology, and … Murphy's law.'

Another stream leading to the Manifestos of the End is green anarchism: anarcho-primitivism, degrowth, and rewilding whose roots go back to the

Romantic movement and primitive communism. Literature professor and philosopher Timothy Morton put the fault of civilisation in the agricultural revolution at the end of the last ice age, arguing that the roots of industrial insanity began with agriculture. Pre-agricultural societies and subsistence societies spent much less time on *work* and much more of daily life on leisure according to cultural anthropologists. From an anarcho-primitivist perspective, the agricultural revolution brought social stratification, specialisation, forced labour, slavery, and alienation not liberation of the human spirit. There is a spectrum of green anarchist hues. Insurrectionists, for example, are deep green/black anarchists who are committed to accelerating the collapse of Western civilisation. Another shade of green anarchism was influenced by critical Marxist theorist Guy Debord who addressed the anomie and alienation from consumerism in *Society of the Spectacle*, one of the provocations and manifestos for the French student uprising in 1968. In the past decade, political economy radicals have transformed the landscape of the discourse on development, particularly the degrowth movement that had annual conferences before the pandemic. The largely academic enterprise brings together radical geographers, anthropologists, regional studies, political economists, and a host of other disciplines and fields who are deconstructing assumptions about progress and development. While not all green anarchist activists and researchers are on board with the *Uncivilisation* Manifesto, many are surely aware of the growing chorus of voices resigned to civilisational collapse.

In the inaugural issue of *Dark Mountain*, after the publication of the manifesto, Kingsnorth and Hine pushed back at critics who called them 'crazy collapsitarians' among other things, including, ironically, 'utopians'. Their response has a strong echo of postnormal times theory:

> We replied that the first thing we were going to do was to stop worrying about how to 'change the world': the world is changing so fast now that the best we can do is to become more observant, more agile, better able to move with it and to understand what is happening.

Kingsnorth and Hine point out that when they launched *Dark Mountain* they were interested in neither utopia or dystopia. The project was never 'a quest for apocalyptic narratives, but rather an attempt to get beyond them.' They do not see a 'cleansing catastrophe' or some kind of apocalyptic event, but rather see it as 'the world we are already living in.' This also echoes science and climate journalist David Wallace-Well's description of coming, but also ongoing, *cascading catastrophes* and his perspective that the collapse, for some populations, has been the story for the last 500 years. The indigenous peoples of the Americas, the Indo-Pacific, and Africa have been victims of civilisational collapse for generations. The elephant in the room is the ongoing wreckage and personal catastrophes faced by the victims of global weirding. For example, in just one climate exacerbated wildfire in the late summer of 2020, the Almeda fire destroyed large residential sections of both Talent and Phoenix, Oregon in which over 2000 individual family homes burned to the ground. While the ongoing crisis in Syria is usually portrayed as a political or geopolitical conflict, the roots of internal conflict have been blamed on climate change, stresses on freshwater sources, deforestation and other environmental factors. These catastrophes falling on individuals and families illustrate how within hours or days, 'normal' life and middle-class lifestyles can disappear, leaving individuals and families homeless and destitute overnight. Waves of environmental refugees are likely to become larger and already have a significant impact on rich and poor countries alike.

Kingsnorth and Hine deny that the *Uncivilisation* Manifesto was intended to overthrow civilisation. They point out that after only two centuries, industrial society has reached the limits of its capabilities; and wonder: why would anyone even bother to overthrow Western civilisation when historical forces are already dragging Western civilisation down. They suggest that the best thing to do when something is falling is to get out of the way; and argue that 'the decline or stuttering collapse of a civilisation, a way of life, is not the same thing as an apocalypse. It is simply a reality of history.' As in palliative care at end of life, there are stages. We are now at the stage of mourning: *Dark Mountain* raises the call to mourn our mounting losses: indigenous peoples, languages, cultures, and non-human species, habitat – and resilience.

Will the *Uncivilisation* Manifesto literally be the Manifesto of the End? It seems unlikely. Postnormal times analysis argues that the speed, scope, scale, and simultaneity of change and the proliferation of technologies, cultures, and identities will continue to generate divergent and sometimes shrill manifestos. There will be manifestos for new gender roles, for political identities, for different types of human/machine combinations, genetic modifications, emerging professions, and myriad of post-industrial aspirations. However, given the complexity of our world, it is hard to fathom how Western civilisation can be sustained. Which suggests that we must try harder to achieve some version of *transnormal* transformation of society before the whole thing 'goes down the tubes.' I hold out some hope that as the reality of climate change, peak oil, and the limits of complexity sink in, we can come to our collective senses and find some transnormal wisdom. We need to develop vastly more creative and imaginative spaces to vision our way to a more sustainable or resilient future that does not require civilisational collapse to get there. However, as so many Manifestos of the End argue, our emerging reality is most likely the unravelling of world order.

POSTNORMAL ADVENTURES

Jerry Ravetz

The evolution of science now proceeds at an accelerating pace. To appreciate how science is changing, an historical perspective is ever more necessary. Otherwise, those with experience just content themselves with moans that 'things aren't what they used to be', forgetting that, as the old Yorkshire song goes, they never bloody were. In my own struggles with, and writing on science, going back well over six decades, I have attempted to think historically. Roughly, that means understanding the conflicts of the present in terms of the unresolved contradictions inherited from the past. This heuristic works very well in some political cases, notably Ireland and Israel/Palestine. I have attempted to apply it to science; and I might as well apply it to my own work – the better to move forward.

My 1971 book, *Scientific Knowledge and its Social Problems*, highlighted my initial concerns about science. The formative problem of the book was expressed in the slogan: 'the activity of modern natural science has transformed our knowledge and control of the world around us, but in the process, it has also transformed itself; and it has created problems which natural science alone cannot solve'. I had accumulated problems and discontents with the standard account of science on very many issues, and I identified the key contradiction as the passage from Little to Big science, or from academic to industrialised science. But, as it happened, my knowledge of industrialised science was extremely limited. I had valuable experience of reflective research in scientific and arts disciplines, and I had a very precious historical understanding derived from my academic work. I could write a very insightful account of the craft work of science, including some quite original material on the obscurities at the foundations of theoretical science. But on industrialised science, I had little more than experience of a rapidly growing university and a deep political commitment, originally Marxist, then shaped by activity in the antinuclear campaign. Also, I already had enough experience of the corruption of good causes so I was not uncomfortable to find similar phenomena in science. However, there are two significant absences from the book. One is that I did not know of the warnings about science in President Eisenhower's Farewell Address, written by political scientist and speech writer, Malcom Moos. That text could have defined, and justified, the critical programme of my own book. But no one in the radical science movement in Britain ever mentioned it; perhaps it was assumed on the Left that nothing that Eisenhower had said could be worth looking at. The other, unrelated but also interesting, point is that my language reflected a lack of awareness of the feminist approach, in that I referred to scientists as 'men'. I don't have a huge burden of guilt over this, as the book was written before the explosion of radical feminist thought; but it is worthy of remark in the cause of historical accuracy.

In the ensuing sixty years, the social problems of scientific knowledge have grown and proliferated, now perhaps more quickly than their solutions. Internally, the challenges of quality assurance, described euphemistically as a 'reproducibility crisis', reveal a corruption in the transmission of the tacit knowledge in the craft skills on which that knowledge depends. The management of uncertainty is crippled by the persistent faith in numbers as nuggets of truth, revealed both in the ubiquitous pseudo-precise quantities and in the unresolved disputes over the techniques of statistical inference. In the external relations of science, the core myth of the beneficence and benevolence of an infallible natural science, creating a fountain of facts for human welfare, is increasingly frayed. The enlisting of the symbol of science in policy debates leads inevitably to the politicisation of science itself, and then to the confusion and hence corruption of its norms. Simplistic policy crusades invoking Science, demonising all who withhold uncritical support, threaten the integrity of science as no overt attack ever could.

Even in the 1960s, I had an insight into a possible solution: a 'critical science' modelled on the philosophies of the French Enlightenment. In my later collaboration with philosopher of science, Silvio Funtowicz, our 1990 book, *Uncertainty and Quality in Science for Policy*, established the basis of a reform of quantification, in the NUSAP (Numeral, Unit, Spread, Assessment and Pedigree) notational system – now widely used in climate

science, hydrology, medical research, and risk assessment. In the Epilogue
to that book, we made clear that this technical reform was a key to the
reform of knowledge as manipulated by a new secular priesthood. A few
years later, we developed the notion of postnormal science (PNS), with it
simple diagram and mantra: 'facts are uncertain, values in dispute, stakes
high, and decisions urgent'. Postnormal science opened windows to the
new realities of science. There are now many movements for the reform
and rejuvenation of science. These work on many fronts, including
transparency, ethics, and democratisation. There is even a renegotiation
of the Cartesian boundaries on reality, as science now shows that whales
and trees think and communicate, perhaps even with us. But as yet there
is no direct confrontation with the forces that are transforming science
into a debased instrument of policy and profit.

Postnormal science has now become a movement of some significance.
It has a history which is well documented in the back issues of the journal
Futures, thanks largely to Ziauddin Sardar, the former editor of *Futures*.
Our paper, 'Science for the Postnormal Age', is the most cited paper in
the history of the journal. It should be remembered that when it was first
announced, the field of radical critique of science was barren. The
Utopian-anarchist imaginings of Paul Feyerabend, Austrian-American
philosopher of science, had become an historical curiosity. The Marxist
critics of the s6091 and s0791 were reduced to a tiny sect. Even to
challenge the prevailing orthodoxy, that all policy problems could be
reduced to comparisons of precise quantities, was itself a radical act. For
my earlier writings, I recalled Lenin's term 'Aesopian language', as a way
of getting past the censor. The radical message of our study of quantities
was well hidden in our Epilogue of *Uncertainty and Quality in Science for
Policy*. But our censor was in our intended readers – the science and policy
communities – so we had to be very tactful indeed. In describing
postnormal science we sneaked in the politics through the technical term
'extended peer community'. And we were careful not to challenge the
puzzle-solving 'normal science' on its own turf; we just said that now
there are big problems where facts are uncertain and decisions urgent.

This caution served us well; we did not scare off potential supporters
who were privately worrying about the way that the official pretence of
certainty was harming science in the difficult policy-science domains. The

growth in readership and influence from the original defining paper was steady and organic, and the paper eventually achieved great prestige. A time-lag of roughly a generation is not bad, for a radical idea. But I have been aware, for quite some time, that this restricted perspective will eventually render the original doctrine obsolete. Whether a renewal will come from within the PNS movement, remains to be seen. But the terms 'corruption' and 'power' never appear in the early writings, and quite soon they will need to be incorporated in any analysis of science that hopes to be relevant.

It is personally gratifying to see scholars mentioning PNS without citing any sources. It shows that PNS has become a meme! It is now taking its place in a variegated and rapidly growing movement for reform in science. It is scarcely a decade since a prominent mathematician called for a boycott of a leading publisher because of their particularly rapacious publication policies. This was the 'spring' for science. Not long after, the problem of quality, which had long been festering, was thrust upon both scientific and lay publics. By the mid-2010, the persistence of discriminatory practices based on ethnicity and gender became an issue within science as in other institutions. With all these campaigns, science has joined the human race. The mystique of the Scientist as a dedicated white-coated bespectacled middle-aged male is gone forever.

But the last decade or so has also seen other radical changes. Accelerating change, globalisation, instant communication, and interconnectivity, and many other factors led, my friend Ziauddin Sardar, to the notion of Postnormal Times (PNT). Sardar show speed, scope, scale and simultaneity as driver of change, generating contradiction, complexity, and chaos. It was not just science that had gone postnormal, Sardar argued, but many other spheres of human activity from politics to governance, economics to finance, social relations to communication. Indeed, postnormality had become the spirit of our time, where facts tended to be contradictory and disputed, values are not just contested but are also in constant flux, stakes impact the planet as well as communities and individuals, and decisions have existential dimensions. PNT too has a simple mantra: 'we live in an in-between period where old orthodoxies are dying, new ones have yet to be born, and very few things seem to make sense'.

There is a fruitful tension between my postnormal science and Sardar's postnormal times. It is really quite common in the development of radical and intellectual movements for the earlier critics to be overtaken by those coming later. The Protestant Reformation had Erasmus and then Luther; the French Enlightenment had Fontenelle and then the Encyclopedistes. The French Revolution had Condorcet and the Gironde, and then Jacobins and Robespierre. Mid-ninetheenth century Russia had Hertzen and then Chernyshevsky, with his fateful slogan 'what is to be done?'. Of course, the radicals did not always shape history their way; after Luther came the turmoil which persisted for more than a century and left Germany in ruins; France went from The Terror to Napoleon; and the Russian revolution produced Lenin and Stalin. If there are indeed some radical defects in our science-based civilisation, we should be aware that they will not simply be put right with piecemeal social engineering. So, we need to be aware of historic errors and ensure that history does not repeat itself.

My own thinking on these issues provides a bridge between the two sorts of postnormal analysis. Some years ago, I realised that my early study of Marxism had left me with a very powerful insight: contradiction. I developed this in a couple of papers in the 2000's, working on the 'characteristic contradiction' of a complex system. The papers received very little notice. It is heartening to see that postnormal times brings contradictions to the heart of its analysis, along with complexity. There are several topics on which a fruitful dialogue between PNS and PNT could now be opened. For example, the role of ignorance in contemporary modes of knowledge production. The possibility of a real decline of science is hardly ever discussed, even among those who warn of the dangers of technology going out of control. Yet history teaches us that excellence of any sort cannot be maintained indefinitely in any local milieu. A Japanese scholar, using primitive data-processing methods, established a seventy-year cycle of scientific excellence, with centres moving through Italy, England, France, Germany, and the US. There are already strong signs of senescence in American science. Could Chinese science take over after American science? We consider how 'classical' Greaco-Roman civilisation gave way to the 'Hellenistic' of the Eastern Mediterranean, itself soon blending with the flourishing Islamic cultures. Could we now be witnessing an analogous development, with emerging foci of creativity, each with their own characteristics, in the mainland and in the 'Confucian diaspora', both practicing Feng Shui? That could be an emerging paradigm, which would go with the shifts in power from the West to the East. Time will tell. Perhaps a renaissance of Islam will be next in the queue for greatness.

Until quite recently, I had been taking a rather relaxed view of my relations with Sardar. PNS has been, in historical context, a window to the new world of science. PNT, by contrast points out how it could all go horribly wrong unless when learn to, as its champions put it, 'navigate' our way out of postnormal times. The difference in style and affect was so total, that they could co-exist comfortably. Quite suddenly I have realised that we are actually well on the way from PNS towards PNT. I am still trying to make sense of it all. So far, I have a collection of themes that require serious attention.

A manifestation that we are moving away from PNS and towards PNT is what we can call 'crusading science'. There is an apocalyptic vision of impending doom, a call to urgent action, a damning of critics as 'deniers' (echoes of the Holocaust), and a citation of evidence that is not merely policy-based but policy-shaped. We have grown accustomed to the apocalyptic declaration of the collapse of the environment, starting in the 1960s with the population bomb, then global freezing, limits to growth, global warming, resources exhaustion, climate change, and now climate emergency. This crusade now shares public concern with the Covid-19 pandemic, for which we face repeated lockdowns, health passports, and perpetual vaccinations. Such declarations not only paralyses agency and hope but have other serious problems. But this is not the place for detailed critiques of these campaigns. I will only make observations based on my own special interest: the management of uncertainty. For climate sensitivity, the crucial link between increase in CO_2 concentrations and the rise in global temperature has an error-bar of $+50\%$, in other words a factor of three. This huge gap in policy-sensitive knowledge persists in spite of decades of scientific resources being thrown at the problem. In policy terms it means that the consequences of an increase in CO_2 can be anything between totally benign and totally catastrophic, and we cannot know until it starts, or does not start, to happen. This annoying feature of the emergency remains concealed in full view; for the mainstream of politics, media, and science, it does not exist.

There is a similar situation with Covid-19. It is known that the mortality rates vary enormously with age and pre-existing illnesses. When an old person, already sick, dies, does this count as a Covid death? In the UK, it is quite simple. For the published statistics, so long as a person has tested positive within the previous four weeks, it counts as a Covid death. Any death with Covid is logged as a death from Covid. The possibility that they were moribund anyway and that Covid was irrelevant, does not appear in the published numbers. And then these are presented to the public daily, with no indication of their uncertainty. Of course, the rate of incidence and mortality from the disease varies strongly; but vital statistics with no hint of their uncertainty and quality are seriously weakened as contributions to knowledge and policy. Indeed, the closer one looks at the statistics for Covid, on issues like masks and testing, the more it becomes like one of Sardar's 'smog of ignorance' – where ignorance is deeply embedded in what we regard as trustworthy knowledge.

It could be argued that in the important issues in the policy domain, science has been subject to hijacking by external interests, themselves with a mixture of ideological and commercial motivations. There is little doubt that this has already happened to a serious extent in pharmaceuticals. To the extent that this analysis is correct, we face some really new theoretical questions. We are familiar with the political and ethical problem of the applications of science to harmful or even evil ends. The H-bomb and Silent Spring showed dramatically that the classical optimistic view of scientific advancement needed revision. But even in those cases, there were extenuating circumstances: the basic scientific research was done by persons who were competent and well-intentioned. Now, by contrast, the research effort itself has arguably been compromised. The crucial evidence for a 'hockey stick' of global temperatures included a time-sequence where two completely different data sets were surreptitiously pasted together; this was the notorious 'Nature trick'. More recently, at the onset of the Covid-19 pandemic, the academic computer simulation model that was crucial in convincing the UK government to do lockdown was revealed to have no documentation of its code, so that it was impervious to scientific criticism until a team of industry experts was brought in to sort it out. We might consider this as an innovative scientific methodology – 'solipsistic science'. And the communal aspect of science, with open, collegial debate between opposing viewpoints, has largely been replaced by the exclusion, even banning of critics, with the slogan 'the science is settled'.

It has all happened with such apparent suddenness, that we are now scrambling around looking for an explanation. Part of the answer will be found in the unresolved social problems of scientific knowledge. Among these, quality assurance is prime. As I discovered in the course of writing my old book, and later found support in the work of W. Edwards Deming, there is an essential ethical element in the operation of quality assurance. As I had previously learned from my Atlantic City tram driver, wherever there's a system there's a racket to beat it. Without a commitment to quality in a community of practice, no amount of regulation, however strong the incentives and sanctions, will be able to enforce it. Who guards the guardians? This general commitment depends crucially on the stature and behaviour of the leaders, and their success in imparting it to every new generation. I saw that the transition from 'little science', where supervisors could be mentors to their students, to 'industrialised science', where sheer numbers made that impossible, presented a deep challenge, which would need new sources of commitment for its resolution.

All this helps to explain how important areas of science can be taken over so easily, whenever it was to someone's advantage to do so. With the loss of commitment consequent on industrialisation, compounded with the confusion of methods, old-fashioned criteria of quality fell into abeyance. The situation was made worse by the belief that science is automatically self-correcting; people in key positions then lowered their guard. In their recent article, 'Policy Making in the Post Truth World', Steve Rayner and Daniel Sarewitz, have pointed out that contemporary science, with its focus on complex systems, has another hazard. With so many 'confounding variables' in any experimental situation, the 'feedback loop' whereby ideas are tested, becomes ever complex and lengthier process. As a result, quality-testing is delayed and compromised; and so inferior work survives longer, perhaps indefinitely longer, and the identification of 'shoddy science' is rendered ever more problematic.

The quality problem has been compounded by the rise of statistics. Particularly in the study of complex situations, statistical methods are the only barrier against the ubiquitous pitfalls of inference. But statistics does not provide a new alchemy, whereby the ore of raw data is infallibly converted into the precious metal of scientific facts. The techniques themselves are vulnerable to quality problems, with incompetent misuse and malevolent abuse common on a large scale. Worse, it has been found that in some fields the scientists don't even know that their corrupted techniques are wrong! There are even deeper levels to the problems, which I am only beginning to explore. The perennial debates among statisticians have gone to a new level, with some now warning that the standard tests of significance are seriously misleading. Teachers of statistics might now be wondering what to put into the curriculum! We might say that statistics has lost the 'paradigm' which uniquely defined good practice. For me, the situation is evidence of an inherent contradiction of/in modern science: namely the founding fantasy that quantitative knowledge is both simple and necessarily true. The way out of postnormal times will not be straightforward.

For me, it is all summed up in a public display in Berlin of a 'carbon clock' which shows how much time there is left before our 'carbon budget' is exhausted and global warming sets in seriously. The Mercator Research Institute describes it as 'That's how fast the carbon clock is ticking' and it displays the remaining time to the nearest hundredth of a second and the remaining quantity of CO_2 to the nearest ton. This is a beautiful example of mathematical gibberish; to express this hypothetical global quantity of carbon budget to one part in a trillion is as near to nonsense as a grammatically expressed statement can come. The explanatory text describes the numerous uncertainties that affect the estimate; but it has occurred to no one that the precision is unnecessary and misleading. And I am sure that most readers of this essay will not see that there is a problem; and it is in this misperception that I see the real civilisational problem: our modern-scientific mathematical language does not distinguish between good sense and pernicious nonsense.

Such a state of affairs is definitely beyond postnormal, but equally perhaps not yet PNT. Is there is key attribute whereby it could be named and thereby identified? Certainly, not all of science has been hijacked. Nor has it all become 'promotional', with policy-shaped evidence, like the science of weight-loss diets or anti-ageing face creams. Perhaps its strength lies in its great variety; thus, we still have the mass of academic researchers enjoying a huge variety of sources of support, leaving room for critics to make their invaluable contribution as an 'extended peer community'. There are also the important movements for reform, ranging from citizen and open science, through to reproducibility, research integrity, decolonising research and similar radical movements. So, can we identify a particular branch of science where the matured contradictions are salient and threatening?

I would like to consider biomedical science, as the integrated research arm of the sickness industry. In the US, this is a very large element of the cash economy, and its performance is generally accepted as low-quality. The contradictions are clear to all: much of the world's best research in the causes of disease benefits from generous public and private benefactions there; but the absence of a healthcare system was cruelly exposed by the Covid-19 pandemic. We might even apply a concept from what I now call 'cacologic systems theory': in that, the principal subsystems have effectively broken away from the main system and pursue their own ends, even though this selfish policy by each, effectively dooms them all. The corruptions of the American big pharma industry, including its tamed regulators, were clearly exposed in the opioids scandal. A single paper from the 1970s was the official, accepted evidence for their safety for all the subsequent decades, until the mounting toll of addiction and death forced a review. Who knows what other abuses are flourishing out there, noticed only by the fringe of critics who are ignored or denounced? Indeed, there are even agencies that provide any result that is desired by their clients. But the claim of systemic corruption in science is, as yet, very rarely made.

If policy-related research is truly in a state of vulnerability to manipulation, then what sort of counter-force could there be? It is less likely to be found within the formal institutions of research. What about external groups? Serious critics tend to be very marginal thinkers or activists. But the elements of a mass base are mainly found on the Right, where commitments are rather more about identity than science. On that side there will be a dearth of elite institutional expertise for all the structural reasons I have mentioned, in addition to the weight of accepted scientific argument. Hence, by default populists and demagogues will be more prominent, thereby furnishing another argument against them by the mainstream.

This situation raises a number of paradoxes, which I believe are significant for our understanding of the crisis as it matures. The original formulation of PNS mentioned the 'extended peer community'; in PNT it is replaced by polylogues, but both emphasise different legitimate perspectives and ways of knowing, akin to the working of a democratic society, characterised by extensive participation and diversity. Examples of this are community activist scientists mobilising against obvious abuses. Lois Gibbs, the American environmental activist, who brought global attention during the 1980s to the environmental crisis at the Love Canal Homeowners Association, is an example. Her efforts led to the creation of the US Environmental Protection Agency's Comprehensive Environmental Response and Compensation Liability Act, now used to locate and clean up toxic waste throughout the US. Another is Erin Brockovitch, who, despite formal education in law, took successful action in 1993 against California's Pacific Gas and Electricity Company - the company's cooling tower system was dumping various toxins into drinking water. But popular-science campaigns are not always so totally simple. Sometimes, indeed, the academic science is correct and the populist outsider is a charlatan and adventurer, like the Soviet agronomist Lysenko. The May 2021 local elections in Madrid was resoundingly won by a right-wing candidate for her defiance of government orders to lockdown. It seems that the experience of the dread disease was not sufficiently intense to overcome the pleasure at conviviality of Madrid's citizens. Could this flaunting of populist rejection of science be a harbinger of a sustained revolt? Sometimes I play with a scenario where the Northern Hemisphere soon has a succession of three cold summers. This could well be a random fluctuation, quite consistent with an overall warming trend. But it would be seized upon by the deniers as a refutation of the dire predictions. In the debate, the mainstream could then be seen to be in the position of welcoming confirmations while rejecting refutations of their theory, a methodology which Karl Popper had identified as pseudo-science. Given the Right-Left split on the climate emergency, this situation could lead to extreme cognitive dissonance among the progressive techno-elite, reminiscent of the effect on the Old Left of the Soviet invasion of Hungary in 1956.

Perhaps we are heading towards postnormal times with its contradictions, complexity and chaos. The appropriate response would be to get ready for another style of science, with its appropriate social and conceptual base, to take the lead. We might look for a clue to the necessary innovation in identifying what has been absent from science as we know it. A candidate for that element is non-violence. In his Oval Office, the President of the United States has memorials of three (non-White) heroes of non-violent social change. Where is science in this inspiring scene? For me, it is conspicuous by its absence, just as non-violence is conspicuous by its absence from any discourse on science. I concluded my radical social analysis in Scientific Knowledge with an invocation to charity, taken from Francis Bacon. Now we might speak of a postnormal consciousness of non-violence, realised in practice through mercy and compassion, thus taking us back to Sardar's own expression of the essential commitment.

EMERGING NIGERIA

Ahmad Adedimeji Amobi

My elder brother was travelling to Saudi Arabia and I would be accompanying him, along with one of his students, to the airport in Lagos. I had only been informed three nights before the trip that I would be joining them. I was going to Lagos for the first time as an adult; and I had to decide what clothes I should wear. I picked my three best outfits and took them to one of our neighbours to help me choose the best. She picked my white *jalabia* that I had abandoned inside the wardrobe because it was over-sized when it was bought for me. But I didn't like her choice. It was not as if I really went to her to choose, I went to her to choose the one I already intended to wear. As she was persuading me to wear the *jalabia*, I kept saying, 'why not this shirt and trousers? It is Lagos for God's sake'. She insisted but I had already made up my mind. I wore my blue shirt and black trousers.

In my southwestern part of Nigeria, Lagos to us is 'abroad'. A small London. If not for everyone, for me, it was my dream to visit the city because talking about Lagos is basically describing Nigeria. Lagos: the most populous city in Africa. Lagos: the commercial state of Nigeria. Lagos: the city you sneak into at night as a dreamless person but would wake up in the morning with a heavy bag of dreams. If Lagos is Nigeria then Nigeria is an analogy. Coined by the British journalist, Flora Shaw, wife of Lord Fredrick Luggard, the last governor-general of Nigeria under colonialism, it was named on 8 January 1897 after the River Niger that runs the length and breadth of the country. It would take over sixty more years before, Nigeria would pronounce itself an independent country on 1 October 1960. But from 1914, when Lord Luggard amalgamated the Northern and Southern protectorates, then created the Lagos colony and Protectorate of Nigeria, Lagos was at the heart, and became the capital until 1991 when it was replaced by Abuja, a purpose-built populous in the geographical centre of the country.

On the day we were travelling, I dressed up well because I did not want to look like someone from Osun state, a state that provides almost no resources for Nigeria. In our car, as we were driving, with places whirling backwards with breeze, I did not know that the trip would take such a form as this, a complete string of sentences and paragraphs. But I was conscious of every place, everything. When we got to Ibadan in Oyo state, the largest city in Africa, John Pepper Clark's poem titled 'Ibadan' drove into my mind. Even though I'd been to Ibadan at least a couple of times, it had never occurred to me to see the city through the poet's eyes:

> running splash of rust,
> and gold-flung and scattered among seven hills,
> like broken china in the sun.

For Clark, Ibadan is a rusty city with beautiful houses. His words bring alive the geography of the city as it bends and rises and explores the shades of the landscape: noise, sellers and buyers, workers, corporate buildings, etc. When we arrived at Academy market, I saw a Close-Up advert on a billboard. My brother told me Close-Up is being produced in Ibadan. He was wrong. Close-Up is a toothpaste manufactured by Unilever, a British establishment in Nigeria.

But things are being made in Nigeria. The Dangote Group, led by Aliko Dangote, Nigerian business magnate and, according to Forbes, the richest person in Africa, manufactures cement, food products, and is the major supplier to Nigeria's drink companies and breweries. Educated at a madrasa and Capital High School in Kano, Dangote is a home-grown wealth creator. He started small, buying and selling sweets, following in the footsteps of his father who was a successful trader of rice and oats in Kano state, Nigeria's second largest state. Dangote Refinery has been under construction since 2016 and is expected to be one of the world's largest oil refineries when it is completed. Abdulsamad Rabiu, Femi Otedola, Wale Adenuga, Folorunsho Alakija also belong to the circle of Nigerian businessmen internationally recognised for their home-grown enterprises servicing a burgeoning middle-class – that is, those who have not decided to emigrate. Nigerian businessmen decry the lack of foreign investment. 'Nigeria is one of the best-kept secrets', Dangote says. 'A lot of foreigners are not investing because they're waiting for the right time. There is no right time'.

By the time we arrived in Lagos in the evening, it was getting dark but the beauty of the city can never be shaded by darkness. It was a different breeze; the aura was soul whelming and voices sounded differently and from every side, bustles and rumbles swarmed over us. I closed my eyes and took it all in; this is Lagos, the city where international talent from Nigeria is born and amplified.

It is a city of music. Omah Lay, acclaimed singer and songwriter, born in Port Harcourt state moved to Lagos to boost his international music career. 'Lagos provided me the exposure to opportunities that I needed to launch my career', he says. Lay is an example of the way in which Nigeria has become globally renowned in music and film. Fela Anikulapo-Kuti, the godfather of music in Nigeria, is regarded as the pioneer of Afrobeat. Afrobeat, the term coined by Fela himself to mean a genre of music that includes the combination of African musical styles with other forms of sound instruments, is internationally revered. All African artists now claim Afrobeat as their form of music – an indelible signifier of the Nigerian culture and Africa at large.

To understand contemporary Nigeria, it is necessary to draw from the past, juxtapose it, and build a connection. The influential capacity of Nigeria is built by the Nigerians themselves and not its government, with the youths being the backbone of it all. Fela Kuti, who died in 1997, was a pan-Africanist and his political activism was expressed through his music, performed in his dialect – Yoruba and pidgin. But the honour is not placed on Fela alone His legacy brought up and inspired a plethora of young artists. King Sunny Ade, the first Nigerian to be nominated for the Grammy Awards, signed with the British Jamaican record label, Island Records, in 1982 and released his album, 'Juju Music', to international acclaim in the same year. Burna Boy won Best Global Music Album at the Grammys for his album 'Twice As Tall'. The first Nigerian to win a Grammy Award, while Wizkid won Best Music Video for his song 'Brown Skin Girl' with Beyonce and Blue Ivy. This attests to the force Nigerians are becoming on the world scale. Once upon a time they were scarcely nominated. Now they are winning.

But the narrative has started to change. Instead of Nigerian artists travelling to secure deals with international record labels, they are now coming back to Nigeria. They realise that Nigeria is becoming a leading light in the global market, influential and with a world audience ready to listen to our music. By 2017, Sony Music Entertainment and Universal Music Group had built offices in Lagos, which the writer Wale Oloworekende declared a 'move widely interpreted as confirmation of Lagos's position as the epicentre of popular music out of West Africa'. Again, in 2020, the global music streaming platform, Audiomack, set up its first international office in Lagos. Spotify followed in 2021, due to the high streaming rate the company was getting in the country. But this isn't about Lagos alone; it is about a state in Nigeria.

It doesn't stop there. The movie industry is also excelling and pushing bars. *Lion Heart*, directed by Genevieve Nnaji, which premiered in 2018, is the first Nigerian movie to be acquired by the giant streaming platform, Netflix. Not long after, it was nominated for an Oscar, but was disqualified because it did not meet the requirement of being 'predominantly indigenous'. Netflix has continued to acquire Nigerian movies and has established a full affiliation in Nigeria as 'Netflix Naija'; Naija is the pidgin form for Nigeria. Lagos and Sambisa Forest in Maiduguri, an area known only for being dominated by the Boko Haram insurgency, are featured in the world-accepted Marvel studio movies: *Captain America – Civil War* and *Black Panther* respectively. Hollywood is developing international movie locations in places grabbing headlines for entirely different reasons.

I grew up in a religious environment. My father was a popular Islamic cleric and I was, at a very young age, introduced to Arabic literacy. Though, my father died before I was born, I came to understand his legacies and tried to build on them. Later, I sought Western education. If my father had been alive, I cannot be sure I would have had quite the same opportunity to be captivated by Western education. When I was a secondary school student, the first Nigerian writer that I came across was Chinua Achebe. In every English textbook that we used, *Things Fall Apart*, Chinua Achebe's magnum-opus book, was mentioned. That was when I started getting curious and hungry to know the writer, even when I hadn't read *Things Fall Apart*. But I knew it was published in 1958; and told the story of Nigerians in the eastern part of Nigeria before and during colonialism, written by someone who experienced it himself. At school I learned that colonialism is an exploitative approach that insists: we can give you something far better than what you think you have. Yes, if colonialism hadn't happened, Nigeria would not be what it is today. Of that there is no doubt. But who is to say whether the violence of colonialism was worth what we have been left with? Colonialism wiped out our monarchical system, traditional beliefs, and institutions. Without colonialism, perhaps Nigeria would have remained a place amenable to people of different cultures. Nigeria as a name may not even have existed.

Nigeria battles with a large wound of corruption that is a remnant of colonialism. How? It is quite simple. Colonialism introduced the exploitative mechanism through which things that belongs to the public can be driven to the pockets of individuals. The people who direct public property into their own pockets think they have the power to do so. Colonial masters might have left Nigeria, but the idea of colonialism still remains. Only now it has shifted: the oppression is not done by colonisers, but exploitation and corruption survive in Nigeria in the hands of Nigerians who guard the corridors of power.

While Chinua Achebe's sequel to *Things Fall Apart*, *No Longer At Ease* grapples with modernity and tradition, idealism and the forces of corruption in Nigeria. There is only one character in the novel, Obi Okwonkwo, with an indigenous name. Christopher, Clara, Mr Green and others, represent Nigerians who have exaggeratedly adopted the culture of their white colonisers. In the 1840s, when British missionaries arrived in Nigeria, religion and business were the colours on their faces. Only one thing is certain, the imposition starts from there because their religion was preached and reformed as offering the only salvation.

As well as Chinua Achebe, Cyprian Ekwensi and the writers of the Onitsha Market stand out as a unique form of popular literature embodying voices from the stalls of Nigeria's everyday markets. The Onitsha Market literature is a genre of moralistic novellas and pamphlets written by students, emerging journalists and taxi drivers, and sold at the famous market in eastern Nigeria, considered to be the largest market in West Africa. It has produced some prolific writers, including Speedy Eric, O Olisah, Thomas O Iguh, and Felix Stephen. These writers expressed the political and social concerns of the people in newly independent Nigeria. What Chinua Achebe does is to go further, challenging the narrative about Nigeria as carved out by colonisers but also holding successive post-independence governments to account. Nobel Prize in Literature winner

Wole Soyinka would continue this discourse, leading to his arrest and two-year imprisonment in 1967 during the Nigerian Civil War, with renowned contemporary writer and activist Chimamanda Ngozi Adichie describing Soyinka as her 'guiding light'. Soyinka's concerns are as relevant today as they were when he was incarcerated. The politics of memory continue to play a pivotal role in all that occurs in contemporary Nigerian society. The injustices of the war that ravaged Nigeria post-independence continue to be denied, and this denial replicates itself in state-sanctioned violence as government actors attempt to suppress alternative interpretations of nationhood by playing on the fear of separation.

It is up to Nigerian writers to continue to use writing as a tool to correct, express and bear witness to voices, emotions and scenes that challenge systematic and institutionalised state-led atrocities. On 20 October 2020, when the Nigerian Army opened fire at peaceful crowds protesting against police brutality at Lekki Toll Gate in Lagos, Nigerian writers and journalists risked their lives to bear witness to the horrific scenes and investigating the truth of the events even when the government of Nigeria persisted in denying it. The massacre captured the attention of the whole world because Nigerian youth wrote and spoke about what they lived.

What happened in Lekki is a metaphor, a summary of the structure of the system Nigeria is presently practicing. In particular, the antics of Special Anti-Robbery Squad (SARS) is noteworthy. SARS is a security body formed out of the Nigerian Police Force. It was set up in 1992 by Simeon Danladi Midenda, and charged with the duties of curbing robbery, motor-vehicle hijacking, kidnapping and crimes. Nigerians experience incessant brutality at the hands of this police unit. Anyone who is dressed in a manner that the officers objected to, or who 'looks' suspicious, would be accused. The unit abuse their powers, using the slightest excuse to question anyone, often brutally. From attire to idiosyncrasy, almost anything could get you into trouble. SARS officers demand bribes from whoever they accused of illegal or immoral activity, and when they fail or are unable to pay, victims would be beaten and brutalised, including women and children.

So, when Nigerian youth trooped out in 2020, risking COVID-19, they intended to end it all. The oppression, the brutality, bad governance, and every other thing that exists in between. It was the first-time young

Nigerians were expressing their suffering to the world and letting the government know they were no longer willing to stand for it. It marked the first fight of Nigerian youth against the entire Nigerian system inherited from the brutality of colonialism, traumatised by the civil war, and beset by corruption and insecurity. And that protest, thrust hands into the eyes of the Nigerian government.

We, young Nigerians, have had enough. While our hope champions intellectual learning, creativity and innovation, the systematic and institutional corruption and injustice serve to crush the dreams and ambitions of talented citizens. This is a nation with the potential to become one of the most influential countries in Africa because of the talent and imagination of the emerging generation. These youngsters have no time for those still chasing the ghosts of a dysfunctional past. Young Nigerians are circumventing the structures of power and authority of the state that demands conformity, and are instead accessing opportunities through social media to gain the attention they need, the attention they deserve. They are tired of the government's lacking appreciation of and investment in talent-building and wealth creation. The government machine only praises those who serve it, oils its wheels and write to maintain the status quo not those who challenge it, hold it to account. The young generation writes not to defend the establish order but to bear witness. Given the oppression and lack of opportunities, it is not surprising that most Nigerians strive to travel out of their country. Everyone seemingly wants to emigrate to the US and the UK, and not return, or even look back at what the country of their birth has done to them. The facilities to nurture one's talent are simply unavailable.

When the businessman Innocent Chukwuma established Innoson Vehicles Manufacturing Company in 2007 at Anambra state, it was boasted that for the first time Nigeria would be producing Nigerian-made cars. But how could an engineering company operate without electricity? It is not that Nigeria lacks natural resources. The country is blessed with oil as well as other natural resources, such as petroleum, flourishing under the earth upon which we walk. But while Nigeria is producing oil, indicators of poverty increase at every level. The second largest country in Africa with natural resources, such as gold, mineral and, of course, oil, doesn't have a refinery and has to export its oil, contract external companies to refine and import it back into the country - at great cost.

Nigeria joined the Organisation of Petroleum Exporting Countries (OPEC), an organisation of just thirteen states in 1971. OPEC aims to 'coordinate and unify the petroleum policies of its member countries, in order to secure the stabilisation of oil markets'. In a November-December 2006 Bulletin Commentary titled 'A special date for Nigeria', the organisation suggested that the country no longer sees itself as just the 'Giant of Africa' but also now the 'Heart of Africa'. The statement was probably true in 2006, when the country was in a better economic condition. But the triangular problems of Nigeria – the corruption, the government failing its citizens, insurgencies from Boko Haram to oil pipe breakers, and farmer-herder conflicts – have brought it to its knees. If Nigeria would qualify as the 'Giant of Africa', which it is, it would not be due to those who govern it. It would be due to the efforts of the young generation.

The current administration of President Muhammadu Buhari set out to fight against corruption and recover Nigerian resources overseas. The initiatives started well, but corruption has eaten deep into the body of the system and eventually, the corruption-fighting administration is also drowning in a pool of corruption. The head of the Economic and Financial Crimes Commission (EFCC), the body charged with the duty of investigating corruption, has been accused of embezzling billions of naira. Naira is devaluing every day. Abduction reports are frequent headlines; and to ordinary Nigerians nowhere seems safe. If the Nigerian government cannot tackle corruption, provide security for its citizens, and cannot guarantee economic stability and growth, where does our future prosperity lie?

In 2019, I watched a Chinese TV series. It was set in San Francisco, USA, in a place called Chinatown. It was the first time I had heard of Chinatown. I was fascinated by the idea of the Chinese in America, and in the series, the Chinese communities exist in parts of America but not always *as* a part of America. I wondered if there is a Chinatown in Nigeria. Google revealed that there is a Chinatown in Lagos. It was officially established in 2001. It is a shopping arena with 300 shops and 200 apartment units, with tall red walls that resemble the Great Wall of China.

Sitting on 20,000 squares metres of land, and expanding, the centre affirms the direct cultural and economic exchange between Nigeria and China. It is also, I discovered, a symbol of Nigeria's love for China. We Nigerians trust anything made in China. Indeed, 'Made in China' has become such a coveted stamp that any product that does not have this label might not sell. This is why some Nigerian-made products are also sometimes labelled 'Made in China'. Hong Kong investors started establishing factories in Nigeria in the 1950s, with one of the first, the Li Group, based in Kano, believed to be the largest private owned business with serial growth every year. China has invested heavily in Nigeria's efforts to combat economy and security issues. In February 1971, under the government of General Yakubu Gowon, Nigeria established diplomatic relations with China, securing mutual direct investment between the two countries. The relationship has grown over the years and China's influence on Nigeria is now pivotal.

When Chinese President Hu Jintao visited Nigeria in 2006, his host and the then Nigerian President, Olusegun Obasanjo, said, 'from our assessment, this twenty-first century is the century for China to lead the world. And when you are leading the world, we want to be close behind you. When you are going to the moon, we don't want to be left behind'. Since then, Chinese companies have boosted the economic standard of Nigeria, building the Lagos-Ibadan expressway, Kano-Kaduna railway lines, Abuja-Kaduna rail, and airport terminals in Abuja, Lagos, Port Harcourt and Kano, helped launch the Nigerian Communications Satellite, and provided the Nigerian Air Force with Wing Loong II, CH-4 and CH-3 aircrafts. In March 2020, China's loans to Nigeria stood at US$3.121 billion, which is 11.28 per cent of the country's external debt of US$27.67 billion. Some have argued that China's interventions in Africa is self-interested, exploitative, and even neo-colonial. I think this is simplistic and serves to perpetuate unwelcome stereotypes of Chinese and African people.

Naija No Dey Carry Last is a book of essays written by the internationally respected Nigerian writer, satirist, activist and political critic, Pius Adesanmi. The essays explore the history of Nigerian politics and democracy. *Naija No Dey Carry Last* is a pidgin statement which can be loosely translated to mean 'Nigeria is not a country of dullards that occupy last positions.' Adesanmi in mocking the mediocrity of Nigeria's politicians, the incompetent of the ruling elite and that shamefully Nigeria is often seen as one of the most corrupt countries in the world. But young Nigerians have inverted 'no dey carry last' to mean a country of creatives, intellectuals, and innovators who are changing the narrative, even when their government does not pay attention or care about their dreams and potential.

After my brother was cleared to board his flight, I was staring at his back and smiling as he walked out of sight. But behind the smile was sadness. I said to myself, Nigeria is losing another talent abroad. It was sad because so many Nigerians want to 'get out of the country' because they believe, 'out there', that is where their talent will reach its full potential – even if they would face racism and other forms of oppression. I recalled the words of Rasaq Malik Gbolahan, a 'Nigerian-based' poet. In a WhatsApp chat, I asked him why he still remains in Nigeria while poets of his generation have travelled overseas. He replied: 'not everybody who writes wants to go abroad'. As a writer, I want to stay in Nigeria. There is a great deal that can be done by staying in the country. The #EndSARS protest is enough of a justification. Aliko Dangote and other successful business owners established their businesses without stepping out of the country. Nigeria is not the giant of Africa for just its population. It is also because of its talented young, its internationally renowned musicians, its writers and intellectuals, its emerging film industry, and its design, fashion, and theatre creatives. We are resourceful, we have resources, we will not be content with the last positions.

'GREATER SERBIA' 2.0

Jasmin Mujanovic

It is perhaps the most dangerous idea in European politics today, and therefore a threat to the entire continental order. And in a sign of the times it's yet another reboot. The government of Serbia, particularly the country's Minister of the Interior, Aleksandar Vulin, calls it the 'Serbian World' (*Srpski svet*). It refers to the stated desire by Belgrade to enact the formal, institutional, and political union of all ethnic Serbs in the Western Balkans. That is, the unification of all Serbs and all 'Serb lands' – territories inhabited by significant ethnic Serb populations in neighbouring Bosnia and Herzegovina, Kosovo, Montenegro, Croatia, and North Macedonia – in one state.

During the Yugoslav Wars, this idea was known by a different name: 'Greater Serbia' (*Velika Srbija*). It was the animating principle behind then President Slobodan Milosevic's wars of conquest and extermination in the region between 1991 and 1999. The apex horror of that initiative was the Bosnian Genocide from 1992 to 1995, which saw the Serbian government and its proxy forces attempt the wholesale removal and liquidation of the country's non-Serb population, with the Bosniak community as its primary target. The aim was to 'purify' Bosnia of the taint of 'Islamisation' (that is, the predominantly Muslim Bosniaks) and annex it to the new, enlarged Serbian polity, along with significant parts of then occupied Croatia.

In the fantastical narratives of Serbian nationalist ideologues like Milosevic and his underlings Radovan Karadzic and Ratko Mladic – both currently serving life sentences for genocide and crimes against humanity following convictions at the International Tribunal for the former Yugoslavia (ICTY) - this entire bloody effort was part of the process of restoring Serbia to an era of halcyon greatness, to a time before the fall of the medieval Serbian state to the Ottoman Empire in 1459. And exterminating the indigenous Muslims of the former Yugoslavia, the Bosniaks and Albanians, was the ultimate form of revenge against 'the Turks' because these communities were improbably portrayed in the Serbian nationalist discourse as the ancestors and collaborators of the hated Ottomans.

The astute reader will immediately notice the parallels between these narratives and anti-Semitic blood libel conspiracies and fabricated documents like *The Protocols of the Elders of Zion*. Like those canards, contemporary Serb nationalism is rooted in a network of quasihistorical mythologies, virtually all of which have as their eventual intent the glorification and justification of violence against Western Balkan Muslims. And like that anti-Semitic credo, these ideas too have resulted in state-sponsored atrocities against these targeted communities.

Still, why are such reactionary ideas salient in a twenty-first century European state, one which is nominally considered as a 'front runner' for EU membership? And what does this phenomenon mean for Europe itself, already in the grips of the tides of a newly energised far-right, and darkened by the shadow of a far more geopolitically influential but likewise revanchist and irridentist Kremlin? Addressing these questions gets to the heart of the malaise of the contemporary Western Balkans, a region still dealing with the fallout of the Yugoslav dissolution, trapped in a decades-long democratic and political deep freeze.

Milosevic's Successor

In short, Serbia's leaders, above all its near-autocratic President Aleksandar Vucic, believe the 'Euro-Atlantic' era - the period of EU and NATO enlargement in the Western Balkans – has ended. This affords them the opportunity, in turn, to resuscitate the Greater Serbia project, a political programme which the country's nationalist establishment and its sympathisers – especially in the influential, and unreformed security and military sector – have never abandoned.

They believe, genuinely and earnestly, that they can engineer Serbia's annexation of half of Bosnia and Herzegovina; that they can formally append the Serb-majority municipalities in the north of Kosovo to Serbia; and that Montenegro will, once more, be brought into a Belgrade-governed union, abandoning its own sovereignty in the process. The exact fate of North Macedonia in such visions is not clear, even if the Serbian intelligence apparatus has historically maintained a deep footprint in the country, and the Macedonian Orthodox Church remains ecumenically ensnared by the Serbian Orthodox Church, whose links to the Serbian state and the country's nationalist establishment are, in a word, intimate. Whether Croatia, despite its EU and NATO membership, would be spared pretensions upon its territory by this expansionist Serbia, as was the cause during the 1990s, is likewise an open question.

To appreciate the depth and sincerity of these convictions – which to the uninformed may seem like crazed phantasms – one must know something about the biography of the country's undisputed hetman, President Vucic.

Serbia's brief period of democratisation – between 2000 and 2012 – effectively ended when Vucic and his Serbian Progressive Party (SNS) assumed the helm from the Democratic Party (DNS). One could even suggest that this process had already ended in 2003 with the assassination of the reformist Prime Minister Zoran Djindjic on the orders of the former commander of the country's Special Operations Unit, Miroslav Ulemek 'Legija'. For its part, the SNS is an offshoot of the Serbian Radical Party, an extremist, far-right bloc which was a thinly veiled appendage of the Milosevic regime during the nineties, and whose members participated in widespread atrocities during the wars in Bosnia and Croatia.

Vucic was a close associate of the Radicals' long-time chieftain, Vojislav Seselj, who was the country's most outspoken advocate of the Greater Serbia concept. Like his mentor, Vucic made his name as a vicious rhetorical pugilist. He famously declared in the Serbian National Assembly, in July 1995, as Serb nationalist forces were in the process of effectively exterminating and expelling the entire Bosniak population from Srebrenica, that his movement's response to any international intervention in Bosnia would be to 'kill one hundred Muslims' for every dead Serb.

Vucic and the Radicals were on the hardest right-wing of an already viciously chauvinist political spectrum; he was a fanatic among zealots. Indeed, the Radicals often functioned to make Milosevic seem like a 'moderate' in the eyes of the international community, while also providing the regime with a modicum of plausible deniability in the conduct of widespread atrocities in neighbouring states, serving a role similar to Karadzic and Mladic, incidentally. Milosevic was the polite, media-savvy face of the regime; the bloodthirsty Radicals were the reality, its *actually existing* policies.

Yet Vucic also served as Milosevic's Information Minister between 1998 and 2000, and he was one of the strongman's ceremonial pallbearers at his funeral in 2006. Substantively, the space between the two was virtually non-existent, and Vucic has remained clear in his commitments to his old master. In 2018, he called the architect of the Bosnian Genocide 'a great Serbian leader'.

And it is a relationship he has sought to emulate for his own purposes. Much as Milosevic propped Seselj as an extremist to make himself appear like a moderate the West could do business with, while his regime advanced identical policies as the Radicals, Vucic has helped buttress Milorad Dodik, the secessionist Serb nationalist leader in neighbouring Bosnia and Herzegovina whose government is almost exclusively financially propped up by Serbia and Russia. Thus, Vucic rarely explicitly advocates carving up Bosnia, but Dodik and his associates do so daily.

After a few years in the wilderness following Milosevic's ouster in October 2000, Vucic returned to political primacy alongside Tomislav Nikolic, another Radical veteran, and their newly formed Progressives in 2012. On paper, the SNS was supposed to be a kind of conversative-populist bloc, which would model itself on the broad spectrum of right-wing European parties, like Germany's CDU or Austria's OVP. The SNS soon emerged, however, as merely a refurbished vehicle for Vucic and Nikolic's familiar nationalist machinations, as civil liberties and media freedoms in the country rapidly declined. By 2017, Vucic successfully side-lined his partner Nikolic, and assumed the presidency himself. Since then, Vucic has even more rapidly consolidated his strangle hold on the Serbian state. He won the 2017 presidential elections with 55% of the vote; his nearest opponent failed to crack 17 percent. In 2020, the entire opposition boycotted the country's parliamentary elections. As a result, the SNS and the its coalition partners – which includes Milosevic's old Socialist Party – have 230 MPs in the 250-member National Assembly; the remaining twenty seats are all occupied by a fistful of tiny ethnic minority parties.

Serbia's Long Nineteenth Century

Serbia is, by all counts, a small state, even by European standards. But nationalism has remained a dominant ideological current in the country's politics since the early nineteenth century, and the country's leaders have long-harboured fantastical plans for Serbia as the leading power in South-eastern Europe. In that sense, the process of state formation and territorial expansion which began for Serbia in the early nineteenth century remains, at least in the imaginations of its political leadership, unfinished. And it is that idea of Serbia as a perennially unfinished state which has historically been the greatest source of the entire Western Balkans' propensity towards instability and conflict.

In 1817, a group of incipient Serbian warlords in what was then known as the *Sanjak* of Smederevo, a territory which today corresponds to Belgrade and parts of central Serbia, won *de facto* independence from the Ottoman Empire and declared the Principality of Serbia. Although the new polity was effectively a vassal state of the Ottoman Empire, as the Porte's hold on the region waned, Serbia's political position improved. Beginning in the 1830s, the Principality began to expand its borders. As it did, the country's population swelled but so did its ethnic, religious, and linguistic diversity. But because the animating principle of Serbia's expansionist policies was one of 'unifying' the 'Serb people', the ruling Obrenović court imposed a policy of Serbianisation on its new subjects.

For predominantly Orthodox and Catholic Christian communities, including the Macedonians, Croats, Bulgarians, and the Vlachs among others, this meant that their safety depended on subsuming their own local and regional identities to the new Serbian state. For Muslim communities, however, above all the Bosniaks and Albanians, no safety was on offer. For them, the new regime meant either forced conversions, expulsion, or extermination. As sociologist Djordje Stefanović writes of the 1870s to 1880s in the newly acquired southeast of the country:

> Despite some voices of dissent, the Serbian regime 'encouraged' about 71,000 Muslims, including 49,000 Albanians 'to leave'. The regime then gradually settled Serbs and Montenegrins in these territories. Prior to 1878, the Serbs comprised not more than one half of the population of Niš, the largest city in the region; by 1884 the Serbian share rose to 80 %. According to Ottoman sources, Serbian forces also destroyed mosques in Leskovac, Prokuplje, and Vranje.

After centuries of rule by the Ottomans, Muslims effectively disappeared from Serbia proper in under a hundred years. This was not entirely unique to Serbia, of course. A similar process of expulsions, killings, and population transfers marked the entire period of the decades-long collapse of the Ottoman Empire which began in earnest in the early nineteenth century, culminating in the Greco-Turkish population exchanges of 1923. But that process did not end in Serbia in the 1920s. It continued into the 1930s and 1940s as the newly formed Kingdom of Yugoslavia – a union of all the South Slavic territories in the Western Balkans, including Albanian-majority Kosovo which had been occupied by Serbia and Montenegro in 1912 and then entirely by Serbia in 1918 – struggled to deal with the competing demands for representations in state which now stretched from the peaks of the Julian Alps to the shores of Lake Ohrid, and all of it ruled by a unitarist Serbian crown.

By the time of the fascist invasion of Yugoslavia in 1941, the country was already effectively on the brink of collapse. Nominally 'pan-Slavic' in character, the Yugoslav regime founded in 1918 had already become a personal dictatorship under King Alexander I in 1929, after the leading Croat political figure in the country, Stjepan Radic, was killed on the floor of parliament by a Serb nationalist from Montenegro, Punisa Radic. Though a degree of political reform occurred after the drafting of a new constitution in 1931, in 1934 Alexander I himself was assassinated by a Bulgarian nationalist revolutionary affiliated with the Internal Macedonian Revolutionary Organisation.

As such, the arrival of German and Italian occupation forces merely provided the catalyst for existing political tensions to dissolve into a torrent of violence across the whole of Yugoslavia. Croat and Serb quisling forces each tried to carve out, in the maelstrom of war, ethnically homogenous and greatly expanded territories for themselves in Europe's new order. Hence while the Ustahsa regime in Zagreb orchestrated a genocidal campaign against ethnic Serbs in Croatia and Bosnia (alongside the usual targets of fascist terror, above all the Jews and Roma), Serb ultra-nationalist Chetniks rampaged across Bosnia, primarily targeting ethnic Bosniak communities.

While it was the communists who finally prevailed in Yugoslavia, and who styled themselves as a multi-ethnic, people's liberation movement, the toll of decades of sectarian conflict – and expansionist fervour in the federation's largest republic, Serbia – was severe. Although the first three decades of communist rule in the region were marked by significant socio-economic progress, the second Yugoslav state was beset by many of the same fundamental issues as its predecessor: it was an authoritarian regime, which struggled to provide democratic and liberal avenues for the country's various communities to advance their interests. And below the officially mandated pledges to 'brotherhood and unity', familiar pretensions remained, even in segments of the ruling communist establishment, especially in Serbia. When Aleksander Rankovic, the powerful former head of Yugoslavia's secret police and the architect of the regime's most severe anti-Albanian policies in Kosovo, died in 1983 his funeral became a kind of mass political rally in Belgrade, with an estimated 100,000 people in attendance, despite official sanctions.

This sclerotic political regime likewise failed to produce meaningful solutions to the onset of sustained economic crisis in the early 1970s, from which the country ultimately never recovered. Following the death of Josip Broz 'Tito' in 1980, Yugoslavia's economy entered a death spiral, which only further exacerbated existing regional tensions. But these only took on their toxic, ethnic edge with the rise of Slobodan Milosevic after 1987. If previous generations of Serbian communists had harboured what the then ruling party's ideologues called 'unitarist' tendencies – a term intentionally meant to invoke the experience of the previous monarchist regime – Milosevic made it central to his appeal to the Serbian masses. And it was he, in the final analysis, who re-invented the Serb nationalist project for the modern period.

Engineering Dissolution

The perverse genius of Milosevic's rise to power was that he, initially, offered two competing political visions, to two distinct camps. To the Yugoslav conservative military establishment, he offered the figure of a resolute commander, determined to crush all anti-regime elements, including those seeking to reform the one-party political regime. Like Rankovic, Milosevic made Kosovo and its Albanian community the locus of his concern over 'separatist' tendencies. To the Serbian public, and ethnic Serbs across Yugoslavia, Milosevic offered the promise of self-determination and protection from a vast Croat-Bosniak-Albanian conspiracy seeking their subjugation in all the Yugoslav territories where Serbs did not themselves constitute a demographic majority. That conspiracy, of course, was entirely the product of Milosevic's media apparatus, and the fevered imaginations of the dissident Serb nationalist elements which Milosevic was simultaneously rehabilitating and bringing into the public. But it was an effective programme all the same.

As Milosevic's populist-nationalist appeal made inroads with the Serbian populace, it raised his legitimacy with the military, which in turn allowed him to be ever more brazen in his political grandstanding. Between 1988 and 1989, he engineered the fall of the governments in Vojvodina, Serbia, Kosovo, and Montenegro through a series of Astroturfed populist mobilisations which his supporters dubbed the 'anti-bureaucratic revolution'. By 1989, he rose to the post of President of the Socialist Republic of Serbia. In so doing, and with his loyalists installed at key posts, he cemented his grasp on the Yugoslav People's Army (JNA), and the expansive Yugoslav intelligence apparatus.

In September 1990 Milosevic's regime adopted a new Serbian constitution – certified through a referendum of dubious legitimacy – which declared the 'sovereignty, independence, and territorial integrity of the Republic of Serbia'. It was an extraordinary step. Serbia had, legally, declared its own independence from Yugoslavia. As it did so, it also engineered, beginning in August 1990, the so-called 'Log Revolution' in neighbouring Croatia, wherein Serb nationalist militants – backed by intelligence operatives from Serbia – seized control of large swathes of the country. In December, these elements declared the 'Serbian Autonomous Oblast of Krajina' and made moves towards its formal secession from the republic.

Milosevic's unilateralism and clandestine aggression in Croatia, and corresponding activities in Bosnia and Herzegovina, resulted in Croatia's (and Slovenia's) own declaration of independence in June 1991. It was a move the regime in Belgrade had anticipated and actively encouraged. Realising that his attempt to seize the whole of the Yugoslav state via the anti-bureaucratic revolution model was doomed to failure in the western republics, Milosevic began driving them toward confrontation. With his control over the country's military and security apparatus, he calculated that he would have the brute force necessary either to force their total submission, or to carve out of their territories Serb-majority areas which he could then fuse to create a Greater Serbia. And where there were no ethnic Serb majorities, as in the case of large parts of northern and eastern Bosnia, Milosevic's forces would create them: through murder, torture, rape, and expulsion.

For all his scheming and plotting, Milosevic's grand plan failed. Slovenia and Croatia handed his JNA and associated Serb nationalist paramilitaries crushing defeats. In Slovenia, the conflict only lasted ten days. In Croatia, it spanned the period between 1991 and 1995, but it ended with the complete collapse of the Serb nationalist project there. In Bosnia and Herzegovina, as in the 1940s, Croat and Serb nationalist forces collaborated to partition the country between the two larger neighbouring states. This too failed but Bosnia was ravaged by the war. Of the nearly 150,000 people killed during the whole of the Yugoslav Wars between 1991 and 1999, 100,000 died in Bosnia and Herzegovina alone. Of these, more than 60 percent were ethnic Bosniaks; and within this community, in turn, just over half the victims were civilians. In fact, just about an equal number of ethnic Bosniak civilians were killed in Bosnia and Herzegovina as the total death toll in the Slovenian, Croatian, and Kosovo wars combined.

The U.S.-brokered Dayton Peace Accords finally ended Milosevic's aggression against the country. And while the result was the most fragmented and complex constitutional regimes in the world - contemporary Bosnia and Herzegovina has some fourteen different governments for a population of barely three million people - Bosnia remained a sovereign and unified state, unlike Milosevic's Serbia. In 1999, his regime lost the last of its four wars, when ethnic Albanian forces, eventually backed by NATO, drove out the rump of Yugoslav military and police from the then Serbian province. In 2006, Montenegro seceded from the state union with Serbia; in 2008, Kosovo became the last of the former Yugoslav territories to declare its independence. Though Kosovo does not have a seat at the UN – due to the Russian veto on the UN Security Council – it is recognised as a sovereign state by all but five members of the EU, and all but four members of NATO, and more than half the UN.

Milosevic set out to create a Greater Serbia. Instead, he led his people into a decade of disastrous losing wars; he made Serbia an international pariah; and he reduced the country's actual territory to its smallest geographic footprint since 1912. He and his programme were, by any conceivable definition of the term, a catastrophe for Serbia, for Serbia's people, and, above all, for all its neighbours in the former Yugoslavia.

An Atlantic Solution

So, why do contemporary Serb nationalist leaders like Vucic, Vulin, and Dodik insist on reviving Milosevic's ambitions? Why do they believe that the 'Serbian World' will end any differently than 'Greater Serbia' did?

Like its closest international ally Russia, contemporary Serbia is a state entombed by its own history. Because the country never actually underwent a process of 'de-Milosevicisation' after 2000, because his collaborators recaptured Belgrade's levers of power after less than a decade of stuttering democratisation, Serbia is today being swallowed whole by the terrible ghosts of its own making. That is as much a threat to Serbia's citizens, and their prospects for a prosperous and peaceful future, as it is for their neighbours.

Bosnia and Herzegovina, Kosovo, and Montenegro, despite Podgorica's membership in NATO, are most vulnerable to Belgrade's revanchist tendencies, and have already been under sustained asymmetrical political pressure from the Vucic regime and its respective local proxies. The recent 'non-paper' scandal which roiled the region – concerning a leaked document apparently drafted by Slovenia's illiberal Prime Minister Janez Janša who is a key regional asset of the Kremlin – and advocated for the creation of a Greater Serbia (and Greater Albania) craved out of the territories of Bosnia, Kosovo, and North Macedonia is but one obvious manifestation of this tendency. As recently as last year, Belgrade also formally advocated for a similar arrangement to resolve its outstanding issues with Kosovo, dubbed the so-called 'land swap proposal'.

These are not idle musings. This is the resurrection of the Greater Serbia project, and especially in light of the all but extinguished prospects for EU enlargement among the remaining Western Balkan states, this is a more coherent 'post-European' future for the region than anyone in Brussels has yet offered. That it is megalomaniacal and would result in another round of bloodletting is not a problem for Vucic's Serbia, which has spent the past decade dramatically increasing its arms procurement and modernising its armed forces – largely through Russian and Chinese benefaction. The point of the project is its realisation. Vucic, a committed radical, wants to deliver the thing that has eluded the country's leaders for two centuries: a modern Serbian imperium. He would like to do it through mere political manoeuvring, but he is investing in the kinetic capacities to follow his mentor Milosevic's example, if need be.

For the West and the broader democratic community, the risks of even a semi-serious attempt at realising these aims are significant. The EU is already encircled by violence in North Africa, the Middle East, Ukraine. It cannot afford to let the Western Balkans, its soft underbelly, slip into chaos. Nor can the US, not in the era of renewed Russian revanchism and Chinese belligerence. There is no doubt that all manner of malign state and non-state actors would use any resumption of conflict in the region, no matter how minor, as a beach head to further destabilise the centre of (what remains of) the liberal democratic order.

The simplest response to such disturbing scenarios is to take away the possibilities for its enaction. And the most effective way to do so is to expand the Atlantic aegis to the remaining non-NATO member states in the region, above all Bosnia and Herzegovina but also Kosovo. Bosnia as, arguably, the primary target of Serbian irridentism since the nineteenth century is the strategic loadstone of the whole region. Clinching NATO membership for Sarajevo would remove the possibility of any kind of credible Serbian aggression against this polity. While NATO membership has not entirely eliminated Serbian interference in Montenegro, it has provided a near impenetrable barrier to the country's absorption by Belgrade. Extending such security guarantees to Bosnia and Kosovo would be transformative, as it would permanently curtail Belgrade to the Drina-Ibar line and finally allow the region a chance to develop politically, socially, and economically without the threat of conflict.

Whether Washington or the European capitals have the vision necessary to push forward with such an initiative remains to be seen. It does not appear likely, in truth. But the longer the Atlantic community neglects this region, the greater the eventual costs will be to roll-back Vucic's neo-Milosevic machinations – especially if he enjoys formal backing from Russia. We have nearly two hundred years of evidence showing that the Greater Serbia idea is one that cannot be attempted, never mind realised, without incredible death and destruction. No one – not the people of the region nor the West – can afford to learn this lesson again.

PRESIDENT OF THE RICH

James Brooks

Where do you stand on the Paris consensus? Or should I say: how far along on the path to agreement are you? After all, as its chief architect Emmanuel Macron explained at its unveiling on 16 November 2020, 'it will be the consensus of everywhere'.

Or is 'Paris consensus' not ringing any bells? That's not surprising; despite being the French president's blueprint for a new world order, it barely made a ripple in the press. The choice of media partner was unusual. The Paris consensus was first outlined in an interview with three students from the École Normale Supérieure – a Parisian *grande école* (specialist university). A video of the interview can be found on the website of Le Grand Continent, the school's geopolitical vanity journal, together with a transcript in six languages. Le Grand Continent was understandably keen to push the boat out for the student-journalist scoop of the century, which landed in their lap during last year's Paris Peace Forum, an annual event for the global political and business elite in the same vein as the World Economic Forum at Davos.

Despite the abundance of world leaders at hand there were no other parties to the Paris consensus. It is a consensus of one – of Macron alone. In the video, which we can tell from the transcript has been heavily edited down to a 33-minute runtime, Macron embarks on a series of free-ranging didactic monologues that his interviewers are too scared to cut in on.

Whenever there is a presidential majority in the National Assembly, as there is now, the French president's job becomes possibly the loneliest, most autocratic constitutional position in any western democracy. Accordingly, Macron has the speech of a man who hasn't tasted interruption or contradiction in a long time. Seated in his office at the Elysée Palace against a dazzling backdrop of gold leaf and mirror glass, expounding his view of the world often barely coherently, Macron's style is oddly redolent of Donald Trump's. It's a different kind of incoherence – much more erudite – but there's definitely a resemblance.

What is the Paris consensus? In Macron's jumbled prolix, it

> means moving beyond the pivotal dates that have formed our politics [1945, 1968, 1989] to question the fixing agent of the so-called Washington consensus, and thus the fact that our societies were also built on the paradigm of open-market economics – of social open-market economies as they were known in post-war Europe – which have become increasingly less socially oriented, more and more open, and which after this [Washington] consensus, became dogmatic and held their truths to be: the shrinking of the State, privatisation, structural reform, opening up of economies through trade, financialisation, with a fairly monolithic logic based on building up profit.

There's one word for all this, of course. Macron is describing the political and economic system that dare not speak its name, but which is globally dominant, and with which he is most closely associated: neoliberalism. But readers who managed to follow Macron to the end of his sentence may remember he spoke of the Paris consensus moving us all *beyond* this paradigm. Why? And how? Here Macron is clearer on the first question than the last. Over the course of the interview, he mentions numerous existential geopolitical threats with which neoliberalism is ill-equipped to deal. The first is climate change. World leaders have not adequately tackled this 'crucial issue' because it has been treated 'as a market externality', Macron says. Only if we 'put it back in the market… with a carbon price, for example' can we make progress. Leaving aside whether carbon pricing is a weapon of sufficient potency to take prime position in the fight against environmental collapse, such a faint dash of intervention hardly moves us beyond neoliberalism. Rather, as a market-based solution, it furthers the neoliberal cause by protecting the market in fossil fuels against more drastic intervention, possibly even total shutdown. Human activity in this particular field is still governed by the market; neoliberalism is alive and well.

The second item on Macron's list is inequality. Here he is not referring to the widening gap, now of cosmic proportions, between the few thousand billionaires whose wealth increases vertically and the uncounted multitudes of the majority world condemned to penury. No, he's referring mostly to the middle class in 'our countries' (Europe? The West?), who 'no longer have any means of progress for themselves'. Without an uptick in their fortunes, these people will start to 'doubt democracy' and be seduced by authoritarianism and closed borders. Macron considers these two things to be very bad, which may surprise the 19,000 people deported by force from France in 2019.

What is Macron's solution for the West's beleaguered middle class? Certainly not socialism, or increased taxation and redistribution. Instead, it will come

> by constructing life courses differently: via education and health within a coun-
> try, but then by a different working of financial and economic movements, that
> is to say by integrating the climate objective, the inclusion objective and ele-
> ments of stability of the system within the core of the matrix.

This is not a purposefully obfuscating translation. Nor has the sense of Macron's words been lost in English. There was none to begin with. And so it goes on. Macron is no more convincing discussing the future of the European Union, or the rise of China, or demographic change in Africa (read: migration to Europe) than he is on the topics above. Should we expect any better of an ex-investment banker catapulted into the highest office without much political experience to draw on? Probably not. The 'Paris consensus' is the sound of Emmanuel Macron vainly trying to repackage the neoliberal business-school bromides that won him the 2017 French presidential election as multilateral solutions for a new geopolitical era.

At least in 2017 he delivered his lines with more panache. I watched him do so on the campaign trail in London. The British capital is home to an estimated 300,000 French people, around a third of whom are registered to vote there, so London was not an unprecedented campaign stop for a French presidential hopeful. François Hollande also held a rally there in in 2012. I don't know what reception Hollande received, but Macron's was rapturous. Which makes sense; he was playing to his home crowd.

As political scientists Bruno Amable and Stefano Palombarini showed in their 2018 book – published in English this year as *The Last Neoliberal: Macron and the Origins of France's Political Crisis* – Macron's electoral success was built on an explicit appeal to a group of people who'd previously been catered to imperfectly by France's centre-right and centre-left parties. The 'bourgeois bloc', as Amable and Palombarini call it, is composed principally of highly educated, senior and/or professionally ambitious white-collar employees. Prior to Macron's daring breakaway setting up his political party in 2016, they might have identified with the centre-left's progressive stance on issues like equal marriage, but been unmoved by leftist calls to maintain France's generous social protection. Or they might have adhered to the centre-right's overt pro-business rhetoric but baulked at its reactionary social attitudes. In both cases the problem was the fit with the offer to the working class in the respective left/right voting blocs. What unified the bourgeois bloc across the political divide was its overwhelmingly positive attitude to the European Union. Or to the *actually existing* EU, I should say. Because while the EU's vaunted status as the guarantor of peace in Europe still resonates with most French people, a majority on either side of the political spectrum have become distrustful of the EU as an undemocratic facilitator of globalised big business. This view first found mainstream expression in the 2005 referendum on the EU constitution, which delivered a ten-point majority to the 'No' vote despite the two main political parties urging their supporters to vote in favour – a sort of Brexit contest *avant l'heure*. Macron's supporters are drawn from the ranks of 2005 'Yes' voters and largely welcome France's gradual political dissolution into the European single market.

Gaining power with an electoral base that excluded the working class would be impossible in many countries as there just aren't enough individualistic middle-class professionals to go round. In France in 2017, the combination of a fractionated political landscape and a two-round voting system made it feasible. With voters split between candidates on the left, centre-left, centre (Macron), centre-right and far-right (two candidates), Macron could ease into the second round with 24 percent of the vote, representing the support of only 18 percent of the electorate. Then, in the second round run-off, up against a candidate – the far-right Marine Le Pen – who elicited more strident opposition than he did, Macron's path to victory was clear. Critics now call Macron 'the president of the very rich' but this is less a taunt than a description of his electoral strategy.

On 21 February 2017, when I went to see Macron preach to the converted, the very rich – or at least those on the career ladder to become so – made up a sizeable swathe of the congregation. Macron tailored his material to suit, remarking in the opening minutes on the domestic French media narrative in which

> going to London is obviously all about making money in the City with a whole bunch of wicked and awful people. [Pause, audience laughter.] Well, you have to make money, not necessarily with wicked and awful people.

A minute earlier, he had thanked 'former colleagues', presumably from his banking days at Rothschild & Co, for attending. Macron was among friends. He was free to engage in the most brazen retail politics to his base with no need to temper his talk for acceptance by a wider audience. His plan to liberalise the economy was presented as it might have been at an investor's meeting. Labour law would be reduced to its bare essentials to make France competitive, he declared, as if most of it detailed pointless impediments to business and not an essential backstop against exploitation. France's wealth tax, meanwhile, would be abolished to 'encourage investment', a justification drawing on the historically bankrupt trickle-down theory of high Reaganomics.

In lieu of social protection, Macron pledged to boost provision of professional training. This was a proposition straight from Walter Lippmann's 'The Good Society', a foundational neoliberal text and one of considerable influence in France. In order to keep up with the accelerating changing demands of capital and remain competitive, the theory goes, people will have to switch jobs several times during their careers and educational policy should adapt accordingly. When Macron gave this idea an airing in London, eighty years after the publication of Lippmann's book, there were murmurs of assent. I doubt whether many of those people believed that *they* would be among the unfortunates struggling to keep pace with capital and retraining for a new job every ten years.

Once in power, Macron fulfilled the promise he made in London to push through reforms 'at the start, quickly, robustly, and take responsibility for them'. Along with the weakening of social protections under labour law and the abolition of the wealth tax, he also moved to end inflation-indexed pensions, cut housing benefit, privatise state assets, along with further actions that align perfectly with the Washington consensus Macron described in late 2020. Many of his reforms were stalled by mass protest or the Covid-19 pandemic, but many made it through.

No government department was left untouched. In higher education, the field I cover as a journalist, the goal was to smooth over the particularities of the traditional French system and retrofit it for global competitiveness. The university system in France is driven by a public service ethos that has localism and egalitarianism at its core. All universities exist to educate young people (most of whom will come from the surrounding area) and produce scholarship, so what is the sense of competition? This is not a question that self-styled 'world-leading' institutions in the UK and US would be able to answer. But that hardly matters because the UK and US decided decades ago that higher education should, like every other field of human activity, operate according to the rules of the market and the UK and US control the hegemonic global discourse.

With its links to 'innovation', the Holy Grail of late capitalism, the higher education marketplace is one from which Macron cannot bear France to be absent. The lack of any French institution in the top tier of any university rankings, largely because of French universities' small size, was a particular bugbear. So alongside other changes aimed at liberalising the sector, Macron pushed through a law to make university mergers easier and then personally intervened to oversee a long fought-over mega-merger to create the gargantuan Paris-Saclay University.

In September 2020, Paris-Saclay entered the Academic Ranking of World Universities at fourteenth. France had finally achieved visibility as a player in the global higher-education marketplace, but not everyone rejoiced. The writing is on the wall for France's former public-service oriented approach and those fond of it know so. When Macron negotiated the Paris-Saclay merger, a group of nine unions joined voices to condemn the president's 'elitist and mercantile vision' for higher education, one 'wholly preoccupied with achieving so-called excellence as measured by international rankings'. Macron's approach at Paris-Saclay would lead to the 'abandonment of the missions of a genuine university, with both training and research, open to and in the service of all people', they said. Such complaints now fall on deaf ears. Macron has consistently marginalised trade unions since coming to power.

Similarly, his willingness to use presidential decrees rather than the usual democratic channels – another Trumpian echo – despite having a healthy majority in the National Assembly, demonstrated an early reluctance to negotiate. Centrism's very name suggests a 'compromise' position between left and right, but that is not how Macron plays it. The speed and force of his reforms, delivered with scant consideration for their effects on the working class or most vulnerable, famously sparked the *gilets jaunes* ('yellow vests') protest movement that overran France for about six months from November 2018. It also cost Macron his absolute majority in the National Assembly, although he maintains control thanks to an alliance with the centrist MoDem party.

Macron's party, La République en Marche ('Onward the Republic' / LREM), was hastily assembled in the year before the presidential election. Its candidates in National Assembly elections that followed the presidential vote included former members and representatives of the Republican (centre-right), Socialist (centre-left) and Ecologist parties. Since taking their seats in June 2017, forty-six LREM representatives have quit the party's voting bloc – a record drop in the history of post-war France. The majority of these dissidents are from the centre-left and were dismayed by Macron's single-minded focus on economic reform and his disinterest in social and environmental policy. Such an exodus partially explains Macron's shift to the right over the course of his presidency. Back in 2017, Macron's status as a former protégé of Hollande, a Socialist, combined with a few strategic overtures to environmentalists, made it possible to imagine him as a centre-left politician. No longer. Macron must now search for the popular and political support that will sustain him in power from those on the right.

But Macron's authoritarian manoeuvres far exceed the law-and-order posturing likely to appeal to right-wingers. The list of examples is long. Since coming to power Macron has moved to enshrine supposedly temporary emergency anti-terror legislation in common law. Measures allowed under the legislation include placing draconian 'control measures' on people without charge or trial. Amnesty International warned that France 'has created a second-tier justice system which targets people based on broad and vague criteria, relies on secret information and fails to offer a meaningful opportunity for them to defend themselves'. During the *gilets jaunes* protests, Macron's interior minister, Christophe Castaner, promoted a harshly repressive policing policy, sacking the head of the Paris police after he told officers to avoid excessive force. After a wave of video footage emerged showing widespread and brutal police violence at the protests and elsewhere, Macron tried to ban the filming of police officers – a move deemed unconstitutional by the legal authorities. He ordered police raids on the leftist party La France Insoumise ('France Unbowed') – his most obstinate political adversaries – and the news site Mediapart, which exposed a number of government scandals. After Le Monde broke the 'Benalla affair', a story involving misconduct by one of Macron's security guards that led to allegations of a cover-up, the relevant journalist and director of the newspaper were questioned by intelligence services. It has also been noted that several of Macron's reforms weaken the independent judiciary to the benefit of the police and public prosecutors, who answer to the minister of justice.

This all speaks to Macron's distaste for the processes of liberal democracy and preference for deployment of executive muscle. Given his habit of painting modern politics as a battle between enlightened internationalist progressives on his side and the dark forces of authoritarian populism on the other, that may seem perplexing. But it makes perfect sense when one considers Macron's diminutive support base and the nature of his political project. On the first point, when the *gilets jaunes* protests began, polls consistently put public support for them at between 70 and 80 percent. The comparison with Macron's score among the general electorate in the first round of the election (18 percent) is telling. Macron is pursuing a political programme in the interests of his minority electoral base – the upper-middle and establishment classes – and instinctively opposed by almost everyone else. He cannot succeed by observing the niceties of liberal democratic politics. Authoritarian powerplay is the only way.

Only in that regard can Macron claim to be at the vanguard of any development in First World politics, beyond what he refers to as the Washington consensus. That term in fact originally related to the economic policy prescriptions favoured by the International Monetary Fund, World Bank and US Department of the Treasury, for so-called developing countries in their hour of need. For many years 'development' meant precisely this – the West ordering majority of the world's nations to adopt neoliberal economic reform and supporting the overthrow of any non-compliant governments. As the anthropologist David Graeber wrote in *The*

Utopia of Rules, his book on bureaucracy: 'whenever someone starts talking about the "free market", it's a good idea to look around for the man with the gun. He's never far away.'

The Washington consensus brought about a second wave of colonisation, arriving hot on the heels of the first. With newly independent states now 'opened up' to Western corporations and burgeoning national workers' movements nipped in the bud, a new era of looting could begin. It did – and it continues to this day. But when your entire economic system relies on ever-increasing GDP and 'a fairly monolithic logic based on building up profit' you must always find new territory to conquer. In the era of globalisation, with the entire world under capitalism's sway, this is becoming harder to come by. And so Western nations must turn inward to unlock further growth. They must continue to liberalise their economies – ensure greater exploitation of workers, cut back social protection, release state capital via privatisation – far beyond anything their populations could reasonably want. This is where Macron's brand of authoritarian neoliberalism comes in. Asked to define neoliberalism in a sentence for non-academics on Twitter, the historian Quinn Slobodian suggested 'the ongoing effort to protect capitalism from democracy.' If the Paris consensus represents any kind of geopolitical vision, it's something like that.

Perhaps this domestic focus can explain, with one notable exception, Macron's apparent disinterest in detailed foreign affairs talk during his Paris consensus interview. Certainly, his own foreign policy stances have been wildly erratic, as if perpetually caught between the principled adherence to universal values that could burnish his image – 'we must defend the Enlightenment', he tells his interviewers – and the hardened realpolitik of commercial interest. Nowhere is this more evident than in his contradictory stances on Russia, which were on full display during the 2019 G7 summit from which Vladimir Putin was excluded. One moment Macron toes the NATO party line by saying that Russia must 'abide by fundamental democratic principles' before any rapprochement could be considered. The next he calls for greater dialogue, urging that 'Russia and Europe [should be brought] back together'. By the end of the summit CNN was reporting that Macron had joined forces with Trump in offering Russia a return to G7 talks the following year.

The notable exception spurring Macron to his habitual volubility during the Paris consensus interview was Africa. Using the kind of language typical of the Davos set, he calls for a 'reinvention of the Afro-European axis'. Only a fool would imagine what he means for this to begin with European reparations for centuries of violent exploitation. Or an acknowledgement that the world's remaining carbon budget, if we are to avoid planetary meltdown, should be preferentially used in Africa, where it is most needed. Or at the very least the cancellation of African debt. None of that, of course – we need to reinvent the Afro-European relationship to reduce African migration to Europe.

Macron has form on this subject. He is among those in the European elite who look at the fragile or collapsing states of North Africa, see the gathering dust-storm of climate change on the horizon, and know that Europe's 'migrant crisis', as it is widely tagged in the European press, has barely begun. Macron is also fond of bemoaning African fecundity. His comments at a 2017 G20 summit were particularly memorable for their judgemental, neo-colonial tone. He spoke of

> demographic transition, which is […] one of Africa's crucial challenges. When, as still occurs today, you have countries with [birth rates of] 7 to 8 children per woman, you can decide to spend billions of Euros there, but you won't stabilise a thing.

In the Paris consensus interview, Macron's discourse on Africa is riddled with omission, contradiction and hypocrisy. He bemoans the fact that 'we only look at Africa through this lens [of migratory flows to Europe]' when it is clear that is his primary concern. He pledges that the 're-forging [of the Afro-European axis] must be based on a Europe that is much more geopolitically united and involves Africa as a partner, on an entirely equal footing' and then boasts that African attendees were invited to the previous G7 summit 'for half of the programme'. When he considers the nature of Africa's challenges and the – we can assume – drivers motivating migration to Europe, climate change gets a passing mention but there's once again greater focus on African fecundity: 'If you take the Europe-Africa region, as one European country demographically disappears, over the same period, one African country appears.' There's a perfunctory pledge to help Africa with economic development 'through agriculture, through entrepreneurship, through education, especially for young girls'. And also one to 'fight the scourge of terrorism' including against 'jihadist groups in the Sahel' but Macron doesn't dwell on the origins of the current Sahel conflict, in which his country has been embroiled for the last eight years.

The Western Sahel came under full French command from the 1890s, but it is hard to govern a largely barren and sparsely populated band of sand and rock that stretches halfway across a continent. A short history of France's involvement in the region was given by Stephen Smith, an African studies academic and former journalist for Le Monde, in the *London Review of Books* early 2021 (Macron has praised Smith's 2019 book on African migration, *The Scramble for Europe: Young Africa on its Way to the Old Continent,* as 'a perfect description of Africa's demographic time bomb'). In his essay, Smith unearths a passage from a 1918 French Ministry for Colonial Affairs report which gives a taste of the colonists' frustration at the recalcitrance of their subjects, and their remedies for it. The goal then was

> to rid the African centre of Muslim theocracies hostile to all civilisation and, with the action of a constabulary force, to secure free passage between the Mediterranean and tropical Africa.

As it turned out, the Muslim theocracies were tough to expunge. The French eventually entered a truce with those they had described as 'bandits' – nomads who, Smith relates, 'had embraced a harsh interpretation of the Quran in the second half of the nineteenth century under the influence of the Senussi Brotherhood, a Sufi order'. Over time these nomads – the progenitors of the supra-tribal grouping now referred to as the Tuareg – became 'keepers of the desert' for the French and a sense of collusion developed. The identification was such that the nomads self-described in Moorish as 'Beidan' – 'whites'.

The era of independence registered as an existential crisis for the nomads, who knew they would lose their favoured position and feared reprisals from the sedentary majorities. Ever since, relations between the two have been tense and involve several Tuareg rebellions against Sahel governments, especially in Mali. Which brings us up to the current conflict. In 2012, a Tuareg rebellion – bolstered by around 3,000 highly armed fighters from Gaddafi's mercenary Islamic Legion army who fled Libya as Gaddafi's regime collapsed – drove the Malian Army out of large areas in Northern Mali and proclaimed the independent state of Azawad. It remained internationally unrecognised for its ten-month existence.

The French military joined the conflict in 2013 in support of the Malian government. After a string of early successes then-president Hollande was acclaimed as a liberator in Timbuktu and Bamako. But battlefield success has been no indication of the conflict's overarching trajectory. In Smith's words, the French expeditionary corps, which number more than 5,000, 'has won every battle it's fought, but it has lost the war'.

The Sahel is the world's new Salafist frontier. Since 2013, fighters have joined the Tuareg from across North Africa as members of several groups now consolidating under the name of Nusrat al-Islam, whose leaders have pledged allegiance to Al Qaida. As Sahel governments succumb to coups and disorder and the theatre of war has expands across the Sahel, the possibility of a French victory looks ever more remote. By now it's hard to gauge what 'victory' could even mean. With opinion in France turning against the war, Macron is desperate to extract France from its grim colonial endgame. Whether he does so in accordance with a three-point plan presented at a Sahel leaders' summit in February 2021 is moot, but sooner or later French troops will depart. The Sahel, or vast stretches of it at least, will fall back under the influence of the Muslim theocracies as anathematic to European powers now as they were in 1918. We can hope that life improves for its inhabitants – more than two million of whom have been displaced internally during the conflict – but that seems unlikely.

The greater tragedy is that conflicts like that in the Sahel are set to increase in number in the coming decades as climate change and food insecurity further destabilise regions already perilously close to crisis. Working off the most conservative climate science (the Intergovernmental Panel on Climate Change reports) the United Nations predicts up to one billion climate refugees by 2050. Where are they going to go?

Macron, meanwhile, has been working on France's commercial pivot, away from the frankly sluggish markets of its former colonies and towards Africa's more promising growth economies. 'We have a special relationship with French-speaking Africa,' Macron acknowledges in the Paris consensus interview, in a tone familiar to anyone who's been dumped by an errant partner. ('You know, you'll always be special to me...') Macron, too, has found somebody new:

I wanted to rebuild a very strong relationship with English-speaking and Portuguese-speaking Africa, and I stand by that. I was the first French president to go to Ghana or Kenya, for example. Or to go to Lagos. It sounds crazy, but that's how it was.

No. It doesn't sound crazy to me. It sounds like denial. Like someone not realising that we do nothing to confront the dizzying existential threats facing 'our countries' – climate change, spiralling inequality, mass migration – by conquering new markets or deploying the airy Davos talk of transcontinental partnerships.

And perhaps, in the final analysis, that's what the Paris consensus is: a commitment to shut our eyes to intimidating reality and stay faithful to the suicidally misplaced imperatives of GDP-growth economics. This may not be 'the consensus of everywhere' but it is certainly the consensus of the US, UK and France – three countries condemned to see themselves as exceptional, even as they live out their late-capitalist post-imperial decline similarly, cannibalising their economies and trapped in the unwinnable wars of collapsing empire.

THE WORLD TREE

Naomi Foyle

Climate crisis, refugee crisis, pandemic. Systemic racism, xenophobia, increasing health and socioeconomic inequalities. State surveillance, drone warfare, robotisation, the rise of AI during an epidemic of mental illness. At the heart of our global nexus of disaster is a terrible sickness: a materialist world view that drives not just science but also the global economy, a narrow vision of reality in which human beings are reduced to isolated and competitive bundles of genes; the mind, self, and God to hallucinations and delusions; and the Earth to a resource to be plundered at the grave expense of the biosphere itself. Covid-19 has revealed just how illusory and lethal are these narratives of radical separation, and to ensure that our post-pandemic world does not return to this warped and toxic status quo, new scientific and political paradigms are required: paradigms of unity, paradoxically multiple, that acknowledge our interconnectedness as human beings, not only to each other but also to the ecosystem and, ultimately, a cosmological force best described as love. This emerging paradigm shift is taking many names and forms of expression: postmaterialist, holistic, complementary, ecological, feminist, intersectional, decolonial, Blakean, polyvagal even, after the vagus nerve that connects the brain to the rest of the body. I would like to honour the lungs of the planet and propose the ancient motif of the World Tree as a living symbol of a post-pandemic new world order worth constructing.

First though, to inspect the axe. Since the Enlightenment, dominant social and political institutions have violently hacked at religious, spiritual, and Indigenous beliefs in the unity and mystery of creation, cultivating in their place a reductive materialism with an outright or implicit contempt for faith and myth, the unseen and the unknowable. The result has been enormous and rapid technological progress, including modern medical miracles, but very slow moral development: while hopeful data explored in the recent BBC documentary *The Violence Paradox* indicates that our species is gradually becoming less physically violent, torture, slavery, and war are nevertheless still integral to the functioning of the global economy, while, as critics of the theory argue, less bloody forms of violence – xenophobia, racism, intolerance, poverty, hunger, and other cruel inequities – are on the rise in our Trump-stamped Brexit era. Science, many would argue, is a neutral tool in this arsenal of evils, capable of generating nuclear bombs or solar panels, dependent on political will. But belief in science has, in many quarters, become scientism – what Habermas described as 'science's belief in itself' – that is, the conviction that we can no longer understand science as one form of possible knowledge, but must rather identify knowledge with science'. And both views – of science as tool and science as saviour – mask the extent to which modern science and the global economy share a materialist worldview, limited in scope and potentially hugely damaging in consequence.

I have written elsewhere about what philosopher Mary Midgley called 'the strange, imperialistic, isolating ideology' that has grown up around science, a process she traces and critiques in her classic text *Science and Poetry*. In brief, over the last five hundred years the world has moved from Frances Bacon's declaration that the role of science is 'to put nature to the question' – that is, to torture 'her' – through Isaac Newton's 'Clockwork Universe', in which God creates the cosmos and then simply sets it ticking, to a thoroughly materialist understanding of reality in which God has been evicted from the building, consciousness is considered an 'epiphenomenon', or mere by-product of the brain, and biologically speaking only genes are considered fundamentally real. Our entire perception of reality is simply a 'hallucination', Will Storr tells us in his *The Science of Storytelling*, an application of the insights of neuroscience to narrative techniques in which writers and readers are referred to as 'brains', fictional characters as 'neural realms', and an ancient myth as a 'classic piece of human bullshit'. This hugely depressing reductionism is entirely of a piece with the language of scientism: ignoring the many ways in which genes and organisms in fact co-operate, for Richard Dawkins and others of his ilk, human beings are just 'robot vehicles' or 'wet computers', slaves to the blind selfish genetic imperative to reproduce. I will return to the broader question of consciousness in a moment, but for now let us just consider the implications of this worldview for economics. The materialist rejection of free will, Midgely wryly notes, would seem to be rather at odds with the rampant individualism and competitive economic and political practices of neoliberalism. More recent research, however, concisely summarised by Joan Walton in her article 'The Entanglement of Scientism, Neoliberalism and Materialism', indicates that in fact Western economics has marched in step with scientism since its inception.

Economics and ecology have the same Greek root, 'oikos', meaning home, and yet far from competently managing our collective household, global economic activity is currently burning up the only planet we have to live on. This ironic discrepancy can be traced to the fact that ecological principles of interconnectedness, biodiversity, and sustainability are entirely absent from the foundations of neo-classical economics. Economics, the nineteenth century co-founder of the modern discipline, William Stanley Jevons declared, is a science that 'must be pervaded by certain general principles ... the mechanics of self-interest and utility'. One might argue that there is, at least, still room in this human-centric science for free will, but thanks to these basic assumptions neoliberal economics now operates according to models in which people are simply considered economic units, who react to stimuli as predictably as motors to switches, and whose human motivations are simply drivers, variables in the equations. Due to the pervasive, secretive global spread of neoliberalism, there is increasingly no way out of these models. As Prof Wendy Brown argues, under the neoliberal regime that has effectively replaced social democracy in the West, 'all conduct is economic conduct; all spheres of existence are framed and measured by economic terms and metrics, even when those spheres are not directly monetised' – we have, Brown concludes, become *homo oeconomicus*.

One just has to look around to see how economic scientism plays out, and to what ill-effects. Throughout the capitalist world, governments, corporations, and mainstream and social media collude to sell people a shiny sense of self, manipulating our innate desires to belong and be loved in order to create nations of consumers: of digital devices, apps, make-up, throwaway fashion, television programmes, the latest prize-winning novel, politicians' lies, high speed railway projects that hack down ancient woodlands in order to shave twenty-five minutes off a journey between

London and Birmingham. Our power to change all these conditions is strictly controlled by economic forces: Western secular democracies are in fact plutocracies, governments formed by those with the most money to pump into not just the electoral process, but culture as a whole. Elsewhere on the planet, things are no better, and possibly worse. Under modern communism, materialism's dehumanising politics are nakedly exposed: in China the individual is nothing more than a chip in the motherboard, a cyborg unit to be constantly monitored for any deviation from standard processing functions, and in the case of the genocide of the Uighur Muslims, wiped clean. Perhaps in its less extreme forms of social engineering China is simply more honest than our own governments: the introduction of 'social credit', a digitised system of rewards and harsh penalties for actions as simple as granting or refusing a neighbour a favour, formalises what under neoliberalism is still chaotic and unofficial, playing out in social media addictions and algorithms on platforms that harvest our data to profit from our emotional needs. In oligarchic and theocratic societies, Russia, the Middle East, and elsewhere, though states may pay lip service to the idea of a transcendent spiritual realm, or even to democracy, in practice they conflate the power of God with that of political leaders, monarchs, the military, religious nationalism, and patriarchal family structures, and co-opt divine authority to serve the selfish ambitions of the elite. Globally, corruption is everywhere, from out-and-out kleptocracies in the Global South, still trapped in the colonial tradition of pillage, to the shameful crony capitalism that has characterised the British response to the pandemic; and from the logging of the Amazonian rainforests to the mining of rare earth metals for endless generations of smartphones, from on-going investment in fossil fuels to sham recycling in British cities, nearly all nations collude in environmental destruction.

All of this fatal damage is enabled by a materialist worldview which considers the planet and other people as resources to be plundered and controlled. Clearly, if we are to preserve a planet worth living on, a paradigm shift in humanity's dominant understanding of our shared reality is required. Tempting as it might be to hearken back to simpler times, though, we cannot turn back the clock. The challenge we have now, as concerned and compassionate human beings, of all faiths or none, is not so much to reign science and economics back in line with more traditional thinking, but to generate a new synthesis: to encourage the next stage of our evolution as a species: the evolution of our collective consciousness to a more complex and comprehensive understanding of the unity and diversity not just of life, but the universe.

Holistic Paradigms

Clearly, I am not the first person to suggest this: my own hard-won hope in the future is indebted to a long chain of visionary thinkers, artists and activists from Hildegaard of Bingen, and William Blake to Ziauddin Sardar, Arundhati Roy and Rebecca Solnit, draws strength from the wisdom traditions of world religions and is encouraged by the inclusive ethos of organisations such as the Muslim Institute, Extinction Rebellion, and the Palestine Solidarity Campaign. Recently, too, I have been attending Zoom events hosted by the Scientific and Medical Network (SMN), a deliberately uncontroversial name for a radical organisation that describes itself as 'a creative international forum for transformative learning and change ... bringing together scientists, doctors, psychologists, engineers, philosophers, complementary practitioners and other professionals in a spirit of open and critical enquiry to explore frontier issues at the interfaces between science, consciousness, wellbeing and spirituality.' While event topics vary from neuroscience to soil regeneration, healing techniques to the paranormal, SMN speakers generally share a common belief in a postmaterialist paradigm, one that might take various names and differ in detail, but can most simply be described as holistic: an understanding that, from nuts and bolts to human minds, everything we are taught to perceive as separate entities is in fact profoundly interconnected. The evidence for such an 'expanded' or postmaterialist science is the subject of a full report and layman's guide by the SMN project The Galileo Commission, which seeks to examine the axioms of science and develop new working assumptions that better fit anomalous data; and – much like the work of Ziauddin Sardar and others on science and Islam – to encourage a cooperative relationship between science and spirituality.

However specifically delineated, these holistic paradigms are postmaterialist because, in their understanding, consciousness is intrinsic to all matter. As discussed, in the materialist worldview, consciousness is considered a by-product of the brain, a localised 'hallucination', a simplistic and reductionist understanding of the mind that debases language and, in its metaphor of the brain as 'hard-wired', a damp computer, leads many materialist thinkers to a denial of free will. I am not denying the insights and discoveries of neuroscience: it is true that the brain does a remarkable job of integrating fragmentary perceptions, but if the picture it creates for us is simply a 'hallucination', then what word should we use for apparitions that are not in fact present in a physical space – or at least, not apparent to others in the room? Science has in fact a better term for this ability of the brain to create coherence – 'the binding problem', a phrase that indicates there are still unanswered questions about what exactly is going on here. In the meantime, though, all the blithe talk of brains contemptuously consigns notions of mind, self, or psyche (let alone spirit or soul) – all of which are useful and commonly understood terms for the human perception of being a being, possessing or participating in an integrated consciousness over space and time – into the bin of redundancy. When materialists also deny free will, they simply fly in the face of experience. If we did not have free will, what would be the point of parenting, education, sports training – indeed, any and all human endeavours? We all know we are subject to many forces beyond our control, and hugely influenced by our formative years; we can also accept that our brains form habits it is hard to break, but we are not wind-up toys. From childhood to old age, we are here to learn and grow, and decision-making is the essence of this process. As children, we need adults to show up for us, to teach us how not to act on impulse, and to nurture our innate moral sense – babies have been shown to understand the difference between kindness and cruelty. Unless we – and our brains – have been so damaged by the lack of such care that we become capable only of violent reaction, we grow to understand that, in mundane activities from dieting to personal relationships, when we do set intentions and apply our will to achieve them, we can genuinely choose to create change in our lives. As we mature, we also realise that, as citizens, we must exercise our collective will to intervene in situations of social and political injustice and inequality. A refusal to acknowledge all this marks out materialism as a right-wing philosophy – and one with selective vision. As Midgley and others point out, even within the materialist paradigm a denial of human agency on the basis of neuroscience does not account for the ways in which brains are shaped by human activity: that is, by things we choose to do.

In a holistic paradigm, though, the nature/nurture Möbius loop between mind and brain runs far deeper than human sentience. In the postmaterialist view, consciousness pervades the cosmos: just as a quantum can be seen as both a particle and a wave, the entire universe is simultaneously both matter and consciousness. Although models and theories of mind differ, as explained in the layman's guide to the *Galileo Commission Report*, 'dual aspect or complementarity models of consciousness are a minimum consensus' among critics of materialism. For many such theorists, consciousness is akin to a field that brains, as complex organs of consciousness, have evolved to both filter and transmit within. In this worldview, the universe is considered one Great Mind, as Michael Gosse recently described it in an SMN talk on miracles, also using Aldous Huxley's term 'Mind at Large' to convey a non-religious sense of what believers know as Allah, God, the Great Spirit, or Creator. Many objections can be raised, of course, to this hypothesis, including the apparent difficulty of inanimate objects: what sense does it make to say that a rock partakes of consciousness? In *The Science Delusion* (2012), his landmark challenge to scientism, Rupert Sheldrake writes extensively on this question, invoking the panpsychism propounded by a variety of Western thinkers including Spinoza, Leibniz, Alfred North Whitehead, David Bohm, and even the materialist Galen Strawson. Panpsychism posits simple and complex manifestations of consciousness: while amongst mortal creatures human beings might represent an apex of self-awareness – no other animal writes anguished love poetry, after all – in this theory the growth of plants toward the light can also be described as sentience – the plant is clearly aware of the light – while at the quantum level the attraction and repulsion of elementary particles might be considered a rudimentary form of consciousness. Sheldrake himself considers that elementary particles are acting according not to laws but habits of nature – such particles can be said to be 'unconscious', not in the sense of being non-conscious, but in the way that we too act unconsciously, 'sleepwalking' or 'on auto-pilot' at times.

Also embracing paradox and ambiguity, psi phenomena and near-death experiences, the new holistic paradigm draws on data and insights gained from quantum physics, and the concept of non-locality, in which – as the Galileo Commission layman's report puts it – 'information is perceived for which no signal-theoretical trajectory is possible'. Again, none of this represents a fundamentally new understanding – the Rig Veda, one of the world's oldest religious texts, attributed to rishis, or poets, who attained their insights though lengthy periods of meditation, observes of the 'cause' of the universe:

> Desire came upon that one in the beginning; that was the first seed of mind. Poets seeking in their hearts with wisdom found the bond of existence in non-existence.

> Nasadiya Sukta (10.129)

The sense here of desire as the seed of 'one' mind resonates with the view that a universal field of consciousness is embedded even in the attraction and repulsion of elementary particles, while the mysterious ability of those particles to appear, disappear, and reappear suggests that a mechanical model of the universe, while useful for engineering, does not answer fundamental questions about life, death, and the cosmos.

If the universe is one Great Mind, though, the greatest miracle of all is the numberless variety and diversity contained within this unity. As Muslims know, the human mind is incapable of comprehending the infinite mystery of creation, and to suggest that we can is the height of arrogance. What our minds are good at doing, though – something neuroscience acknowledges, as Will Storr explains in his language of 'hallucinating brains' – is creating metaphors. As Midgley argues, collectively-held metaphors are critical not just to our understanding of the world, but the future we are co-creating. Far from being pieces of 'classic human BS', as Storr would have it, early cosmologies can provide us with powerful and accurate metaphors for the nature of the universe, understood by our ancestors, and mocked at our peril. At a time when the biosphere itself is at risk, as a non-scientist I find myself reaching for metaphors that have stood the test of time and are capable of bridging the abyss of the Anthropocene – the current geological epoch in which human activity is fatefully impacting the Earth – into a more balanced understanding of our place on the planet and in the universe. Few such images offer themselves with more dignity, strength, generosity, and beauty than the tree. Indeed, as Noble Ross Reat points out in his absorbing essay 'The Tree Symbol in Islam', in the Qur'an the tree is itself a simile for language:

> [A good word is] like a good tree, firmly rooted, [reaching out] with its branches towards the sky, yielding its fruit at all times by its Sustainer's leave' while 'the parable of a corrupt word is that of a corrupt tree, torn up [from its roots] onto the face of the earth, wholly unable to endure (14: 23-26).

Needed more than ever, at this time of climate crisis, to absorb the carbon dioxide we are still pumping into the atmosphere, the tree is also a vital symbol and guardian of ecological health. As the beloved Palestinian poet Mahmoud Darwish put it: 'the tree is forgiveness and vigilance'. Both the Qur'anic verse and the poet's words suggest that the tree is far more than a relatively cheap air filter or source of food. Through its verticality, its majestic height and depth, its visible and invisible aspects, its branching nature, its roles in many vital ecological processes, the tree is an ancient and universal metaphor for humanity and our relationship with the universe. The tree represents our individual psyches, human families, systems of thought, and taxonomy. In classical Islam, as Ziauddin Sardar notes in *How Do You Know*, in relation to the ethics of science:

> … the living, organic character of knowledge was compared to a tree, and various sciences were regarded as so many branches of this single tree . . . [but] should a branch of a tree grow indefinitely it could potentially end up by destroying the tree as a whole. Knowledge cannot be pursued for the sake of knowledge: it must have an enlightened social function.

Beyond even such a versatile and comprehensive image of human knowledge and endeavour, though, stands the vaunting symbol of the World Tree, a transcendent image of the profoundly interconnected and conscious nature of the Universe itself.

Trees of the Garden

To climb the World Tree from a starting point here on our damaged Earth, ecological values stressing humanity's dependence on the Earth and all Creation have been espoused by every world religion and for many

Muslims will already form the basis of a personal world view. Throughout the Qur'an, imagery of watering a garden is repeatedly invoked as a metaphor for God's grace and power:

> And you (Muhammad) see the earth barren, but when We send down water on it, it thrills and swells and puts forth every lovely kind of growth. That is because Allah, He is the Truth, and because He gives life to the dead, and because He is Able to do all things. (22:5-6)

In this Surah and others, the garden represents not only sustenance and beauty, but a sacred marriage of earth and sky; not just Allah's generosity in feeding humanity's stomachs and senses, but also Allah's promise of paradise to our faithful and eternal souls. Judeo-Christian gardens have similar resonance, and within all Abrahamic holy books, individual species of trees have their own particular roles and places. The Biblical forbidden fruit is not specified in the original Hebrew, and in rabbinical discourse is associated with a range of fruits from figs to pomegranates, apricots or lemons; but after Albrecht Durer's 1504 engraving of Adam and Eve, and due also perhaps to a confusion over the Latin translation of the 'Tree of Knowledge of Good and Evil' (in which 'evil' is *mali* and 'apple' *mala or malum*), the apple tree – in European folklore, a magical bearer of fruit of eternal youth – came to dominate Christian interpretations of Genesis. In the Qur'an, the date tree is often invoked as a sign of Allah's generosity – praised not just a source of daily nourishment, its fruits have the quality of manna, feeding Maryam at the time of the birth of Jesus. Also adorning the Surahs are the fig, the pomegranate, and the olive tree, each to be grateful for, and the fruits of their harvest shared with the poor. A Biblical symbol of peace and landfall after the flood, the olive is also considered sacred in the Holy Land for its immense longevity: on my last trip to Palestine in 2018, I was taken to see an olive tree known to be over five thousand years old. Gnarled, fissured and twisted as a thrust of arthritic hands, yet massive, an orchard unto itself, the tree is still in full leaf, giving its shaded interior the humbling quality of an ancient sanctuary. Located in a small farm near Bethlehem, this magnificent being is guarded closely by the family who understand clearly both its vital importance and the existential threat it faces. Central to the landscape and economy of the Occupied West

Bank, and therefore regularly uprooted by the Israeli army, the olive tree
has become a political symbol of Palestinian endurance.

Rooted deep as it is in human history, with its awesome height guiding
our imaginations to the heavens, the tree is also a transcendent symbol, an
ancient and universal icon of cosmic order. As Reat eloquently discusses,
this mythic pre-eminence is hardly surprising: large, living, immovable 'yet
supple, the tree became a model for human architecture and a model of
divine architecture'. As Darwish also has it: 'the tree is a standing prayer,
directing its devotions upwards.' In Islam, Reat explains, verticality is
strongly associated with spiritual progress and while the tree plays a
relatively minor role in the Qur'an, in the Hadith, the mystic literature and
Islamic art and architecture, the Islamic World Tree grew, as it had
elsewhere, to take on the cosmological significance of the divine *axis mundi*:
in a chaotic universe, a pillar of stability, shelter and sacred presence.

I will return to the Islamic texts shortly, but the mythic symbol of World
Tree, of course, long predates Abrahamic religions, and a short
consideration of its global reach and historical depth may help ground more
recent theological manifestations. Perhaps the earliest written account of a
World Tree comes from Ancient Sumer, in the myth of the Huluppu-tree,
one of many Sumerian myths that have come down to us on cuneiform
tablets dating from 2000 BC, though perhaps telling much older stories.
Thought by scholar Samuel Noah Kramer to be a willow, in this chant-like
creation myth, 'a single tree, the Huluppu-tree / was planted by the banks
of the Euphrates', where it is uprooted by a storm and rescued from the
river by the young goddess Innana. As Diane Wolkstien elegantly translates,
Inanna, Queen of Heaven and Earth, plants the Huluppu tree in her holy
garden, only for a serpent 'who could not be charmed' to nest in its roots,
a fearsome Anzu bird – depicted in Sumerian art as an eagle with the head
of a lion – to breed in its branches, and the 'dark maid' Lilith to make
herself at home in its trunk. Weep as she might, these unruly interlopers
will not leave Inanna's tree, and neither will her brother Utu come to her
assistance. At last, she calls on Gilgamesh to help her. The hero arrives with
his bronze axe, with which he kills the serpent, frightening off the Anzu
birds who fly off to the mountains, and Lilith, who 'smashes' her home and
flees 'to the wild, uninhabited places'. Gilgamesh then uproots the tree and
his men cut off its branches. From the trunk of the tree, he carves a throne

and a bed for his 'holy sister' Inanna, and in gratitude she fashions him two objects unknown to modern scholars but surmised to be symbols of kingship: from the roots of the tree a *pukku*, and from the crown, a *mikku* (both of which Gilgamesh later loses). Wolkstein gives a fascinating and insightful Jungian analysis of the myth, in which the three trespassers represent Inanna's own lawless fears and desires, which must be recognised and surrendered before she can take authority of her own self, as symbolised by the tree. But Wolkstein also points out the cosmological implications of the myth, in which this singular tree represents the conflicting dualities of male and female power, 'consciousness and unconsciousness, light and darkness, and the power of life and the power of death'. The tree not only embodies Heaven and Earth, Inanna's domains, but also, in its roots and wild trespassers, the Underworld, ruled by her sister Ereshkigal: it exceeds a metaphor for the coming of age of the goddess, and is arguably an *axis mundi* and map of the cosmos.

As Reat discusses, the World Tree is a dominant motif in the cosmologies of Africa, Asia, and the pre-Columbian Americas. Among other examples, he cites the Mbocobis of Paraguay, 'who speak of a tree by which the dead climb to Heaven and the Herero of Damaraland in Africa [who] hold a certain species of tree sacred because it is the ancestor of man and animals'. In his popular *An Illustrated Encyclopaedia of Traditional Symbols*, J.C. Cooper describes the Iranian Cosmic Tree with its seven precious metal branches, the Hindu Cosmic Tree, said to have sprung 'from the Cosmic Egg floating on the ocean of chaos', the Chinese Tree of Life, or Tree of Sweet Dew, which 'grows on the summit of the sacred mountain Kwan-lung'. Aboriginal Australians also consider trees to be sacred ancestors, and particular trees feature in their social and spiritual life as 'birthing trees', where women have for generations given birth and buried their placentas. Also known as 'directions trees', suggesting a role in the mapping work of Aboriginal songlines, these particular trees are supposed to be culturally protected by government order and the recent felling by the Victoria highways department of a directions tree on the land of the Djab Wurrung provoked enormous grief and anger. An entire book could be written about these ancient and still living cosmologies and having searched both Amazon and the British Library catalogue, I am surprised to see that apparently no one has yet done so in English. Given the limitations of space, I hope I will be forgiven for focusing next on a tree close to my own heart. Having recently taken a DNA test to discover I am barely English at all, but a mixture of Celt, Iberian and 20 per cent 'Viking' genes, I became fascinated over lockdown by Yggdrasil, the giant ash at the centre of the Nine Worlds of Norse mythology.

As attested in the Poetic Edda and the later Prose Edda, Yggdrasil is a meeting place for the Gods, who gather there daily for their *things*, or assemblies, but also the site of their home world, Asgard. How the Nine Worlds — homes also to the Vanir (or sea-gods), Elves, Dark Elves, Dwarves, Jötnar (often translated as 'giants'), human beings and, in Hel, the dead — physically intersect with the tree is never made clear. Though some illustrations depict the various realms floating in its branches or roots or encircling its trunk, and the Eddas describe the rainbow bridge Bifrost that connects Asgard to Midgard, the world of human beings, the relationship is clearly a metaphysical one. The Eddas do reveal that Yggdrasil is a 'friend to the sky', reaching high into the windy heavens, and has three roots, each ending in a well or a spring. Of these, the Well of Urd, home to the Norns, three giant-maids who spin the fate of all beings, is sometimes said to exist in the sky, adding yet another layer of complexity to Yggdrasil's ability to unite Heaven, Earth and Underworld. The fact that the human beings of Misgard are said to be descended from a man named Ask (Ash) and a woman named Embla (Elm), further demonstrates the depth of the Norse view of tree as *axis mundi*.

Yggdrasil also shelters a host of other beings including a brotherhood of stags whose names all begin with 'D', the hawk Veðrfölnir, who sits between the eyes of an unnamed eagle perched in its branches, an ouroboric serpent surrounding the trunk, the dragon Niðhöggr, 'Dread Biter', who gnaws at the tree's roots, and the mischievous squirrel Ratatoskr, who scuttles up and down the trunk relaying like shiny nuts of gossip the eagle and dragon's insults and grumbles about each other. These details suggest both the might of the tree, and its vulnerability, and indeed at the time of Ragnarök, the 'twilight of the Gods', Bifrost is broken, war erupts between the Nine Worlds, and Yggdrasil is burned and charred and disappears along with everything else into the Void. Arguably reflecting pagan fears of the advance of Christianity, this bleak eschatology is offset in later iterations of the myth with a vision of resurrection in which the Earth is renewed, green and fresh, the dead god Baldr returns from Hel and – perhaps speaking to the endurance, after all, of Yggdrasil – a man and woman emerge from their hiding place in the woods to repopulate the world.

Although practically synonymous with 'the World Tree' in the popular European imagination, Yggdrasil's roots run deep, and many scholars believe it derives from earlier and broader shamanic traditions. Ygg, meaning 'terror', is one of the many names of the god Odin, and because the tree is the site of Odin's twofold initiation into magical power, its name (also possibly meaning 'yew pillar' or 'pillar of terror') is commonly translated as 'Odin's Horse', a kenning (or Norse word-play) for 'gallows'. The reference to death reflects the self-sacrificial nature of the two initiations: once when the god sacrifices an eye in exchange for a drink from the Well of Mimir, whose waters contain the knowledge of the cosmos; and also when, in order to learn the secrets of the runes that the Norns carve into Yggdrasil's trunk, Odin pierces himself with his own spear and hangs upside down from the tree for nine days and nine nights, his head in the Well of Urd. As well as Christ and the Hanged Man in the Tarot, these stories connect Yggdrasil to the cosmology and practices of Siberian shamans, for whom the tree was a pathway between the human and the spirit realms. Some scholars argue that this trail leads to ancient Korea, where the tall thin branching shapes of the delicate gold Crowns of Silla have been interpreted variously as the World Tree, mountains or reindeer antlers, themselves also a feature of Korean shamanism.

Similar stories and practices, researched by the gnostic writer Aethyrius, are found in Turkic culture, Mongolia, Finland, and Hungary, where shamans in the Magyar tribes that migrated from Siberia in the tenth century, accessed spiritual sky-realms by climbing Világfa, which means precisely 'world tree'. Aethyrius points out the common features of eagles and serpents in many of these myths, and also notes that in many of the tales the *axis mundi* is rooted in a mountain. Though in Greece and other regions the mountain then came to displace the tree, despite the dominance of Mount Olympus, 'medieval folk stories from Greece restore the tree as the pillar that holds up the world (adding a crowd of goblins, the kallikantzaroi, who are perpetually sawing at its base)'. Cooper corroborates this observation, citing among others the Chinese Tree of Life, or Tree of Sweet Dew, 'variously the peach, mulberry, plum or the bamboo', which grows at the peak of the sacred mountain Kwan-lung; the Iranian white haoma, the celestial tree growing at the top of Mount Alborj; and an Islamic Cosmic Tree, which 'grows at the top of the Cosmic Mountain and represents the whole universe'.

Cooper's *An Illustrated Encyclopaedia of Traditional Symbols* has a bibliography but no footnotes, and it is difficult to source his brief remarks. Reat's account of the Islamic World Tree, though, is admirably clear. In his scholarly but immensely readable article he accounts for four distinctive and significant Qur'anic trees – the Infernal Tree, which grows in Hell and sprouts fruit akin to demon-heads (37: 63-6); *Sidrat al-Muntaha*, or Lote Tree of the Uttermost Boundary, a species of plum which stands veiled in inexpressible beauty 'near the garden of promise' (53: 13-18); the Tree of Knowledge, which in Islam takes on aspects of the Tree of Immortality (20: 120-1); and finally the tree of the Lamp verses, the 'olive neither of the East nor West' (24: 35). He then demonstrates how, in the Hadith, mystic literature and Islamic architecture, these Qur'anic trees are integrated into the Islamic *Shajarat al-Tuba*, or Tree of Bliss that stands – in an inverse of the Infernal Tree – in the centre of Paradise. Reat observes how two different Qur'anic images of the lote tree combine in the *Shajarat al-Tuba*, the singularity of the *Sidrat al-Muntaha* fusing with the heavenly location and 'spreading shade' of the 'thornless lote trees' of the Surah of the Event. In the Hadith, one tree is said to stand in Paradise, 'in whose shade a horseman would be able to ride for hundred years'. The tree's beneficence is all encompassing: according to a hadith, souls abiding in its shade 'are clothed in clothes from the sleeves (that is, flower calyxes) of the tree'. The *Shajarat al-Tuba* is also said to be the source of four rivers: one hadith identifies these as 'two concealed and two revealed' rivers, respectively of Earth (the Nile and the Euphrates) and Paradise, while according to Cooper, they are all four supernatural rivers, running with water, milk, honey, and wine. According also to Cooper, because olive oil is burned in lamps that symbolise the Light of Allah, the Tree of Bliss must be the olive which, being 'neither East nor West, but therefore central, represents spiritual blessing and illumination'. While acknowledging the possibility of this interpretation in his discussion of the Lamp verse, Reat notes that trees depicting feeding lamps on prayer rugs are generally stylised or other fruit trees, and also cites a hadith traced to 'Utaba in 'Abd al-Salma, in which a

Bedouin asks the Beloved Prophet what the Tree of Bliss looks like, only to be told 'it does not resemble any tree of your Earth'.

As Reat explains, in the *Mathnawi* of Rumi various aspects of the Islamic World Tree are also firmly associated with the Tree of Immortality, sought desperately by a king's envoy, who is finally told (and told off) by a Sheikh:

> O Simpleton, this is the tree of knowledge in the sage . . . it is a Water of Life from the all-encompassing Sea of God. Thou hast gone after the form, though has gone astray: thou canst not find it because thou hast abandoned the reality. Sometimes it is named 'tree' sometimes 'sun'; sometimes it is named 'sea', sometimes 'cloud'.

The clear lesson here is that immortality cannot be attained as a physical condition, but only through a spiritual or metaphysical union with the essential and eternal Oneness of all things. Significantly, the Tree of Knowledge is *in* the sage – it represents personal qualities of wisdom and humility, an openness to the divine flux of life that human beings should aspire to and can achieve. Rumi's Tree of Knowledge differs from the one in the Old Testament in that its fruits are not accursed, and it is not jealously guarded by God. But the Tree of Life and the Tree of Knowledge of Good and Evil have significance in the Judeo-Christian tradition far beyond their roles in Genesis. *The Torah* is often referred to as the *Etz Chaim*, Hebrew for 'tree of life', a concept visually represented by the Menorah and in Jewish mysticism by the Kabbalah with its latticework of ten sephirot connected by twenty-two paths. The sephirot Chokmah, or 'Wisdom', named Sophia in the Christian tradition, is considered female and lauded in *The Book of Proverbs* in arboreal terms: 'She [Wisdom] is a tree of life to them that lay hold upon her, and happy is everyone that holdest her fast.' (*Proverbs* 3: 13-18). In a similar vein to Surah 14, *Proverbs* also reminds us that calm and kind words are the fruit of the tree of wisdom: 'A soothing tongue is a tree of life; but perverseness therein is a wound to the spirit' (*Proverbs* 15:4). In Christianity, the cross is also considered a symbol of the Tree of Life, with Christ as its fruit. And in both traditions – in the non-canonical Jewish *Book of Enoch* and in *Revelations* – the Tree of Life is said to stand waiting for all of us in Paradise, no longer forbidden but waiting to nourish the souls of Jews whose names are written in the Book of Life, and Christians who do God's commandments. Returning to our contemplation of the *Shajarat al-Tuba*, we can hear echoes of these other Abrahamic trees in the *Qurrat al-'uyun*, in a passage traced to Abu al-Laith as-Samarqandi, upon which Reat believes Ibn Arabi modelled his famous concentric plan of Paradise, with the Tree of Bliss at the centre:

> The Prophet said, "In Paradise there is a Tree of Bliss whose root is in my dwelling place and whose branches shelter all the mansions of heaven; nor is there mansion or dwelling place which lacks one of its branches. Every branch thereof bears every species of fruit that has been in the world, and every flower that has been in the word blossoms on that branch but more abundantly and splendidly than the fruits of the world, and fairer than its flowers. And the Tree of Bliss bears grapes, every cluster of which is longer than a month's journey, and each single grape is as big as a swollen water skin ... Each of the blessed has his own branch with his name inscribed on it.

Here the celestial tree *is* the Book of Life. One is reminded also not just of the Christian notion of the Father's many mansions, but of the Aboriginal birthing trees, which are closely associated with the children born beneath them and identified by ancient carvings, and the marvellous tree told of in Guiana and Bolivia, that bore all the food stuffs in the world, until man chopped it down and flooded the planet with the water stored in its trunk. In Holy Books, with their images of a heavenly tree, in Indigenous people's defence of their land, in a walk anywhere beneath trees that delight us, we are reminded that it is not yet too late to repair the damage.

Infinite Love

Wherever it appears – whether with roots in the soil and heavenward branches, or inverted like the Tree of Bliss as depicted in Ibn Arabi's Paradise and the domes of mosques, drawing spiritual nourishment from sun and sky and spreading its branches over the faithful – with its elemental connections to earth, air, fire and water, animal and bird life, the World Tree is a healing and unifying symbol, integrating the Heaven, Earth, and the Underworld, growth and decay, life and death, the seen and unseen, order and chaos, the individual and the family, male and female, disparate cultures and faiths, the human psyche and the cosmos. In the Sumerian myth, the Huluppu tree, carved into a throne and a bed, represents the authority and fecundity of the sacred feminine, achieved in partnership with masculine power. In the Norse tradition Yggdrasil represents not only a balance of heaven and hell, but also male and female – magic in Norse culture was associated so strongly with women that male practitioners could be ostracised, giving Odin's initiation a transgressive quality that resonates with the growing understanding of gender fluidity in our own time. In Revelations the Tree of Life gives forth a different fruit each month, while its leaves are for 'the healing of the nations', metaphors which, in our time of global polycrisis, suggest not just the need to celebrate our shared humanity, but the critical importance of trees to fields as all-encompassing as carbon capture, biodiversity, and mental health.

The need to plant trees as literal hedges against climate crisis hardly needs argument: trees are being planted on a mass scale by all forward-thinking governments, and their ability to inhale and store carbon is also now being explored in the construction industry, in the form of super-strong cross laminated timber being developed at Cambridge University. But as Roger Leaky of the International Tree Foundation explains, to call trees the lungs of the world is an understatement: as well as exchanging oxygen for carbon dioxide, trees also function as planetary kidneys and a skin, regulating the flow of water and gasses between the atmosphere and earth; as intestines, exchanging nutrients between the soil and vegetation; and in their role as homes to countless creatures, as the hearts of complex ecosystems essential to the planet's health and our survival. The key role trees play in our own wellbeing is also well-documented, and it is striking that the long-disparaged 'hippie' practice of 'tree-hugging', came to enjoy new respect during lockdowns when human hugs were disallowed. Any one of these topics deserves a book of its own and still would not exhaust the topic of trees: Zeshan Akhter, for example, in 'Wild in the Forest', her philosophical essay on conservationism for the *Nature* issue of *Critical Muslim*, unearths the colonial history of British forestry. To conclude, though, with a return to the themes under discussion here, in the search for a new post-pandemic and postmaterialist paradigm, trees, I believe, also have much to teach us about economics and consciousness. Although considered thus far in terms of its verticality, with its cylindrical shape the tree also embodies circularity. This too has cosmological significance: Reat points out that Ibn Arabi's Plan of Paradise reflects yet transcends the concentric rings of the solar system. But considered as circular, the healing reach of the World Tree motif also extends to global economics. The key threat neo-classical economics poses to the planet lies in its insistence on the possibility of infinite growth on a finite planet, a catastrophic notion thankfully challenged by the recent invention and rapid growth of 'doughnut economics'. Devised by Kate Raworth in 2012, doughnut economics is a holistic and sustainable economic model in which the classical line graphs are replaced with a visual graphic of three concentric rings around a 'hole'. The inner of the three rings represents human activities which must take place within two boundaries: a social foundation and an ecological ceiling; the hole in the middle represents shortfalls in meeting social needs, while around the doughnut lies the fatal zone of 'overshoot', where planetary systems begin to fail. Though the iconography of this regenerative and distributive model needs to depict a hole at centre – and indeed doughnuts are tempting, fattening, and reassuring luxuries with which to brand a new economics – it strikes me that perfectly healthy and indeed venerable trees can be hollow. The hollowing process in fact represents a cyclical symbiosis, whereby fungi feed on deadwood at the centre of the tree, releasing nutrients that enable the tree to live longer and, in the case of storms, to bend more easily with the prevailing winds. I wouldn't agitate for a mass change to 'doughnut' in reference to Raworths' fundamentally ecological economics, but personally, from now on I will envision a tree growing through those sticky chocolate rings: a vertical axis that connects us not to endless material growth, but ancient wisdom and infinite love.

Finally, for those seeking a postmaterialist paradigm for consciousness, what better metaphor could there be than a tree? To reflect again on the ubiquitous notion that the human brain is a computer, consider that metaphors are only strong when the vehicle, or image, closely resembles the tenor, or subject of the trope. Are there any hard wires in our heads? Are we formed of right angles, toxic rare earths? With our solid but watery trunks and branching toes and fingers, our mortal bodies, with their fungal infections, age-lines and visceral responses to the weather, with the blossoming of our talents and the fruits of our labour, which do we more resemble, a laptop or a tree? The comparison might seem to break down at the key point of our cognitive abilities, which computers mimic and in their speed exceed. But if we are willing to grant a form of consciousness to AI, why wouldn't we do the same for massive organisms that are increasingly understood to communicate with each other? Growing research into the 'wood wide web' suggests that trees are also the brains of their ecosystems. In a recent interview with Yale Environment 360, German forester Peter Wohlleben, author of *The Hidden Life of Trees*, discusses how he began his career treating trees as commodities, but has come to view them as 'social and highly sensitive' individuals. Trees, he notes, have 'brain-like' roots that can distinguish their own species from others and transmit nutrients to their own saplings and sick family members. With the help of fungal networks, tree roots can also emit electrical signals to alert others to insect infestations, allowing healthy trees to build their defences. Trees, Wohlleben has observed, can also remember droughts, and learn to store more water as a result; form 'friendships' by growing in spatial harmony with other trees; and seemingly make individual decisions about when to drop their leaves. All these observations point like a twiggy finger to sentience, but also evoke the image of our own long straggly vagus nerve, which vine-like connects our brains, lungs, hearts, and digestive tracts, and challenges the idea that human consciousness is located, like a hard drive, only in our skulls.

Rather than 'wet computers', then, I propose that we call ourselves 'ambulant trees', and when speaking of our emotional and cognitive activities replace the reductive and mechanical term 'process' with verbs like 'photosynthesise', 'absorb' and 'cross-pollinate'. Above all, we can learn from the slow sentience of trees: we valorise computers for the speed of their calculations, but to save the biosphere and create societies in which all can thrive, we must all slow down: travel by train, electric scooter, bicycle, and foot; communicate in person, in dialogue rather than antagonistic sound bites. As we seek to overcome the increasingly tendentious nature of public discourse, we can also learn from the stately silence and soothing whispers of trees.

As I hope this essay has persuaded you, to hold the tree close is also to embrace our cosmological inheritance as human beings, to accept our dependence on the planet, and our place in a vast mysterious universe that perhaps is conscious but may be better described as consciousness itself. In such a universe, 'miracles' are simply evidence of the profound interconnectedness of all observable phenomena. Let me end then, with a short account of a miracle: a personal and unverifiable story as are all such 'anomalous events' that by their nature fall outside the remit of materialist science. During the long 2021 UK lockdown, I struggled like many people, and although counting myself fortunate not to have suffered illness or financial hardship during the pandemic, the isolation, long nights and increased workload got to me. Around February, I entered counselling, began a gratitude journal and began to pray and mediate more regularly. Still, I was not feeling much better: in April, I still found myself weepy and shaky. At the start of May, though, I went for a walk on the Downs and, returning though Rottingdean, decided to duck through an entrance-way to a walled garden for a quick nosey. I was met by a tree I later identified as a Japanese maple. My first reaction to it, though, was wordless. At the sight of the tree's elegant form, its tessellated foliage a delicate sphere of blue sky and red leaf, the centre of my chest burst into a warm liquid glow. It was a sensation I had last experienced in a Zoom meeting in January, when my five-year-old niece in Canada spontaneously told me 'I love you' – as if my heart was a pool and a golden penny had dropped into it. As an instantaneous response to the tree, it felt like a summons, a sign I belong to a beyond human family, to all of nature, and indeed to the Universe. Since then, although angered and upset by events in Gaza and Kamloops, I have not been depressed or anxious, but literally 'light-hearted', strangely able to remain buoyant in our turbulent times. The Tree of Bliss, I understand deeply now, grows and blossoms in each of us.

PUNCHING UP AND DOWN

Andrew Brown

The point of a public stoning is that everyone in the crowd has to pick up a rock. It is a team building exercise. At the end of the cathartic murder, all are equally guilty, which implies that they are all also equally innocent and quite convinced of their own righteousness. That is why Jesus's intervention in the New Testament story of the woman taken in adultery is so devastating. He stops the stoning of a clearly guilty woman by saying 'Let he who is without sin cast the first stone.' The question disintegrates the crowd into individual people, individually responsible. This is much more subtle than it first appears. It is not a demand that only the sinless should exercise power. That would be impossible. But it is a reminder that even when we act as part of a crowd, or an army, a movement or even a newspaper, we do so as unique individuals, personally responsible for our actions.

I think this is a helpful way of thinking about Twitter and the other forms of mob cruelty with which the world now entertains itself online. To mock those less powerful is no longer an individual act of scorn but a collective one. Social media has made collective punishment easier than it has ever been. Even in societies that practised merciless public stigmatisation and shaming, like seventeenth century England, where criminals might not only be executed with enormous cruelty in public, but subject to lesser, brutal humiliations – having their noses split, or merely being placed in the stocks – these treats for the public were reserved to special occasions. But on Twitter, every day is now an opportunity to shame and mock and stigmatise. Obviously, it is better to be the victim of an online storm than a public execution. Still, Twitter can destroy people's lives and livings as thoroughly as a spell in the stocks could do.

I myself take a shameful pleasure in a Twitter account called 'Maomentum', which mocks unsparingly the Corbynite faction of the Labour Party. This morning, for instance, it explains that 'Can't help feeling that this Harry and Meghan interview is a conveniently timed distraction away from Richard Burgon's alternative budget.'

It's very funny sometimes, though the jokes repeat, as they must, because the politicians being mocked repeat themselves endlessly as they return to irrelevance. The horse being kicked here is not just dead but decomposing. Perhaps if you were a Labour member and felt trapped beneath this decomposing corpse, the matter would feel more urgent. But for me it is simply entertainment. It's not even hatred, though it can feel like that to the recipients. It's something less personal and far more crushing.

I know something of this from the other side, so to say, when I was editing the *Guardian*'s 'Comment is Free' Belief section, and we published some reasonable pieces of serious thought about religion, not least Ziauddin Sardar's experiment in 'Blogging the Quran'. This was in the early days of webbish optimism, when it was supposed the comments from readers were something desirable in themselves.

So, every attempt at expounding a religious position would be met by a storm of derision. Mostly, the authors were arguing with the voices in their heads, a condition that afflicts rationalists especially when they are trying to prove how rational they are. But this did not stop them at all. There was one commentator from Northern Ireland who posted more than 10,000 comments in the first five years of the site, all of them pointing out in one way or another that religions were evil lies. There were two things remarkable about this man: he was obviously intelligent and well-informed about Christianity at least, both in theory and practice; also, he only ever posted during office hours. No doubt, from the perspective of a bored office worker in Belfast his attacks on religion appeared to be punching upwards. He would think so, as many reasonable people do who had lived through thirty years of low-level civil war between Catholics and Protestants and seen that the only way to get the two sides to even begin to talk was to reconceptualise them as 'Nationalists' and 'Unionists'. So long as the conflict remained religious, and thus embedded in community identities, it also remained existential. But in the context of the Guardian's site, or at least of its commenters, he was punching down at the pathetic remnant who clung on to the hope of a respectful hearing for religious beliefs.

This kind of disproportion between the small and powerless group that you feel yourself a part of and the tremendous shadowy power that appears to threaten your victims is not entirely new. It's based no doubt on the same dynamic as leads many bullies to believe that they are just defending themselves. But that doesn't make them any less awful to be bullied by.

Like so many of the bad habits of social media, this started in the print media, when that was a playground open only to journalists. One of the secrets to success in journalism before the web was to make your readers feel part of an elite that was in on a secret. This allowed them the pleasure of despising all the unenlightened rubes. This was always part of the charm of *Private Eye*. The nicknames it discovered, or bestowed, on the royal family – 'Brenda', 'Brian', and so on - gave a sense of intimacy that none of the official royal reporters could aspire to. Of course, this was often confined with vicious unfairness and wild factual inaccuracy, but that hardly diminished its power in an age when you could justifiably suspect that a lot of the official reporting on politics and power was just as inaccurate, and deliberate in its concealment of some brutal realities.

Another of the progenitors of online abuse was the 'gonzo journalism' of Hunter S Thompson. Before him there had been the 'New Journalism', which attempted to convey the realities of the world by breaking out of the straightjackets of American newspaper conventions, but Thompson's only real subject was himself. He offered readers the direct experience of a wholly unfettered ID the inventive aggression of his language, fuelled on rage, cocaine and late-night drunken readings of the *Book of Revelation* is still astonishing today. But there could only really be one Hunter S. Thompson – and that was the man as he represented himself in print, not the physical avatar, who long outlived his creativity until the last thing he wrote was a note complaining that life was no longer any fun and he shot himself over a bottle in his kitchen.

Like every good media idea, Thompson's was copied, and the copies mass produced. The result was a school of print journalists who were neither reporters nor analysts. They were voices – 'influencers' before their time. They flourished especially on papers like Andrew Neil's *Sunday Times* where knowledgeable specialists were disparaged as 'fans with typewriters'. The schtick was that the new influencers were just like you'd be if you dared, only better and more powerful. They were relatable. Most were alpha males, of the Jeremy Clarkson/Piers Morgan type, but there were a couple of alpha females, like today's Alison Pearson (whose podcast title is 'Planet Normal'), all using the same, jeering, bullying voice in their complaints against the world. And then there was Julie Burchill, whose entire schtick was that she was frighteningly hip. What she thought this week, you'd be thinking in a year's time, but by then, of course, she would have moved on to something else.

This kind of journalism was of course brutal and painful to receive. I know that I myself wounded one Archbishop of Canterbury so much by my reporting and commentary in the *Independent* that his wife cancelled the family's order for the *Church Times*, for which I also wrote, and his son wrote to me in personal terms complaining of my cruelty. But it never consciously occurred to me that I was more powerful than my victims. That did not happen until I went freelance, and picked up a gig for the *Guardian* interviewing unimportant people. I loved it. And I decided that I would practice what I called 'after sales service' and drop people a line after the story had been published, asking if they were happy with it.

Those who are not journalists may be surprised that this doesn't happen as a matter of routine. All I can say is that in most cases of opinionated journalism it's unthinkable, and would be considered deeply unprofessional. There is one respectable reason for that behaviour: when you're writing about powerful people, they will do everything possible to twist you in directions favourable to their purposes. Political journalists, trade journalists, sports journalists, and, above all, celebrity journalists, are treated simply as conduits, or sewers, through which the product of PR departments can reach the public. And, if they rebel, they will be punished with loss of access. And many times, when people do say something revealing and true to a journalist their immediate instinct is to lie and deny that they have said it. This is why there is such a strong professional inhibition against the pre-editing of copy (and why it is so seldom admitted that the great majority of news is managed anyway).

Of course, the less respectable reason is that those who have been bullied like to bully everyone weaker. So, you try what you can to see what you can get away with. There are libel lawyers to protect you from the most egregious mistakes; and the career of Boris Johnson shows that what most editors most want from a journalist is readers, not accuracy. This is another way in which the nastiness of social media was foreshadowed by the analogue antisocial media of the Nineties.

So, we practised drive-by journalism, but I had decided to stop at the scene of the accidents and talk to the pedestrians. The response was humiliating. One woman, as it happened a scientist who was an ex of an old friend of mine, pointed out three ghastly howlers in the four paragraphs I had written about her work – and these were wholly unintentional and the piece as a whole was intended to be a friendly boost: she had worked on one of the earliest flu vaccines. I took to checking very carefully that people meant what they thought they had meant before I typed anything serious.

This kind of discipline used to be imposed on national journalists by their training on local papers, where you were liable to meet the subjects of your story in the shops or on the buses that both of you used. But for opinion journalists none of that applied. They worked behind screens, as even reporters increasingly would. The reporter had once been a man with a shorthand notebook stuck in a pocket where he could always get at it; they were to become keyboard warriors long before the net democratised the process for everyone.

I learned, or at least I hope I did, from the practice of after-sales service. From 2000 onwards, I was much more conscious of the reality of the people I wrote about. No doubt I caused a lot of pain, but most of it, from then on, was intended.

But just as I was cleaning up my own tiny act, the bad habits once available to only a tiny minority of journalists were becoming available to all their readers, and the media themselves were encouraging this every way they could. This was based on two misunderstandings which nearly killed the traditional media industry. The first was to suppose that all they were doing was printing onto electrons, rather than paper; in fact, it was entering an entirely new business, in which the advertising which had so long supported them would all go to Google and Facebook. The second, related mistake was to suppose that 'content' was an undifferentiated mass from the advertisers' point of view, so that the more you produced, the more advertising would grow to surround it. The result was a few terrible years when every media executive believed that readers' opinions, or 'User generated content' in the jargon, would be a cheap and profitable substitute for real journalism. It could never have been financially profitable, of course: the costs of proper moderation far exceed the notional benefits of advertising.

What's maddening is that it might not have been quite so toxic; reader content might even have been profitable in terms of news and insight, in the way the readers' letters are. After all, there are always some readers who know more than the writer about any particular story; the trick is to isolate them from overwhelming majority who only think they do. But that is not a discrimination that any AI yet can make or encourage. It requires human editorial skills. No one was prepared to invest in them. So, the habit of angry contempt spread more widely as technology made available to almost everyone the peculiarly vicious habits of mind which had until then been confined to paid journalists. Suddenly all the ink in the world was green.

The giant advertising companies known as social media know this perfectly well, and profit from it deliberately. Facebook's internal policies about permissible personal abuse have been published and what they amount to is that if you have been a subject of five or more media pieces in the last two years, or if you have been elected to any office at all, no matter how humble, or even if you are a journalist, you are yourself 'a public figure'. That means that Facebook allows things to be said about you that are 'meant to degrade or shame, including, for example, claims about someone's sexual activity': posts like that are only removed if they are about private figures. You can call for the death of 'public figures', providing you don't tag them, so they are unaware of your exhortations. Similarly, content which 'praises, celebrates, or mocks their death or serious physical injury' is only banned if they know about it. So, if you don't like this piece, it's fine to demand my death by torture, so long as you don't tag me in the post.

Where does this leave us? One possible route is suggested by the career of one of the most skilled and successful opinion journalists of the last few decades, Julie Burchill. She has never, so far as I know, reported on anything except the state of her own mind. The outside world is of interest only in as much as it provokes some reaction in her. She got her start in rock criticism, where the only use for recognised standards is to overthrow those of the week before. Drop a mind like that into Twitter and it's like dropping a lump of sodium into a bath of acid: it flames and stinks and skitters round in circles until it is all gone. In Burchill's case the end came with a public apology to Ash Sarkar, British Bangladeshi intellectual and political activist and senior editor at Novara Media, a left-wing, alternative media organisation, whom she had accused on Twitter of all manner of crimes. This is worth reading because the lawyers extorted from her a pretty full list of the harms that come from the bullying overlap of journalism and social media:

> I wish to make clear on the record that I do not believe, have never believed and never intended to make any allegation that Ms Sarkar is a promoter, supporter and/or sympathiser of Islamists or fundamentalist terrorism or to suggest that Ms Sarkar condones paedophilia in any way. I also now understand that it is blasphemy for a Muslim to worship Prophet Muhammad and I had no basis for stating that Ms Sarkar does so. I accept that there is no truth in any of these allegations, and I recognise that such comments play into Islamophobic tropes and did so in this case.

> I also accept that I was wrong to continue to tweet to and about her after that date. I should not have sent these tweets, some of which included racist and misogynist comments regarding Ms Sarkar's appearance and her sex life. I was also wrong to have 'liked' other posts on Facebook and Twitter about her which were offensive, including one which called for her to kill herself, and another which speculated whether she had been a victim of FGM. I regret that I did not pay much attention to them at the time. On reflection, I accept that these 'liked' posts included callous and degrading comments about Ms Sarkar and I should not have liked them. I can confirm that I have deleted all my posts and tweets and likes about Ms Sarkar.

> I have also now seen messages that were sent to Ms Sarkar following my posts about her which are abhorrent, and I wish to make clear that I do not condone any such messages. I did not know when I published my posts that Ms Sarkar had previously received death threats and other violent threats and abuse, some of which emanated from a far-right conspiracy theory circulated about Ms Sarkar during summer 2020, of which I had not been aware.

So, you threw a few rocks maybe just to show your disapproval of vice and no one could have been more surprised than you when the target of your virtue was buried in rubble and horribly dead. The first paragraph is about the rocks that she threw herself: stuff she wrote and, in some sense, meant at the time; but the subsequent paragraphs are mostly about the effect that other people had on her original actions. In this they catch the dynamics of the crowd exactly.

The instinct among progressives is to blame this kind of thing on the Right, and on authoritarian or xenophobic impulses. But this won't wash as a complete explanation of the phenomenon. For one thing, the Left, is every bit as capable of spite and hatred, even if most of it is directed at other sections of the Left – as in the @maomentum Twitter account. Still, the complaints made from the Right about 'cancel culture' in universities do have some merit, especially in the US. Once opinions have been weaponised in the struggle for status within shrinking fields like academia, other people's opinions can be used to justify some remarkably vicious persecution. And this points up a very important feature of social intolerance, which is that it often takes place within very tight little environments, where the ruling orthodoxy can be entirely at odds with that of the wider society. An extreme example is the way in which Jehovah's Witnesses can be 'disfellowshipped' and cut off from all their friends and family merely for adopting some of the beliefs which are in the outside world wholly uncontroversial: eating pork, or believing in blood transfusions, for example.

But you do not have to be as tightly organised as a religious sect for this kind of orthodoxy to become stifling in any small social group. I remember a private discussion at the *Guardian* where some of the lead writers were playing a game: which opinion do you hold which, if known, would finish you off at the paper? Someone replied that they really didn't care very much whether fox-hunting was legal, one way or another. That won the game outright. It was a real breach of the taboos of the tribe. Yet to anyone outside the building it would have been a perfectly normal and acceptable reaction.

Whether your cause is fox hunting, trans rights, white privilege, humanism, Islam, or Christianity, it's possible quite genuinely to feel you are part of a persecuted minority and to react as part of a persecuting majority. Obviously, this is an exaggeration of a well-known human tendency to self-righteousness but it's not, I think, something that you find in every culture. Some have been entirely undisturbed by the cruelty of the majority and happy to think it was legitimised by divine command. This is certainly been true of stable slave-holding societies. But the things about slave-holding societies, and other, lesser forms of authoritarian rule, is that it is always clear in them where power and legitimacy lie. The needle on the moral compass points unerringly to power. If anyone is genuinely punching upwards in such a society, they are taking a risk that is impossible to overlook. That is why old-fashioned Jewish jokes, or those that prospered under Communism, are still funny.

But in the West today, the very idea of authority is contested. It's not that there are no authorities, but that there are too many. In the sort of watered-down existentialism that most people take as common sense today the only ultimate arbiter is your own inner self. This leads to a complete dislocation of the traditional ideas of Right and Left, which are based on disagreements about an agreed arrangement of power. It also leads to an enormous resentment against the world, one entirely justified by the underlying axioms. If you walk around trying to believe that 'You can be whoever the fuck you want', to quote a T shirt I just saw on a provincial high street, you are going to be constantly frustrated by the failure of the world around to acknowledge your luminous self-importance. And of course, you're going to feel part of a persecuted minority, because on those terms you always will be. It's a kind of perpetual adolescence held up as the model for all human behaviour.

In this light, the whole question of 'punching up' or 'punching down' becomes unanswerable. We can of course analyse how power works in particular social situations, and who can force whom to do exactly what. In those situations, it is possible to decide whether a joke is a gesture of defiance or a bully's jeer. But out on the internet, we are all only lashing out, throwing stones and screaming into an enormous void where no one else can be heard screaming.

ARTS AND LETTERS

FIVE POEMS AND A SHORT STORY

Salah Badis

The Nif: Complaint and Dignity in Algeria

On February 10, 2019, Abdelaziz Bouteflika announced his fifth presidential candidacy, and six days later protests erupted in Algeria, sparking the Revolution of Smiles. The protagonists of Salah Badis' short story meet in front of a dysfunctional ATM in one of Algiers' richest neighbourhoods, and a conversation between strangers unfolds.

I was standing at the cash machine outside the municipal post office in Hydra, surrounded by fellow citizens, all of them in their fifties and sixties, and all of them – all of us – staring at a man whose card had just been swallowed.

'Maybe there's a problem?' someone from the group ventured. 'Maybe there's no money in the machine?'

The man pointed at the person who had used the machine before him and said that it had swallowed his card too, though neither of them made a mistake when entering their PIN, and neither of their cards were expired.

One of the bystanders began to grumble. He was saying something about 'surprise', that these days the only surprise is when we're surprised.

The others started to mutter along with him.

My friend and I had been waiting to withdraw cash. The misfortune of the two men ahead of us made up our minds: we wouldn't risk it. We told the woman behind us in the queue that she could come forward and take our place. She looked to be in a rush, desperate for cash, and had clearly decided to take a chance. The two victims, meanwhile, went into the post office to try and recover their bank cards, now languishing in the steel belly of the machine.

The woman successfully withdrew money, and amid the general astonishment, newly emboldened, we stepped up and withdrew our money too. The grumbling man, waiting for his turn to enter the post office, was still talking.

'Nothing surprises us anymore. I mean, forgive me, but a person should be able to use a cash machine without worrying about whether it's going to work. How are Algerians meant to have any faith in their bank cards? We might be the only country in the world where a facility like this isn't up to standard. They say we like to feel the cash in our hands, but that isn't the case. The problem is that we are unable to put our faith in our institutions: you give your worldly riches to them and they hand you a card with a magnetic strip that is promptly swallowed by a broken machine.'

I went over. He was addressing everyone, but when he saw that I was paying attention he began speaking to me directly. He was tall and elegant, soft-spoken, switching easily between fluent French and formal Arabic, like all bilingual speakers in this country. He had a way of speaking that solicited sympathy: there was a slight catch in his voice, the kind that makes his listener want to give him a hug, to console him. He was wearing a mask, and so was I. No one here wanted to look reckless, like they didn't care about safety guidelines and social distancing. If it wasn't for his hair, just a few grey streaks across his head, he would have been the very image of the writer Amine Zaoui, whose jet-black hair still defies old age.

But who is Zaoui? Dear reader, Zaoui is an Algerian writer, 'a writer of complaint and discontent' – which is to say, he grieves over the past. He has been writing since the 1980s and must now be in his sixties. He started out writing in Arabic, then switched to French after fleeing the civil war and going to live in France. Later, he returned, and remains active in Algeria to this day. He writes a weekly column, posts copious commentary on Facebook (every post accompanied by an author's photograph), participates in French- and Arabic-language cultural events, and for the past decade has published novels at the rate of two a year, one in Arabic and one in French.

I first encountered him as a young boy, when he was presenting a radio show about literature and culture, and for all this time Zaoui has kept up his complaints about the decline of civilized values – urban and urbane – in the face of encroaching Bedouin barbarism. In support of his thesis, he cites Ibn Khaldun and deploys French sentences of great complexity. He has lost track of himself in a maze of his own characters and obsessions – sexy aunts, incest, the family legends of Jewish-Muslim families who can trace their lines back to al-Andalus, old manuscripts entombed in the shrines of saints in western Algeria—and is now like a man who has wandered into the desert to collect gemstones and jewels, only to end up, pockets weighed down with stones, without any idea how he will ever get back again, or what he will do with what he's found.

My friend wandered away to make a phone call. The Zaoui lookalike was still talking.

'You must excuse me, but you could be my son's age. Some of us have seen so much in this country.'

He leaned in, closer now than would have been usual even before the pandemic. 'We saw Khaled Nezzar return and we didn't bat an eyelid when they started calling him a hero and cleared him of all charges…'

He straightened up, but his voice stayed low. This was a proper conversation now, the cash machine quite forgotten.

'I live here, in Hydra, "home of officials and the wealthy", and I know each and every one of them. I see them living their normal lives, not the lives you see on the television.'

My friend finished his call and rejoined us.

'When I see the state of my country today, I despair. What are we missing? What do the advanced nations have that we don't? I've wasted my life here, and when I think back, to 1994, say… How long ago would that be?'

'Twenty-six years,' I say.

'Exactly right. You were probably a little boy. You wouldn't remember.'

'I don't, to be honest. That's the year I was born.'

'Good God. Younger than my own children.'

I said nothing.

'Not that age means a thing!'

'Of course.'

'Anyway, I think it was 1994 that I wasted the opportunity of a lifetime.'

For a moment he fell silent, then: 'I got offered a job in Poitiers. You know it?'

I nodded at my friend, and said, 'He lived in France, though he's back now. The only thing I know about Poitiers is that it was the furthest west the Muslims went in Europe.'

'There's been growing levels of police violence there,' added my friend. 'All over France, really. There's a law they're trying to get through parliament that would make it an offence to take footage or photos of the police...'

Interrupting my friend's brief speech on police violence in France, and recovering his temporarily broken flow, the man resumed. 'In any case, I was offered work in Poitiers: a job and a home and a car. My children were still young; they could have adapted to life there. Do you know what I said?'

'You said no, and came straight back home?'

'Exactly. I said no and came home, despite the civil war and all the killing. "Never," I told them. "I'll never live in France. The *nayf* wouldn't let me."'

As he said this last sentence, he touched his nose, hidden beneath his mask.

'I regret it now, of course. How could I leave a life like that and come back here? I regret it.'

'You regret your *nif*?' I said quickly.

'What? I regret my naiveté, I'm saying, the patriotism which led me to...'

'But you didn't say patriotism. You said *nif*. They're different.'

The man smiled. I couldn't see his whole expression, of course, but I could see it in his eyes.

'Look,' I said. '*Nif* is one thing and patriotism is something else. I don't believe in patriotism and you never mentioned it. You said that you regret your *nif*.'

He sounded flustered. 'I was young, of course. Maybe I didn't know what I was saying.'

'But why would you say it at all? Is there something personal between you and France? Some family vendetta? Or was it just that they colonised us?'

'The colonialism, I suppose.'

'And has the history of colonialism somehow changed since? Why the regret? I've got no issue with people living in France, but it makes more sense to me that they decide where to live on rational grounds, rather than this colonialism business that clearly isn't even convincing to you.'

Let me take a moment here to explain what *nif* means. It is a word in Algerian dialect. Everyone knows what it means, but they never explain it; or rather, you'll never find anyone able to define it with any precision. Well, first of all, it comes from *anf*, the standard Arabic word for nose. We say, 'He's got the *nif*,' meaning that someone thinks a lot of himself. In classical dictionaries *anafa* or *unfa* is defined as 'pride,' and disdainful people are referred to as *shumm al anouf*, which is to say, 'sniffy.'

Now, all these nasal terms derive their meaning from the fact that the nose is one of the highest features on the human body. If water reaches our noses, we drown and we die. When we fall, we do all we can to avoid landing on our face so that our nose does not strike the ground. To 'rub someone's nose in it' is to humiliate them. Which is why the man became flustered when I asked if he regretted the nif that had taken hold of him and made him reject the offer to live in France. It is why he preferred to say that he regretted naive patriotism rather than admit his slip of the tongue.

'I was travelling a lot back then,' he said. 'We used to believe that we could change things for the better.'

'What did you do?' asked my friend. 'You used to travel a lot; your neighbours are officials and generals. Did you work for the government?'

'Ah.' The man hesitated for a moment, then said, 'You could say that, yes. But I wasn't a government employee exactly. I'm an engineer.'

'Maybe that's why you feel such despair,' my friend said. 'It's not easy to live next to all this negative energy and remain unaffected.'

Astonishment dawned in the man's eyes.

'Now,' said my friend, 'how does that poem go?

Never serve the Sultan, ever,

Never join his company,

Secure your interests and endeavours,

Take only what God gives to thee...'

There was silence. The man wanted to say something. He apologised for rambling on. He was a good man, despite his endless complaining, so we said, no, quite the contrary, it had been a really interesting conversation, and we wished him the best.

When I got home I called my friend and we talked about the man, about his complaints and his regret at missing the chance to settle in France. My friend said that he had wanted to make the man understand that we were young men, that even though our lives were more insecure, financially and psychologically, than his own had been, we still had hope for our country. My friend said that he himself had left France to return to Algeria because there was no life there, no opportunity.

Later, I went to the website of the Al Maani online dictionary and began searching through the entries for anf, nose. I was looking for any possible connections with the Algerian nif, but to my surprise - the same surprise that always accompanies any voyage through the classical dictionaries - I found that among the words derived from the root word anf is anifa, which means 'to complain'.

Translated from Arabic by Robin Moger

Pirates of the Sea

The pirates have been straggling in Algiers
for three centuries.
You can see them with their tattooed arms,
and their skin burnt by the sun.
standing by the beach
Wetting their feet
To keep them from growing roots on land.
Their swords were taken away from them and their ships destroyed,
Their castles became museums haunted by the wind,
And their cannons were placed
in the plazas of dull French towns.
People forgot their names,
denied their right to ride the seas,
dispersed in harbours and beaches:
porters, gamblers, and beggars
dancing in the street weddings,

And sleeping in the open air

A damned lineage that neither dies nor breeds.

Running away

The drowned of the sea aren't the only ones
Who wish to reach the beach.

We, too, who live in Algiers,
Wrestle with the waves of people and vehicles,
Looking for the shades,
Spending our money on water bottles,
Distilling our time on the asphalt,
Looking for a parking spot,
As the radio presenters throw up in our ears,
And our knees crumble of all the driving.

We spend our days dreaming of the beach,
A beach on which we can throw the fatigue
we have accumulated inside the eyelids, pockets,
shoes, and on the foreheads.
We dream of escaping the heat of the asphalt,
To the coolness of the water,
Like the whales who attempt suicide, and fail each time.

The Summer of All Dangers

'Summer is a pleasure in Algiers'
We used to say.
The calm mornings' breeze,
the few cars on the road,
sandwiches, bottles of cold water,
and off to the beach,
before the sun ignites and burns,
And swimming, till midday.

The sun is an orange of fire,
That a hidden hand squeezes all day long,
on our backs.
The summer now stretched
more than three months,
the Aurassi Hotel that we call
"The air conditioner of the city"
Is not the most prominent landmark there, any longer,
And it didn't make our summers less hot in any way,
The city's features are changing,
And you haven't come back, yet.
You spend your summer, on a so far away place,
Where there is no sea.

We still are impressed by the sea,
We spend our days watching it,
From our houses' terraces,
As if we hold eternity
As if nothing is happening in here, anyway.

The Highest Man in the City

You haven't come back from your emigration, yet
And the Minaret that is being built on the corniche
for two years now, is still "Under Construction".
They say it would be the highest minaret in the world!
I do not know whether it's true,
but I'm sure that the highest man in the city, today,
Is the operator of the crane building that minaret.
He oversees everything from his place.
He can even wave to the bored boats
anchored in Marseille's harbour,
on the other coast.

I do not know when the mosque is going to open,
nor do I know when you'd come back,

but people here
doubt that they'd be able to hear the muezzin's voice,
When he calls for prayer.

A Monster

My daily rhythm changes;
I set my biological clock
according to your time settings.
And when you are busy,
I lie on the large spaces
of time difference, due to time zones,
And I sleep.

Between us: a continent and an ocean,
books and gossips,
and love that depends on internet coverage's
on and off,
and that lives as long as
our phones' batteries live.
And when technology's power dies,
our flesh surrender to the monster
That you call: yearning.

The parcel of books that you had sent me
Hasn't arrived yet.
The postman says:
it could be lying in the heart of one of those boats
anchored in the middle of the sea.

The boat hasn't reached the harbour yet,
And we are not pirates, any longer,
to go and to get it back.

Translated from Arabic by BH

TWO POEMS

Halimah Adisa

Your Daughter is Hurt

Your daughter is hurt.
She takes advice that breeds
no connection to her happiness.

As a child, her age shames her.
She compromises things that should make her love.
So, instead of loving, she takes Truth into her vein.

As she grew, you taught her to grow beyond
the ways that should connect greatness.
But what practical route does she take?

You made her live on the cotton fields
and, while she associates, they say
She's blunt — bad for stating preferences.
Have you forgotten she carries Truth in her vein?

You should have shown more of the way, mother.
So, why did you let her sink?
You didn't teach her to swim by the lake.
Why didn't you teach her that men only love girls who can give them their
guts?
Why didn't you tell her that friends
will unlove her and feel insecure if she protects her world?

Why didn't you tell her that suitors will get caught up if she puts her head
up high?

Why didn't you tell that
the universe in every person
she meets will want to take a turn
in the flesh of what she preserves.

Your daughter's heart is
a big room for chaos.
Her soul tortures.
Her stomach, a battle field of pain
Her mouth of impeded words —
heart litters loneliness.

What heart is free from affliction
if not a child's.
Lord, make her wear it.

The He(ART) of Giving

I don't know what dad saw
that made him drop some money into a man's bowl.
I was too little to understand.

I talk of stories I have heard about giving
and once, it seems so unclear to me.
When you help, aren't you helping yourself too?

Would you say you don't think of the benefit
you'd get when you drop some notes into a beggar's bowl?
You've been told that the giver receives.
So, a beggar helps you secure a seat in paradise — your help is being
reciprocated.

You open a restaurant. Why?
To help. You feed people and their hunger flee for a while—a fire that
flickers.
You get your promise—you receive.
And those people help you secure a seat in wealth.

You start a transport business to convey people to a destination—they pay.
You help them through and you get your promise: they help you secure the
path and like

Armah would have it, nothing destroys the soul like its aloneness.
You build an industry.
You are so kind that you employ the unemployed and you get your
promise: their brains for your growth.

Now, I see what dad saw:
A pot of gold for a giving he(art). And whosoever gives, gets more in
multiple.
Could daddy be resting in paradise now, because he got a seat secure for
him?

DISPLACED LIVES

Sari Omer

Sari Omer is a Sudanese photographer based in Khartoum. He was born in 1981 in Riyadh, Saudi Arabia, before returning to Sudan for his schooling. After graduating in Fine and Applied Arts from Sudan University of Science and Technology, Omer worked with NGOs such as Oxfam and the Sudanese Youth Union.

Omar's photographs capture everyday life in the Sudan. 'I want to display', he says, 'the beauty and complexity of my homeland to the world'. Between 2013 and 2019, he visited every camp for internally displaced persons in Darfur and Sudan to document the plight of refugees in the region. His work has also explored women's rights and the issue of female genital mutilation in Khartoum; and he has depicted human rights activism in Sudan for the UN. One of the most respected and admired photojournalists in the country, Omar is one of the founders of the Sudanese Photographers' Group. He is now the official photographer of the Sudanese prime minister.

The following images are snapshots of the lives of displaced people in Darfur and Sudan. You can see more of his images on Instagram @sawrasari.

A group of young people in Khartoum, in a sit-in during the peaceful revolution in Sudan. The sign behind them reads: 'If you do not gain freedom and peace, do not leave your place, for your comrades died to gain your freedom'.

A worker in the manual textiles industry in which the palms clap is used, in Khartoum, Fatah locality. She manufactures manually and sells to improve her financial position.

A group of men in Wad Hajam village, South Darfur, working in the
manufacture of palm fronds products for the local market

A group of women in the village of Wad Hajam, South Darfur, during
a lecture on the Revolving Fund of the United Nations Development
Program in 2018

A worker in the local brick industry in the city of Al-Jarif West, on the bank of the Blue Nile. He arranges bricks on the ground to obtain enough heat from the sun.

Abou Karina local market, east of Darfur

A woman from South Darfur makes yogurt in the traditional way,
Al-Firsan Village

The National Bank of Egypt
building in the ancient city of
Sawakin.

REVIEWS

THE ORDER OF COVID

Kanchana Mahadevan

The coronavirus pandemic has disrupted, levelled and altered life in radical ways. It has stymied economies, politics, society, and cultures by inhibiting personal physical contact; it has levelled the rich and poor by exposing the frail infrastructure of commodified health systems; it has redefined the public and private spaces through work from home, video conferencing and virtual spaces, while emptying out campuses, offices, and parks. Even as the mysterious virus eluded cognition, sparking off a trail of conspiracy theories and conjectures, it heightened scientific research by seeking explanations into the virus's genetic sequence and the search for vaccines. Yet in the midst of such levelling, the elusive global trajectory of the coronavirus also spotlighted inequities. Not everyone had the privilege of working from home productively; women struggled to balance jobs with personal lives, children grappled with the loss of company. In the absence of urban public transport, migrant workers in India walked for days on end – often unsuccessfully – to their rural homes. The lack of access to laboratories, libraries, and field data hindered knowledge creation that was not related to the grand narrative of the virus. Vinay Lal's *The Fury of COVID-19* draws together these tensions of the pandemic's new world order. It details the specific ways in which the raging coronavirus has changed the human condition by weaving together history, politics, and philosophy, situating the disease in the context of cultural histories. Vinay Lal's characterisation of COVID-19 as a 'singular ineluctable fact' upholds that nothing similar has transpired in human history.

Pandemics receive the attention they do often because of the larger contexts and interests in which they are embedded. For the most part, pandemics that have been highlighted are those that have impacted the Western world. Lal cites a protracted list of pandemics spanning the twentieth and twenty-first centuries, such as the plague, the Spanish Flu,

H2N2, H3N2, HIV, SARS, H1N1, MERS, the Ebola. Yet all of them have not received the same degree of attention. Many of them are 'forgotten pandemics', despite their intensity. The reasons vary from post war fatigue with disease and death, as was the case with the Spanish Flu that broke out after the First World War, and the H2N2 or the Asian Flu and the H3N2 or Hong Kong Flu that occurred after the Second World War, the Korean War, and the threat of a nuclear war. But there was also a tendency to remember and narrate diseases related to the world, particularly the Western world, rather than a region, as the Ebola pandemic revealed. COVID-19 has impacted Western nations, as much as, those in Latin America and Asia; it has, therefore, been characterised as unique.

Vinay Lal, *The Fury of COVID-19*, Macmillan, New Delhi, 2020.

The earlier pandemics did not bring the world – its economy in particular – to a total halt, in the manner of COVID-19. Lal notes how norms of physical distancing, masking, and partial shut downs did prevail during the Spanish Flu. But then trade continued and public interaction was not completely prohibited. COVID-19's singularity does not allow for taking refuge in the comfort of universalisms. It is not a particular event that can be classified under a universal concept such as 'pandemic' with which it shares essential features. Rather, COVID-19's connection to other analogous episodes in human history is nominal and could be understood as what philosopher Ludwig Wittgenstein terms as 'family resemblance'. In this tenor, Lal chronicles an array of phenomena that have repeated and reinforced themselves in the context of the present pandemic. These include quarantine and isolation, stress on hygiene and cleanliness, discrimination against the socially vulnerable, imperialist governmentality, nationalist responses, weak health systems and the active role of the transnational body, the WHO in proclaiming pandemics, often in collusion with pharma industries. The chapter on 'Who's Responsible: The WHO and Medical Internationalism' is a rare account of the interventionist role of WHO whose internationalism is curtailed by American nationalism.

The Fury of COVID-19 cautions against naively invoking the history of pandemics for set answers to these challenges. 'Family resemblance' notwithstanding, the present pandemic has led to heightened state intervention, adjournment of trade and public movement. These phenomena are symptoms of the world being brought together through disease. Lal cites the French historian Emanuel Le Roy Ladurie's accounts of how the plague, the invasion of the Americas, and the flu are all versions of 'microbial unification'. This enhances the specificity of the challenge facing the human condition in the current crisis. He questions the approach of finding 'global solutions' to 'global problems' in the spirit of a global modernity; and recommends working with the 'partial guidance' of history to situate the present pandemic in specific cultural contexts to examine how forces such as the political, social/cultural and economic (among others) mediate it. This implies that some of the ways in which one can cope with the pandemic might also emerge in specific cultural contexts.

The book argues that the paucity of modern approaches to the pandemic is evident in the separation between cognition and feeling central to the dominant scientific explanatory paradigms, which have proved to be insufficient. Lal notes that allied phenomena such as governmentality or capitalist consumption that have segregated reason and faith, as well as, individual and community, cannot speak to the pandemic's ability to interconnect the world through disease. The Western imperialist tendency to track the origin of the virus in a specific geographic context - often the East - is rooted in the need to understand a phenomenon that speedily multiplies as it connects. He notes how the fourteenth century Italian writer, Giovani Boccaccio, regarded the plague as originating in the East 'before it unhappily spread Westward'. This tendency, rooted in the Greek historian Thucydides' account of the 430 BCE plague in Athens, has persisted to date, with AIDS and Ebola being similarly understood as originating in Africa in representing dictatorships, lack of civilisation, and poverty. It is in this tenor that the coronavirus was disparagingly called the Chinese virus in Italy and the US.

However, not all accounts of the eastwardly turn stigmatise in such an explicit fashion. For instance, in the play 'Indian Cholera' by Henrik Wergeland, cholera originates in India and spreads across the globe by levelling the rich and poor, along with Europeans and non-Europeans, as a punishment for the British colonisation of India. This too is an attempt to master an inexplicable pandemic through moral retribution in the spirit of the kind of modernity that Lal admonishes. A non-retributive perspective on pandemics can be read even in Boccaccio who cites habits of avarice and unbridled consumption as ushering in the plague, on a note that parallels Lal's similar critique of the neo-liberal assumptions fuelling the COVID-19 pandemic. In its first wave, COVID-19 often bypassed poorer nations in the East but afflicted the poor racial minorities – including Native Americans in the US – in the wealthier nations. However, in an unpredictable move, its second wave assailed poorer countries such as India as well. The difficulties of predicting its trajectory reveal that one needs to think beyond linear movement when considering COVID-19 (or any other disease for that matter) as one can discern patterns that intertwine and zigzag, rather than flow unidirectionally.

It is against such Eurocentric readings of maladies, as originating in the Orient, that Lal adopts a decentred approach by turning to the diverse unfolding of the pandemic in varied geopolitical contexts (each of which has its own histories of disease). The various chapters in the book take us through the different parts of the world to unearth the notable contextual forms of COVID-19. They also bring out how each context has capabilities to cope with the disease that emerged from its own cultural histories of responding to pandemics. The colonial history of plague in India frames Lal's discussion of the largest exodus of migrant labour walking back to their home villages from cities due to a sudden lockdown announcement in April 2020. History repeated itself – albeit in a gentler form since transport was available – one year later with the second wave. Lal outlines the communitarian efforts to contain the disease in one of the largest slum settlements in Asia: Dharavi of Mumbai. His discussion perceptively reveals how the absence of caste hierarchies helped the various communities of Dharavi join together to handle the virus on a more caring mode. Dharavi has continued to remain stable with a few cases through the second wave, demonstrating that social vulnerability to disease can be overturned through solidarity. The personal involvement of both health workers and the community are crucial in tackling a pandemic. A similar communitarian model was used in Kerala but it is conspicuously absent from the book.

How different western nations reacted to the pandemic depended on their cultural history and notions of freedom. The history of plague and the large elderly population in Italy led to the moral problem of prioritising treatment based on age. Was Italy 'too hasty in sacrificing the old to the young' Lal asks; is there a hidden social perception of dispensability? Similar questions are raised in relation to national histories, identity and imagery that shaped responses to the pandemic in the UK, France, Sweden and the US. Measures of lockdown in the UK, for example, were met with resistance in the name of the 'inalienable right to go to the pub'. France did not undertake using mobile phone applications to track people with coronavirus as this was seen to be against their cultural investment in liberty. However, unlike the UK, France did not think of its freedom as insulated, but as an example for the world. The nations of the European Union witnessed widespread lockdowns of their borders that were earlier open to each other. Lal cites Sweden's 'light touch' approach of keeping public places open despite the increasing onset and fatalities of the virus as resulting from their dependence on decisions made by their state health bodies rather than political leaders. It is a society with 'high trust' in health experts and social welfare provisions, which, for Lal, is also true of both, Norway and Denmark, who imposed restrictions unlike Sweden (many closed their borders to Sweden due to their policies that led to the spread of the coronavirus). Sweden differed from other Scandinavian countries in not having been occupied by other powers (such as German or Soviet) as a result of which it developed a historical political culture of maintaining neutrality through the world wars. In the United States, Lal cites critics – often from the far right – of state promoted lockdown as invoking cultural constitutional vocabulary of rights and freedom in the name of the 'American way of life'.

Lal suggests that one cannot write off the protests against lockdowns such as those witnessed in the US as extreme right anarchism against the state or even simply white supremacy. Anarchism has been used by the Left as well. Moreover, the protests are attempts made by people to express their will and act in the public domain. One would have to contend that they were oblivious to the spread of disease and did not heed scientific warnings. Yet, argues Lal, one cannot be dismissive of the presence of an alternate way of thinking in such protests.

However, *The Fury of COVID-19* could have devoted some attention to the persistence of more democratic public protests for racial equality, such as the re-emergence of the Black Lives Matter movement after the killing of George Floyd or the farmers' protest movement in India. How can one relate progressive movements such as these with the right-wing demonstrations against wearing masks or vaccines? Or can one alternatively read them as attempts to seek social justice under conditions of inequality and the long interlude of the pandemic? Moreover, in the various closures of national borders to avert the spread of disease, Lal discerns rising nationalisms and weakening globalism of bodies such as the African Union, the EU or the UN. He chastises Brazil's President Bolsonaro and the Philippines' President Duterte for not following the norms to prevent the spread of the virus suggested by the WHO. Bolsonaro and Duterte are indeed deeply insensitive in their responses to the pandemic. However, such a judgement cannot invoke the WHO as a yardstick precisely because of its own politicised and centralised hegemonic position. Lal devotes a whole chapter to documenting the questionable position of the WHO, which postures as a supranational body while also being controlled by the national interests of the US. He asks (perhaps rhetorically) whether the UN can transform itself or whether new forms of internationalisms could arise in a post COVID world. Such a question, however, is tangential considering the perennial hovering of nationalisms underlying international institutions.

There is nothing unique or original in the WHO regulations on pandemic practices of quarantine and physical distancing when one turns to cultural stories and myths. Lal demonstrates non-Eurocentric legacies by showing that quarantine does not necessarily originate in the context of the plague of 1346 as a foundational moment. Hindu deities such as Lord Ram and Lord Jaganath had practiced quarantine during their vulnerable periods of exile and sickness. There are references to quarantining the ill in the Old Testament and Jesus fasting for forty days, as well as, the Catholic Lent period of forty days. These discussions draw our attention to the persistent isolation of the poor and quarantining of the socially vulnerable through cultural imagination. They also underscore the difficulties of locating an original pandemic, such as the plague in Europe, as a paradigm for the entire world.

Given its investment in non-bureaucratic perspectives on the pandemic, one wishes that the book could have highlighted the critical literature in

India during the various periods of the pandemic in the nineteenth and twentieth centuries chastising social inequities, lack of access to healthcare institutions, and British governmental controls. Even before Albert Camus' *The Plague*, which has become a ubiquitous reference point in pandemic writing, writers and activists questioned the relationship between pandemics and imperial policies. For instance, the social reformer Pandita Ramabai's letter to the paper *The Bombay Guardian* from the Plague Hospital in 1897 is a scathing critique of the lack of sanitation and safety for women under 'the heartless unjust' British rule. Similarly, the 1938 short story, 'Quarantine' by Rajinder Singh Bedi, portrays the difficulties of care givers in a village in India during the nineteenth century. Bedi sums up the chilling plight as one in which the 'plague was terrifying indeed but quarantine was rather fatal'. Many preferred to hide the disease in fear of being quarantined in plague shelters that segregated the sick from the healthy. The story is told from the perspective of a doctor who narrates the unsanitary and squalid conditions under which he worked alongside a sacrificing caregiver William Bhagav. Bhagav swept and sanitised the shelter, enabling patients to convalesce and recover. However, when the disease finally receded, his work was neglected. The doctor was honoured, even though he did not take the kind of risks that Bhagav did. The story brings out the doctor's sense of remorse and worthlessness in a world that does not acknowledge caregivers. It also documents the insensitivity of quarantine as a law to contain illness. Interestingly, in Bedi's story, Bhagav is a Christian who does his good deeds out of love for Jesus. On a more bitter-sweet note, in his 1938 autobiography, *A Life Misspent*, Suryakant Tripathi Nirala, a giant of Indian literature, describes how his 'family disappeared in the blink of an eye' during the influenza epidemic and narrates how this loss opened up a new relationship transcending societal norms of caste, class, and sexuality. Some of Munshi Premchand's works have also cited the struggles with epidemics and disease during the colonial period. These resources become particularly significant as one clings to the word – often through memory – in a world rife with the casualties of closed libraries and bookstores.

These literary works resonate with Lal's wider meditative chapters on the philosophical dimensions of the pandemic, which examine the relationship between human beings and nature in the large context of neo-liberal consumption. Lal articulates the paradoxical predicament that human beings face by being alone, devoid of touch, and yet having the normative task of connecting with one another. 'One of the greater calamities of COVID-19', Lal writes, 'is that, contrary to what we are ordinarily called upon to do when confronted with a grave disaster, it demands of us that we isolate ourselves from others, build fences, and forgo the often intimate and unspeakably beautiful pleasures of touch'. Touch, Lal observes, is the most central dimension of human life, especially taking the feminine dimension of touch into consideration in contrast to the masculinity of vision. However, his belief that ancient traditions and systems (including Indian) emphasised touch overlooks that most philosophical systems, both Indian and Western, have prioritised vision. After all, the classical systems of Indian philosophy are termed as *darshana* or vision. Moreover, in the Indian philosophical traditions, perception itself has been foundational only to a few systems of thought. Feminists, in both Indian and Western traditions, have argued against the canonical neglect of the perceptual lived experiences of women.

A central claim in the book is the loss of direct touch in a period of abject isolation. But is the phenomenon of touch necessarily immediate and direct? One could very well follow Maurice Merleau-Ponty, the twentieth century French philosopher, and acknowledge that there is always a gap, a distance in the phenomenon of touch. He notes that between one's movements (feeling one's hands) and what one touches there needs to be a 'kinship' whereby they don't merely operate in an abstract domain, but in a grounded 'tactile world'. On Merleau-Ponty's account, touching is never immediate, but a mediated overlap with crisscrossing exchanges between three distinct experiences of touch: the ephemeral and nebulous (as rough or soft), concrete things, and the touch itself as a thing among others (when one's hand touches the other that palpitates objects). Touch, then, takes place in the midst of inhabiting the world and apprehending things. It is never direct or immediate but presupposes a 'chiasm' as Merleau-Ponty notes of the material sensible dimension and the figurative conceptual aspect that circulate, entangle, and are reversible. Thus, the hand both senses and is sentient. It never moves in a single direction, nor instantaneously. There is, instead, a coming together and communication between three diverse experiences, none of which coincide with each other. Hence, touch functions through gaps and mediations. The pandemic makes us aware of the mediated gaps of touch, as we connect with people through masks, physical distance, telephones, and computer screens. Lal could have explored how the coronavirus has expanded the chiasm of touch in new modes of inter-corporeality, rather than annihilate it.

The disease as we encounter it has left us alone. It rules out face to face communication, for the time being at least, in the café, the bookstore, and even the classroom. The clinics overflow with patients hindering an interactive and therapeutic doctor-patient relationship. For the most part we are all in solitude. Some modes of solitude are overcrowded without ventilation, while some others are well-spaced with impeccable cross ventilation. Yet we are physically distant from the world of public affairs, from each other. Lal's book addresses the possibility of being social in solitude; of understanding, following Žižek, the paradox of Jesus asking Mary Magdalene not to touch him when she recognises him after his resurrection.

The Fury of COVID-19 demonstrates that meditating during the corona crisis entails thinking alongside diversity (geographies, politics, cultures, and ecologies). Philosophical thought – on a widened ecological mode - is not separated from the religious and the mythological. Rather, it brings together human beings with flora and fauna, spirits and memory. Reading *The Fury of COVID-19*, with its wide-ranging ruminations on Gandhi, pedagogy, Cuban health-systems, and human canine-bonds are interwoven with the larger theoretical issues. I was reminded of Cheryl Strayed's reflections in her 2012 book *Wild*. Strayed narrates her reclusive wandering through harsh weather and landscapes, as she reflects on her losses (having lost her mother to cancer and being unable to forge constructive relationships), memories, and feelings. She sets off on a 1,100 miles solitary trek across the wilderness of the Pacific Crest Trail in the United States to find others and her own self in the process of being alone. On a similar note, Lal documents how the involuntary quarantine has mandated us to think. In locating thought in the simultaneous cultural axes of diverse geographies, Lal reveals that the thinker is never alone. But rather, in an overwhelming company, whose horizon is populated with the familiar visible figure of human beings, as much as, the unfamiliar invisible COVID-19.

SOFT IMPERIALISM

Shanon Shah

In 1952, the British authorities declared a state of emergency in colonial Kenya, precipitating years of violent warfare. Thousands of Kikuyu were detained in internment camps on suspicion of supporting the Kenya Land and Freedom Army, known as the Mau Mau – insurgents infamous for attacking European settlers. British forces sought to purge these captives of what the colonial authorities characterised as mental anguish caused by the shock of modernity. The de-programming agenda involved inmates being forced to build their own prisons, including chambers in which they were tortured by the British.

It's a period of history that is unfamiliar to many British people, especially since the Empire did all it could to suppress any information about this dirty war in Kenya. Instead, the period of the insurgency saw glossy, big budget films produced, such as *Simba*, a 1955 'African Western' directed by Brian Desmond Hurst – best known for *Scrooge* (1951), his adaption of *A Christmas Carol* by Charles Dickens – and starring matinee idol Dirk Bogarde. The film depicts the British as victims of the Mau Mau's supposed savagery, with no honest accounting of the atrocities perpetrated by colonial forces upon thousands of natives.

I learnt about the Mau Mau Uprising – and the British propaganda in response – only very recently, through the 2020 BBC documentary *African Renaissance: When Art Meets Power*, written and presented by Norwegian-born British journalist Afua Hirsch. It enraged me, but it also made me thankful for the BBC. I watched this entire series in the middle of a lockdown in which the British government repeatedly refused to acknowledge the disproportionate impact of the coronavirus pandemic on ethnic minorities, while continuing to pursue its hostile environment policy towards immigrants. I felt comforted by the BBC's willingness to support this truth-telling about the dark side of the country's imperial past.

Robert Winder, *Soft Power: The New Great Game*, Little, Brown, London, 2020.

But what game was the BBC was playing with my consciousness? Was it informing me about history through impeccable research and engaging storytelling? Was it helping to create an alternative image of Britain for me, one that welcomed self-reflection, self-correction, and a commitment to moral improvement? According to Robert Winder, former literary editor of the *Independent*, it was probably doing a bit of both. The BBC was using creative communications and culture to ensure that, despite several truly disturbing developments in British politics, I still had warm feelings about some elements of Britain.

As Winder puts it in *Soft Power*, the BBC 'is trusted because it is the voice of Britain, but not the mouthpiece of its government'. It is an exemple of Britain's 'soft power', which for Winder is not something that can be manufactured by governments but which is nonetheless a crucial measure of 'whether a country is liked'. This is Winder's formulation of the American political scientist Joseph Nye's idea of 'soft power', as 'the third great player in international affairs, tucked in behind military and financial prowess'. In other words, politicians, official foreign policy and even military prowess are not the only determinants of a country's international standing – elements such as 'cheerfulness, politeness and humour' count, too.

The book's introduction illustrates this with an anecdote of Japan's 2-0 quarterfinal defeat to Belgium in the 2018 World Cup. Rather than wallow in dejection, the Japanese footballers 'gave a ceremonious bow to thank their supporters' and later, in the safety of their dressing room, 'they showered, rolled up their sleeves and…tidied up'. Their handiwork made the global news headlines. They had collectively emulated the tidiness guru Marie Kondo, making the world fall in love with Japan – the 'classy', 'true champions' – as a *nation*.

In the book's first half, Winder concentrates on the West, devoting the bulk of his attention to the US, the UK and France – the first an existing and the latter two former imperial powers. For Winder, immigration, opportunity and Hollywood are some of the pillars of American soft power. Britain has the aforementioned BBC, the Monarchy (think of the popularity of the Netflix series *The Crown*), the English language and literature, and the British Council. France has food, wine, *haute couture*, art, and the legacy of its Revolution. But these countries are also facing threats to these traditional elements of soft power. For instance, strident militarism overseas and bitter internal political polarisation have undermined the US's global likeability, while a mishandling of Brexit has marred the UK's reputation.

This cataloguing approach is carried through the remainder of the book in its overview of the soft power credentials of other world regions. However, the formula of listing the pros followed by the cons of soft power in the first half is reversed once we get to the Gulf. Winder opens here with the Islamic State's destruction of the ancient Assyrian ruins of Nimrud, Iraq, in 2015. This, according to him, is merely one of the many ways that the Middle East squanders opportunity after opportunity to make itself universally likeable, whether through religious militancy, mismanagement of petroleum reserves, and a lack of democracy. Even Turkey, with its burgeoning industry of hit television serials, sabotages itself by continuing to jail journalists amid growing nationalist, authoritarian expressions of Islam.

The tone shifts again in the chapters on India and Africa. With India, Winder takes great pains to establish that 'imperialism had been an inexcusable imposition'. Yet, much of the chapter refers to the anti-colonial arguments made by the Indian politician Shashi Tharoor as a launching pad for Winder's litany of rebuttals about the country's colonial legacy. Religious sectarianism, for example, pre-dated the arrival of the British. Rather, colonial administrators such as Warren Hastings had 'genuine' affection for India and Indians. Meanwhile, Rajendra Prasad, the first president of India, paid homage to 'the historic tradition and democratic ideals of British rule'. Finally, there is the 'sad truth' that 'if Britain had never set foot in India, the latter would probably have been colonised by someone else – by Holland, Portugal, Russia or (most likely) France – just as it had, in the past, been colonised by the Mughal empire'. The mixed and inconsistent motives of the Raj, argues Winder, might even have helped to germinate the seeds of modern India's soft power, such as through the European 'discovery' of the *Bhagavad Gita* and other treasures of Eastern mysticism.

The formula of acknowledging colonial violence whilst offering imperial apologia also structures the chapter on Africa. The argument is made, for example, that the continent's slave trade long pre-dated European arrival. And European enslavement of Africans, whilst writing 'an evil new page in this evil old story', gave Africa some new effective soft-power tools – including the birth of 'new musical genres', and a corrective to dominant historical views of how civilisations emerged. And the West is hardly the sole villain in the continuing exploitation of Africa – China is now flexing colonial muscle in the region, too.

Winder's many examples of soft power in different parts of the world are engagingly narrated and meticulously researched. But his global survey often seems random and selective. The problem is not the accuracy or range of facts presented, but the way in which they are assembled.

There is the puzzling issue of the analytical units that Winder applies to his chapters. The first two chapters, titled 'America', are really about the US, whilst South America gets lumped together with Australasia in a very brief chapter towards to the end. Entire or multiple chapters devoted to nation-states – Britain, France, Russia, India, China, and Japan – sit alongside a single chapter covering an entire continent ('Africa') and a bunch of other regions ('Southern Europe', 'Central Europe', 'Northern Europe', 'The Gulf', 'World on Fire: South America and Australasia'). It is also a struggle to make geographical sense of why Egypt and Turkey are included as part of 'the Gulf'.

In the Epilogue, Winder mounts what comes across as a defence of the book's lack of cohesiveness. Soft power, he concludes, cannot be measured or weighed in a simple way. It is 'broad', 'elusive' and 'too ambiguous' as a concept. It is a 'process' rather than a tangible entity – 'a new great game' that nations are now understanding afresh in a world gripped by the coronavirus pandemic. But this is an analytical copout. It also turns the concept of soft power into too much of a shapeshifter. For example, Winder refers to soft power as 'storytelling' and 'collaboration' in parts, as simply 'not propaganda' in others and, somewhat tangentially, as now being undermined by 'identity politics' when it should be used to foster global 'interdependence' in an age of Covid-19.

So, what is soft power, really? And if it's that difficult to pin down, then why devote an entire book to it?

Soft power *is* a fuzzy concept, but maybe a helpful way to think about it is not through a shopping list of archetypes, or even stereotypes, associated with discrete 'nations'. The 'nation', after all, is an idea that is constantly being constructed, challenged and redefined through various means, including through arts and culture, political propaganda, and the machinery of the state. In the efforts of nation-states to project influence, social scientists do in fact distinguish between the 'hard power' of compulsion through military and economic means and the 'soft power' of culture and communications. To say that nation-states use both 'hard' and 'soft' power, however, is simply a truism. What would be more useful is a demonstration of the actual application of 'hard' and 'soft' modes of power in different circumstances or historical moments. In other words, *who* is exerting power – hard, soft, or both – and *why*? And, so what?

To return to Britain's response to the Mau Mau Uprising, soft and hard power elements were both present. The British were indeed using military force, including against civilians, to protect the multiple layers of economic exploitation – a core characteristic of the hard power of colonialism. But cultural and communications tools were also instrumental in justifying Britain's human rights abuses in Kenya, through African Westerns such as *Simba*. By Winder's criteria, the film does not qualify as 'soft power' – the involvement of the War Office, the Colonial Office, and the white settler organisation Voice of Kenya, in its production, clearly make it propaganda. This is a slippery slope, however – government involvement notwithstanding, the film was produced by the Rank Organisation, a major film studio that produced other classics of British cinema such as *Brief Encounter* and *The Red Shoes*. The boundary between soft power and propaganda can be porous.

That the Mau Mau Uprising and its aftermath was prominently discussed in a documentary shown on BBC Four is a matter of public interest, especially at a time when calls for racial justice are deepening. This is what mattered most to me as a viewer. In this sense, Winder is right to say that the reputation of the BBC as a public broadcaster lies precisely in its independence from the British government.

Arguably, though, soft power is not just 'tucked behind' military dominance and financial prowess. There is instead a symbiotic relationship between military, economic and cultural interests. Each feeds the other, just as each is fed by the other. Winder himself points out the *par excellence* example of the evolving relationship between the Crown, the East India Company, and the cultural Orientalist forays that contributed to the formation and maintenance of the British Raj.

This tripartite relationship continues. As Winder rightly illustrates, Britain might have lost its political Empire, but it continues to exert considerable global influence through the soft power of cultural symbols, including television, cinema, popular music, literature and sport. What is slightly more neglected is the role of corporate power in maintaining Britain's global influence, which is reinforced rather than overshadowed by its 'special relationship' with the US.

And so, it is true that the British Council, the BBC and English Premier League football all still contribute significantly to Britain's 'likeability'. But a disproportionate focus on these factors renders invisible the revolving door that allows ministers and civil servants to waltz between the public and private sectors. It is this systemic fusion between corporate and political power that enabled, for example, the Department for International Development to grant contracts worth millions of pounds sterling to British companies under the guise of providing humanitarian aid to Iraq.

Meanwhile, this framework of humanitarianism allows Winder to defend the role of institutions such as the British Museum and the Louvre in continuing to own and house historic treasures from the Middle East. Because look at what would happen when they were left in Iraq – they'd only get blown up by terrorists. It's a compelling argument with practical implications.

It also illustrates how the hard power of imperial ambition can still find legitimacy through the tools of soft power.

ARCHITECTURAL TRANSFERS

Iason Athanasiadis

When Umayyad Caliph al-Hakam II decided to expand the Grand Mosque of Cordoba, in 965, he faced a problem: mosaic-making knowhow had disappeared from this part of southwestern Europe half a millennium before, when the Romans were driven out of Hispania. Without it, al-Hakam II's prospects of emulating his ancestors and recreating the kind of splendid, Byzantine-style mosaics attained in Damascus' Umayyad Mosque were slim. So he sent a message East to Constantinople and Byzantine Emperor Nicephorus II, asking for a little capacity-building support in order that he might create, in his dynasty's Andalusian exile, a reminder of its Syrian homeland.

The emperor of Byzantium complied, sending over a skilled mosaicist, several Syrian apprentices and assistants, and several sackfuls of gold cubes. The resulting delicate mosaics survived the mosque's conversion into a cathedral and remain incrusted to this day on the Mezquita's *mihrab*.

Diana Darke, *Stealing from the Saracens: How Islamic Architecture Shaped Europe,* Hurst, London, 2020.

Muslim caliphs in western Europe sending aid requests to Christian emperors living within Asia's sight line is the kind of heretical anecdote relished by Diana Darke, and heavily populate *Stealing from the Saracens.* Her book traces an iconoclastic architectural narrative across time and space, pausing at exotic buildings, vanished and extant: desert palaces, Crusader and Ayyubid castles, and the Nilometer. But most of all, she uses religious architecture, churches, monasteries and mosques, to summon up a geography of architectural influence drifting westwards from the

Christian and Muslim East, to evolve creatively in the cosmopolitan Mediterranean ports remaining immune to orthodoxy.

From a simple third-century house-church in Mesopotamia's Dura Europos to Antioch's long-lost Domus Aurea (Golden House) cathedral, and from St Simeon's elaborate basilica in northern Syria to the glittering mosaics of Ravenna's San Vitale and Constantinople's Hagia Sophia, the Abbey of Cluny and the onion-domed and Islamically-ornamented St Mark's in Venice, Darke weaves a narrative of how 'the history of Western medieval architecture, like that of Western culture in general, cannot be written without reference to the lessons learnt from Islamic culture, whereas the history of Islamic medieval architecture can be written largely without reference to the West.' Combative, compelling and occasionally reductionist, *Stealing from the Saracens* is very much a product of its polarised time. It began life as a tweet even as Paris' Notre Dame smouldered, then detonated into a viral social media sphere blogpost, before reaching us in final book form to shed light on our blind spot about just how much Western architecture owes to Eastern wisdom.

A former resident of Damascus who channelled her love for old buildings into buying and restoring one in the ancient city's Medina, Darke spiritedly uncovers the scale of eastern contributions to the Western building tradition, and especially the Gothic style, which she sets out to prove has roots that at different times were called Moorish, Saracen or Arab. Along the way, she brings alive a cast of mostly anonymous characters, whose activities illuminate a not-so-distant world when itinerant artisans, pilgrims and knights regularly crisscrossed the Mediterranean, diffusing architectural innovation from east to west. The characters popping from the pages illustrate a more fluid region than we imagine if we accept the commonplace view of an antique and medieval Mediterranean polarised between Byzantine and Catholic Christianity on the one side, and the Abbasid, Fatimid and Andalusian Muslim empires on the other. There are knights returning from the Holy Lands who, inspired by the sight of mosques, may have been responsible for the minaret-like pointed spires atop that period's Romanesque churches; a community of forty Venetians permitted to live and trade in Damascus in the fifteenth century; and a Norman period of rule in Sicily during which the rulers spoke Arabic and developed a Romanesque Gothic hybrid they then exported on to France.

Just as today, when confrontations claims the headlines behind which business partnerships, romances and other consensual transactions persist, life in the medieval Mediterranean continued despite all obstacles: Italian traders made market openings, itinerant artisans and stonemasons from Syria sold their skills in countless European construction sites (as did Michelangelo to the Ottoman court in Istanbul), and in Poitiers a mystery pilgrim deposited a souvenir statuette of Simeon, the Syrian stylite and saint, that s/he had picked up nearly 4,000 kilometres away. All of this activity happens around the rim of the world's most central sea and a historical reflecting pool of cultures. The book's primary locale is not arrived at by chance: religions mould cultures, and wherever these interact they generate new evolutions in architecture. Unsurprisingly then, the imported architectural innovations first affected littoral regions such as Muslim Andalus, the trading cities of coastal Italy, Norman Sicily and Crusader Cyprus, which were some of that era's most intense contact zones.

Andalusia's Umayyads absorbed the Hispano-Roman legacy and added their own irrigation and agronomy knowledge to affect a great agricultural revival. Pointed arches emigrated northwards from Cairo's Ibn Tulun Mosque to make a first European appearance in the cathedral of Amalfi. Recessed niches and stained glass passed from Fatimid mosques to Palermo's syncretistic Martorana church. And the archivolt – extinct on the Continent after the Roman period – was resurrected in Romanesque architecture, apparently via the Persian city of Ctesiphon. It would also have been in Seljuk buildings in Iran as well as in the ports of the Black Sea and in Anatolia, that Venetians saw and copied the geometric brickwork pattern subsequently replicated in their own city's buildings, perhaps Europe's most Oriental.

Finishing the book, one is somewhat left with the impression that the Muslim World bequeathed to the West much of its key architectural elements, and that the greatest role in this process was played by cultures that existed in what today is Syria. Undoubtedly, this owes much to *bilad al-Sham*'s extraordinary location on the coastline acting as Europe's liquid gateway, where the civilisations of Asia and the Far East interacted with the Caucasus and the Arabian Peninsula. The vivid mélange of cultures surviving and mixing in this territory over millennia, produced a sustained and mobile tradition, whereby artisans, holy men and sponsors traded influence with neighboring cultures. Darke reminds us that it was the Syrian Julia Domna, daughter of the high priest in the famous Temple of the Sun in Emessa, who is said to have lobbied her son Caracalla to issue his famous decree of 212 extending Roman citizenship to all free men of the empire, sweeping away all distinctions between Romans and provincials. Such were the numbers who subsequently took advantage of this, that first-century poet Juvenal complained that 'the Orontes has long since been emptying into the Tiber'.

Darke argues that fifth-century monasteries in today's Jordan are the only places where cloisters were glimpsed, before reappearing centuries later during Charlemagne's time in European church architecture. Similarly, the Syrian niche appears in Palmyra (in itself a unique blend of the Assyrian, Phoenician, Babylonian, Persian, Egyptian, Hellenistic and Roman traditions), before reappearing in Europe's Gothic cathedrals. She conjures up Christian monks from Antioch swamping fifth-century Ravenna, the Syrian benefactors of the city's famous San Vitale and Sant'Apollinare basilicas, and the architectural style of the Muslim Umayyad dynasty spreading across North Africa to colonise the Iberian Peninsula. Although Syria exports little architecture today, this tradition of fanning outwards to create anew can still be glimpsed in the small businesses and artistic wealth that fled civil war-wracked Syria since 2010, to fertilise North Africa, Turkey, and Europe.

But *Stealing from the Saracens* is also an enjoyable urban romp through some of the world's once-glorious, now-sidelined cities. We are steered from Samarra to Cordoba, Edessa to the Duchate of Amalfi, and Famagusta to Cadiz, a Phoenician colony with the claim to being Europe's oldest city. Venice is the book's real star, not least because she was the only city whose adoption of Islamic styles was a deliberate and willing choice, unlike in Spain, Sicily and Cyprus where it derived from periods of Muslim domination. The Venetians saw the great multi-faith cities of the Islamic world – Cairo, Alexandria, Damascus, Tripoli, Tyre, Antioch, Aleppo and Jerusalem – as 'prosperous, colourful and civilised', so adopting Islamic styles for their buildings was a conscious and complimentary choice. It might also have been a new and bold identity by which to project their independence by defining themselves away from Rome and the Pope. Whatever the reason, the Eastern architectural borrowings included covering the canal-facing windows of Venice's palazzos with modesty-preserving *mashrabiya* screens, and crowning them with Damascene-style screened-off roof terraces. The contemporary version of St Mark's bulbous, hollow double-domes shared the appearance of those in Cairo, and were similarly made of lead-covered wood. Venice's main church also contained geometric-patterned stone window grilles, relief panels in the style of Egyptian Fatimid wood-carvings, and an ogee arch relief. Another element anchoring the relationship with the Muslim world, was Venice's glassmaking tradition, which developed out of factories and workshops in Alexandria and Tyre, and Byzantine and Arab craftsmen who came to the city to develop some of the finest *cristalo* ever made.

The breadth and range of these exchanges demonstrates how progress in scientific knowledge, much of it rescued from the annals of obscurity by translators shifting texts from Greek into Syriac, then Arabic and onto Latin, shaped architectural developments. Without the advances in geometry, fractals and algebra, domes could not have gone from being supported on clumsy, buttressed pedentives to resting on elegant, barely-visible squinches; nor could a new, immersive perspective like the equilateral triangle view inject a sense of unity and wholeness into a space. It was the knowhow developed between the knowledge depositories of ancient Greece, Persia, and India that resulted in slimmer, gravity-defying spires, elegantly-uncluttered interior spaces, and buildings constructed around the magical 8:13 Golden Ratio.

After reading about architectural developments traced back to Mesopotamian, Byzantine, and Sassanian architectural influences, or about how Euclid's discoveries buttoned onto seventh-century innovations in India to create stabler, less-cluttered spaces, one might wonder at the prominence of 'Islamic' in the book's title. Given the huge range of civilisational, scientific, and cultural inputs that went into the 'gestation whirlpool' travelling northwest, is the focus on just the Muslim aspect not disorienting, especially given the outsized influence of pagan, early Christian architecture, and secular scientific developments?

Darke's selective reading of architectural history glosses over some chains of transmission in favour of others: heavily quoting Wren but not mentioning that he saw the Arabs as merely a chain of transmission: 'After we in the West had lost both, we borrowed again from them, out of their Arabic books, what they with great diligence had translated from the Greeks'. Darke identifies a variant of 'Turkish Gothic' in the masterful thirteenth-century Divrigi hospital/mosque complex built by the Seljuks, but there is nary a mention of the totally Gothic cathedral in the Armenian city of Ani, a few hundred kilometres to Divrigi's east. Granted, Darke's argument that Muslim empires often provided conducive and permissive intellectual environments for the kind of knowledge advances needed to propel architecture forward is powerful. But she cites just as many if not more examples of advances and transmission being spurred by non-Muslim communities and contexts, or even of knowledge transfers occurring due to populations moving away from Muslim rule to avoid onerous religious minority taxes, such as the Byzantine Christians who fled the Islamic conquest of Syria, or the fifteenth-century emigration of Constantinopolitans to Italy following their city's conquest by the Ottomans.

This is very much a book that sets out to right a longstanding injustice, namely of the scant recognition offered by Christian Europe to the Muslim world for the numerous architectural, scientific, and design debts owed to it. So the focus is more on how the Mujedar tradition of Andalus flowed into Gothic architecture or the Cairene inspiration behind Venice's bulbous domes, and less on, say, the appropriation by the invading Umayyad kingdom of Spain's Hispano-Roman legacy, or the Iranian, Fatimid, Ayyubid, and Crusader sources of Mamluke architecture. And even though Darke quotes archaeologist Warwick Ball that 'ancient Near Eastern architectural forms had a tenacity which survived superficial Romanisation and still survive in the form of Islamic mosques to this day,' she does not pursue this to its logical conclusion which would have required a title summarising a more ecumenical flow of influences (although admittedly a book titled *Borrowing from the Greeks, Indians, Persians, and Muslims: How Eastern Architecture Shaped Europe* might have made less of a splash).

In a corner of the eleventh-century Byzantine Kapnikarea church in central Athens, there is a small Arabic inscription in Kufic script that asserts *al-Mulk li-llah* (Sovereignty is God's). Rather than a Muslim statement of superiority inside a Christian sanctuary, the inscription is probably the product of itinerant Muslim stonemasons and therefore of the syncretistic Islamic-Byzantine decorative language that developed in the course of cultural exchanges between the Fatimids and Byzantines. It might even be read as an ecumenical summons. Darke's compelling book serves as a reminder that we are always better when facing outwards.

RISE AND FALL

Iftikhar H Malik

Ibn Khaldun comes immediately to mind when reading Justin Marozzi's *Islamic Empires*. The eminent Tunisian historiographer saw the city as an ultimate culmination of civilisational processes but also a nemesis of tribal *asbiyaa*, which could easily destroy the achievements of a civic society. Marozzi covers the fifteen centuries of Muslim history by focussing on fifteen cities. A gigantic project! But vulnerable to selectivity and even reductionism. The volume benefits from a combination of primary and secondary source-material and follow-up visits. It is often not too far away from reminding its readers of the repeating cycles of violence that wreaked havoc on urban spaces by ruthless individuals in their unscrupulous quest for power.

The chosen cities, while being the foci of political and cultural attainments, periodically fall prey to killing sprees with unrestrained slaughters and wanton destruction. In other words, violence has not been an unfamiliar reality; it happens too often and that too at the hands of fellow Muslim stakeholders as if it was instinctive, especially when it would routinely degenerate into vengeful campaigns against siblings. A work of this nature and genre could easily lead a reader to conclude that it is yet another specimen of Neo-Orientalism. But the book's vistas are laid out quite skilfully making such a generalisation difficult. Still, the text raises a pertinent issue: what went wrong? The answer is in the selective nature of the contents and details often rushing from heyday to hellish times, nudging the reader towards some uniquely *Muslim* penchant for self-destruction, where achievements of a few are wiped out by masquerading successors. Each city here embodies a journey towards hard-earned actualisation owed to some creative pioneer yet its grievous dissolution also seems to be waiting in the wings; and thus, the cycle of progression and ultimate regression happens with mundane regularity.

Marozzi's selection, as he acknowledges in his prefatory remarks, is often personal and discretionary but with a certain intent to weave these fifteen micro stories into a macro narrative.

We begin with Mecca, 'the mother of all cities'. Marozzi is not so sure about the centrality of Mecca as per Muslim beliefs and narratives since the city is almost absent from the Quranic text. Neither does he find any elaborate commentary in any contemporary non-Arab texts. Certainly, with the abrasive Saudi behemoths operating as history erasers - rightly mourned by Marozzi - locating the multi-layered history of this city has become even more problematic. The Wahhabi irreverence for past heritage and unbound Saudi eagerness to draw in money from eager pilgrims may not minimise the city's religious significance though the former has triumphantly destroyed Mecca's frugal but pristine identity. Like Ziauddin Sardar's *Mecca*, Marozzi too narrates atrocities and extremities perpetrated on the Ka'aba by the claimants of Muslim power, often from the very Quraysh tribe or from amongst the Peninsular clans operating as highwaymen. However, challenged by many lesser-known heroes such as Abdullah Ibn Zubair – Abu Bakr's grandson whose severed head was put, by the Umayyads, on Sanctuary's entrance – Meccan travails predate its current Wahhabi guardians and spoilers. One may have several gripes with the Ottomans but there is no denying the fact that they ensured peace in Mecca, Medina, Jerusalem, Antioch, Karbala, Kufa and Samarra, an achievement that their predecessors and successors often failed to accomplish. Even when challenged by Sunni bashing Safawids and Shi'i busting Wahhabis, Ottomans thwarted such volatile encroachments. Like the present-day Saudi monstrosities enfeebling and even the dehumanising Ka'aba, Marozzi's searchlight on Caliphs Abdal Malik and Walid bin Abdal Malik redefining Jerusalem and Damascus, respectively, remains pertinent, as it takes into account their construction of the Dome of Rock, Al-Aqsa and the Umayyad Mosque. Marozzi reminds us of the Jewish and Christian roots of these sites, which elevated Islam to a higher pedestal in those two traditional centres of theological and political power. Damascus, even more than Jerusalem and certainly a world apart from Mecca, was not just a theological centre; it was a cultural hub with its unique political magnificence. Jerusalem had almost become a backwater with Damascus and Antioch assuming a higher profile - under both the Byzantines and then the Umayyads – whereas 'culture was never part of Mecca's centripetal attraction'. Following Hisham's disastrous invasion of Constantinople in 717–18, several latter descendants of Abdal Malik, excluding Umar bin Abdalaziz, fell victims to drink and debauchery, allowing Abbasids a bloody march over them. A younger and solitary Umayyad prince, Abdar Rahman, managed to escape the assassins and fled to distant Cordova to begin a new chapter in the history of Iberian Islam.

Justin Marozzi, *Islamic Empires: Fifteen Cities that Define a Civilisation*, Allen Lane, London, 2019.

The first Abbasid Caliph, as-Saffah (literally, 'the blood shedder'), true to his name and vehemently helped by Abu Muslim Khorasani and his Persian followers, almost wiped out the entire Umayyad upper cluster in 750. The dynastic capital now shifted to a new site in Mesopotamia. Mansur built the first-ever planned Muslim metropolis, Baghdad, which under Harun and Mammun attained a unique eminence in the world of letters and arts. Cairo, another new city founded by the rival Fatimids did try to reach that transcendent status, yet demographic realities of their predominantly Sunni subjects, the Crusades, and then the Ayubis, sealed the dynasty's fate, the way Baghdad fell miserably before the Mongols in 1258. Mansur's planned Round city had gained wider acclaim including from the ninth century hard-to-please philosopher, Jahiz. The House of Wisdom, led by Central Asian polymath, Al-Farabi, reached its zenith making this era as the pinnacle of science and philosophy: 'a world scientific centre comparable to that of Rome in law, Athens in philosophy, and Jerusalem in religion'.

Meanwhile, Cordova evolved into a cosmopolitan and equally tolerant city of the Umayyads where Abdar Rahman III and Hakam II established the golden period of the Andalusian caliphate. Its intellectual pursuits made it almost equal to Damascus and Baghdad. Reportedly, during this era, just in one Cordovan suburb 170 women earned their living by copying manuscripts whereas 60,000 works were being produced annually across the caliphate. Hakam II, like Harun and Mammun, was a bibliophile along with being a patron of music with Zaryab leading the list among the luminaries. The Cordovan eclipse like those of its Asian counterparts was equally volatile and tragic until Muslim Spain came to be confined in and around Granada at a time when the Crusades had already been unleashed by Europe's clerics, counts, and the monarchs, and Jerusalem, and for that matter the entire Levant, found themselves 'lubricated with blood'. After defeating the Byzantines in 1071 in the Battle of Mazikert, the Turkic Seljuks gained an upper hand, hastening appeals from Constantinople to fellow Christians followed by the papal bull of 1095 commissioning the First Crusade.

Islam's erstwhile civilisational centres had started to move further west with Cairo, Fez, and Tripoli emerging as the new urbane constellations of literary and intellectual pursuits. Cairo, established by the Fatimids, was the new Baghdad and though shaken up by the Crusaders, gained a renewed vitality under Salahud Din. The Fatimids were now eclipsed by the Ayubis who were followed by the Mamluks until the Ottomans under Selim captured all these Arab cities in the Middle East and North Africa. Earlier, Mehmed II's youthful energy, military acumen, and immense resourcefulness had ensured the conquest of Constantinople from the Byzantines and the successive victories over the Venetians, Genoans, Safawids, and the Mamluks made the House of Osman to be the largest empire of its times banishing the sordid memories of the Mongols and Tamerlane. Marozzi goes into details in describing the decisive campaign by Mehmed in the summer of 1453 to capture the fortified city upon seven hills and its fall leading to the evolution of this Roman metropolis into a new and no less dynamic centre of Muslim imperial power. It was in 1571, that the Battle of Lepanto deflated the myth of Ottoman invincibility though they recovered from it within a few months to help England defeat the Spanish. Constantinople's writ remained almost invincible until 1683, when it unleashed its fury against Vienna resulting in an unrelenting retreat.

The Ottomans had rivalled the Safawids for a while though successive victories especially their acquisition of Tabriz pushed the latter further east to build a new capital by the River Zayndarud where Shah Abbas I, like Mansur centuries before him, built afresh his prized capital of Isfahan. Its main square called Maidan features the royal palace, Lutfullah Mosque and the Shah's Mosque, built during the successful reign of Abbas, enshrining some of the unique architectural features taking Islamic art to new artistic heights. Like the Ottoman mosques, hans, and bazaars, Isfahan boasted some of the rarest gems in aesthetics in early modern era and the Si-o-see Bridge, with its thirty-three spans built by Abbas, has rightly been described as 'the stateliest bridge in the world'. This city of traders, scholars, and urban planners soon became a rival to Constantinople in every aspect, from diversity of its population to cherished monuments. It began attracting a handsome number of visitors from across the world boasting thirty-three churches and several synagogues, soon to be called 'Nisf Jahan' (half of the world). However, like elsewhere, the seeds of its decline and dissolution of a very exclusive Safawid empire soon overshadowed this city of splendid madrassas, gardens, boulevards, and exceptional bridges. Abbas's successors endlessly engrossed themselves in wild drinking sprees and incessant acts of debauchery, ensuring a pervasive decline at a time when Russia and then Britain began to impose their unilateral conditionalities on decadent monarchs, already losing space to Shi'i clerics.

Isfahan and other Muslim metropolises before it witnessed a familiar rise and fall in their career as did Samarkand following its total decimation by the Mongols until the shepherd-king, Tamerlane, resuscitated it. Known to the rest as the wrath of the world, Tamerlane devastated cities and empires all the way from Anatolia, Levant, China to India bringing wealth, artisans, slaves, scholastic rarities, and animals to turn his metropolis into the grandest in the world. Its madrassas, parks, mosques, and cemeteries like Shah-e-Zinda not only benefitted from the unlimited resources bestowed by Tamerlane but also from the diverse skills of Persians, Indians, and the Turks who augured some of the most impressive monuments, ornamented by azure, ribbed blue domes, guarded by slim minarets, and surrounded by well-planned gardens. Elaborate frescoes, Quranic inscriptions in Kufic script, and a generous use of multicoloured, floral tiles and marble saw their enduring presence in future buildings in Herat, Persia, and India making Timurid legacies more than an invasive chapter in the ever-changing history of the Muslim world. Tamerlane believed in his divine mission as the sword of Islam though millions of his victims happened to be his own fellow believers. Samarkand, after the Shaibanis, might have lost its erstwhile glory as did Bukhara, Herat, Balkh, Khiva, and Kabul, yet its formidable Timurid imprints such as the Registan Square, Bibi Khanum Mosque, Shah-e-Zinda, and Amir's own magnificent mausoleum – like the

Dome of Rock and Abbas's Maidan complex — guarantee a cherished profile to this city of sultans, scholars and saints. Tamerlane's atrocities are papered over by an emerging Uzbek nationalism though contributions by Gohar Shad Begum, his daughter-in-law and the grandson, Ulugh Beg, went a long way in rekindling a latter renaissance in Bukhara, Samarkand and certainly in Herat where the Queen had opened schools and orphanages for girls. Also in Herat, the Chagatai Turkish literary doyen and now a national poet of Uzbekistan, Mir Ali Sher Navoi, wrote his classics along with building institutions on both sides of the Oxus. Navoi died just three years before a Timurid prince, Babur, ventured into the town after being expelled from his native Ferghana and Samarkand, but was equally disappointed with the libertine and even infantile idiosyncrasies his cousins pursued in Herat.

Marozzi is fascinated by Emperor Babur's ingenuity, forthrightness and courage. A refugee prince conquered Afghanistan with his sheer will and charisma, followed by laying the foundation of the Mughal Empire in India. A daring Babur had ventured into India through the Khyber Pass, passing though the 'rippled mountains with dimpled slopes shading from ochre to slate-grey to white' and happened to witness a different sea of humanity in the Sub-continent. Rich in possessions but poor in aesthetics, Indians baffled his sensibilities though his masterly handling of the local Afghan and Rajput rulers, despite their massive armies and numerous elephants, affirmed his daring. A devout gardener and naturalist, Babur designed several gardens in Kabul, a city that he deeply admired due to its climate, diversity, and fruit, allowing our scholar-king to hold his joyous parties and compose frank but lucid autobiography. Babur's nightlong parties featured wine, opium, and poetry recitals yet would never hamper his fighting and daredevil skills. His frankness and superb rendition prove unparalleled as is evident from his *Tuzk*, which relates the narratives of his bi-sexuality and escapades with the literary giants of the time. Kabul, unlike its more recent incarnation, following the decades of civil wars and foreign invasions, was a city of temperate weather, tolerant population, and diverse cultures where Babur had found his lost Samarkand and even willed to be buried in one of his gardens in the Afghan city.

Amongst all these cities with their generous shares of glory and ghastly experiences, it is Fez that seems to have been the most resolute in its consistency in retaining some of its original institutional and cultural products. Tucked away in the heart of Maghreb, the cherished city flourished owing to benefactors such as Moulay Idriss, Fatima Al-Fihri, and certainly the Marinids—the last proving the Mughals of this Moroccan metropolis. Fez was rejuvenated and even redefined by Sultan Abu Inan, whose reign elevated the city to be rightly defined as 'the Athens of Africa'. A city of knowledge, saints, artisans, and innovation, Fez with its warrens of narrow streets, kiosks, silversmiths, *zawiyas*, and numerous madrassas is definitely a medieval museum where despite the inflow of tourists and their eager guides, the cacophonic medieval enterprises, and even life styles have refused to prostrate before an arcane and clueless modernity. This city both baffles and inspires sleuths treading the heritage trails amidst its inhabitants who for countless generations have negotiated an existence that prided itself through eminent brains, traditional artisans, and unique commodities (not forgetting the famous tasselled fez cap!).

The last section of *Islamic Empires* is devoted to chapters on Tripoli, Beirut, Dubai, and Doha to show a rather different set of factors at work at these predominantly Muslim cities where historical, religious, and economic crosscurrents helped engineer their demographics and landscapes, though not always peacefully. Beirut evolved from a small scenically located harbour in the post-Crusades era to a more cosmopolitan and strategic port city since the advent of Napoleon in 1798, followed by the emigration of the Maronite Christians from their hillside villages. Growing Christian demographics gradually decreased the Muslim population in the city whose Sunni, Shi'i, and Druze communities shared strong linkages with Syria. The Ottomans ensured the evolution of modern schools, banks, and boulevards in the town, which further expanded with the establishment of the Syrian Protestant College latterly known as the American University of Beirut. The city became the vanguard of modernity in the Middle East, where vibrant press, literary circles, private banks, hotels, and clubs mushroomed attracting European investors and affluent Arabs until, 'the playground of the Middle East' fell on bad times and like Kabul, Tripoli, Baghdad, and Damascus, suffered a grievous civil war.

Marozzi's Italian father was born in Beirut in 1938 and engaged in trade in Tripoli. Marozzi himself lived or reported from several cities featured in this book giving it a personal dimension. During his childhood, Tripoli, with its white houses facing the Mediterranean and hemmed in by a brown desert, held its own mystique often overshadowing its past as a centre of pirates under a nominal Ottoman authority. Dubai, from a small hamlet of inhabitants engaged in pearling and fishing, transformed itself into an ultra-modern city of consumerist cosmopolitanism, as did Doha with an ever-growing expatriate diaspora forming new hierarchical societies. These novice Muslim cities, role models for others in the region, exist as new utopias patterned as Las Vegas in the heart of the Muslim world.

Like the empires, the cities anchoring Marozzi'a narrative have had their rise and decline, with recent years characterised by stagnation, congestion and contestations often unleashing civil wars and external invasions. The fact that Kabul, Isfahan, Jerusalem, Beirut, Samarkand, Damascus, and Tripoli refused to wither away despite all the extremities, is borne out by their multi-layered lives brimming with joys and pains. The spatial mobility and steady expansion of these fifteen cities provide formidable reminders of their historicity since they continue to experience transformative forces at work under the panoply of the Westphalian nation state system. From Mecca of towering blocks to Dubai and Doha of lofty skyscrapers, the multi-directional onslaught unleashed since the imperial times, continues with its progressive and nihilist trajectories.

ET CETERA

}

ON WORLD ORDER THINKING AFTER BLM

Peter Mandaville

As a graduate student in the mid-1990s, I had a fleeting fascination with the World Order Models Project (commonly known as 'WOMP'). Established in the mid-1960s and led by Saul Mendlovitz, WOMP took as its goal the imagination of possible alternative world orders. Its purpose was both scientific—in that it aspired to an objective accounting of the various forces that shape world order—and normative—in that it committed itself to identifying and working toward preferable alternatives with respect to questions of peace, justice, governance, ecology, and identity on a planetary scale. I was drawn to two aspects of the project in particular. First, the sheer scale on which it conducted its work. I had always been attracted to big picture, macro level scholarship and it didn't get much more macro than WOMP. Second, and probably more important in my mind, was the fact that the network of scholars comprising WOMP included figures from Asia (Rajni Kothari), Africa (Ali Mazrui), and Latin America (Gustavo Lagos and Horacio Godoy)—in addition to contributors from those world regions, such as North America (Richard Falk) and Europe (Johann Galtung), more commonly associated with generating and enforcing the prevailing world order.

I was at the time a student of International Relations (IR) and found myself deeply dissatisfied with the exclusively Anglo-American foundations of the discipline. Why, I asked myself, does a field of study that purports to explain the whole world consist exclusively of theoretical paradigms—and rather dull ones at that—developed by white men of

European heritage? While it would take me a few years to discover the intellectual home in critical theory that eventually permitted me to recognise that the entire enterprise of IR was little more than the expression of a specific conception of world order masquerading as an academic discipline, I could already tell something was very wrong with my chosen field of study. What I found so startlingly admirable about WOMP (which operated adjacent to rather than within IR discourse) was that it involved a conscious effort to ask black and brown people what kind of worlds they actually wanted to live in. And while WOMP—perhaps impossibly ambitious in its vision—certainly attracted its fair share of critics, its work was nonetheless imbued with a deliberate and critical cosmopolitanism otherwise absent from social science scholarship in the 1960s and 1970s.

Now by the time I discovered WOMP it was already essentially a moribund effort, with its final official volume of essays appearing in the early 1990s. While some of the project's contributors are still with us— such as critical IR theorist Rob Walker (associated early in his career with the final stage of WOMP activity), Asia specialist Samuel S. Kim, the venerable, irrepressible Richard Falk, and even Saul Mendlovitz himself (the latter two both now in their nineties)—none of them still identify as WOMPers. In the meantime, IR has started to get a little better in terms of redressing its inherent Eurocentrism. Along with Stephen Chan, I made a modest intervention on this front with a 2001 edited volume *The Zen of International Relations: IR Theory from East to West*. Of far greater significance is the Routledge book series *Worlding Beyond the West*, edited by Arlene B. Tickner, David Blaney, and Inanna Hamati-Ataya, which created a stable platform for IR scholars looking to study the international from diverse regional and cultural perspectives. Landmark critical studies such as Robert Vitalis' 2015 book *White World Order, Black Power Politics: The Birth of American International Relations*, also helped to systematically exposed the racist origins of IR as a field of study. But collectively all this work has barely made a dent in the discipline's thoroughly European scaffolding.

Large scale world order thinking also seems to be out of vogue these days for any number of reasons: resurgent nationalisms and local identities; the indeterminacy of the forces currently shaping (or denaturing) world order; the advent of postnormal times, as described by Ziauddin Sardar and others, where the combination of a breakdown in previously held assumptions (regarding science, causality, normative consensus, etc.) and a trend away from the very idea of certainty—all seem to militate quite decisively against world order-type thinking. So where does that leave the latter-day WOMPers, those of us still wondering about and hoping for the possibility of imagining alternative and more just world orders?

First let's be clear: the current discourse is hardly lacking in narratives that nod towards possible ways of understanding just-over-the-horizon world orders. Conventional IR scholars who think about world order as a function of polarity (that is, the distribution of power in the international system) are obsessed with 'emerging powers', as captured in the popular BRICS (Brazil, Russia, India, China, South Africa) formula—an acronym originally coined, incidentally, by a Goldman Sachs asset manager. As early as 2004, Joshua Cooper Ramo, Co-CEO of Henry Kissinger's consulting firm, speculated about the advent of a new 'Beijing Consensus' to replace the withering 'Washington Consensus' that had traditionally defined the policy orthodoxy of liberal financial institutions such as the World Bank and the International Monetary Fund. In recent years, predictions about the decline or disintegration of the liberal international order have prompted a flurry of post-ism, with academics and pundits alike placing us variously in a dawning post-liberal, post-Atlantic, post-American, or, most intriguingly (to me at least), a post-Western age—the latter framework described most comprehensively by the Brazilian-German political scientist Oliver Stuenkel in his 2016 book *Post Western World*. By and large, however, these are mainly accounts of shifts in the locus of geopolitical and geoeconomic power rather than efforts to posit *preferred* worlds à la WOMP.

Perhaps the closest we come to such a thing today is to be found in multilateral development policy. While they are not explicitly presented as such, it is possible to discern in the benchmark goals and indicators of the UN's two successive frameworks for global cooperation, the Millennium Development Goals and the Sustainable Development Goals, bits and pieces of what intergovernmental deliberation has yielded by way a proposed direction for world progress (for example, increased enrolment of girls in primary education; the eradication of certain communicable diseases). This is something quite different, however, than an actual vision for world *order*. And we still have the field of future studies of course, but it operates today as a diffuse global network of scholars sharing a broadly defined tradition of analytic orientations and methodologies and tied together in a loose organisation, the World Future Studies Federation. This is something quite different from the visionary and structured research program that defined WOMP.

So where does this leave us when it comes to the question of world order thinking? Is systematic effort to analyse, propose, and steer the world toward alternative models for organising political, economic, ecological, and cultural life on a planetary scale still relevant? Is it still possible, even? What would it look like? How would we generate the agenda around which such an endeavour could be organised? At the risk of sounding like I'm woefully mired in (at best) early 1990s thinking, let me hazard the suggestion that such work is not only possible today but actually quite desperately needed. The argument I want to make about why this is the case has nothing to do with a specific commitment to large scale progressive research programmes, systems theory paradigms, or WOMP-ian methodology. Rather, I think we need a new round of world order thinking because recent shifts in global political consciousness mean that it may be possible for the output of such an effort to be heard and used in ways that were not possible previously. Let me elaborate.

The past half decade has witnessed an unprecedented irruption of public awareness, engagement, and activism around various forms of systemically embedded exclusion and injustice. The Black Lives Matter (BLM) and #MeToo movements, for example, have forced the beginning of a long overdue reckoning with regard to the normalised racism and patriarchy/ misogyny that lie at the foundations of many core institutions and practices in modern life. We have finally named and are talking openly about things we used to not see, turn a blind eye to, or—even worse—consciously perpetuate. While I welcome the increased mainstreaming of anti-racism, feminism, and LGBTQ rights as a sign of progress in addressing those specific forms of injustice, I am even more excited about what they have enabled in terms of people being able to recognise, understand, and talk about the nature of structurally and culturally encoded exclusion more generally.

As a result of this opening, we are starting to see a proliferation of organising, coalition-forming, and allyship. Black Lives Matter making common cause with groups combatting Islamophobia who in turn advocate on behalf of immigrants and indigenous peoples. Much of this is happening within individual countries (such as, in the examples just cited, here in the United States) and tied, appropriately, to specific demands for legislation or policy reform. But the communication, engagement, and organising also crosses borders generating new or significantly expanded transnational movements—all of which aggregates over time into a broader sense of global political consciousness regarding the exclusionary nature of the present order.

Now this is not to suggest that the organised expression of mass discontent at the prevailing world order (if, by that, we mean primarily post-WWII international liberalism) is anything new. From the protests of 1968 to the emergence of the World Social Forum, or the Occupy movements of the 1990s and early 2000s, we have seen episodic mobilisations to combat the alienating effects of global capitalism and the racism that underpins it. And of course the genealogies of these more recent protests intersect with historical efforts—some of which, such as the abolitionist, anti-colonial, and suffragette movements, date back centuries—to interrogate and challenge an emerging world order whose self-mythology of freedom has always been premised on various forms of systematic disenfranchisement, exclusion, and violence. What I see as different now is the fact that these conversations are starting to include segments of the majority, political dominant population in countries such as the United States who previously never would have regarded the causes in question as having anything to do with them or their lives.

So how might this relate to and inform a new impetus for world order thinking? My logic on this point is very straightforward: in the face of growing and increasingly widespread recognition of the systemic nature of exclusion and injustice, there is an opportunity to leverage that consciousness by linking it to a renewed effort at highlighting the macro level ('world order') overlay that reinforces multiple forms of national and local disenfranchisement around the globe. To some extent this is the kind of analysis that thinkers like Michael Hardt and Antonio Negri sought to provide in their *Empire* trilogy (and the subsequent, related *Heretical Thought* series). While the very particular theoretical provenance of their work—combining elements of post-structuralism and neo-Marxism—

limited its ability to resonate with broader readerships, it would not be inaccurate to say that what I have in mind for a new world orders project is something like a more accessible effort to leverage newly woke communities within what Hardt & Negri call the Multitude that would provide those constituencies with a research-driven blueprint for political organising and advocacy such that their ongoing mobilisation to address local and national drivers of injustice can simultaneously speak to and begin to reshape macro level structures. All of this informed by a theory of change premised on the mutually reinforcing interaction of bottom-up and top-down vectors for action and reform.

While the pretexts and examples I have relied on to build my case so far draw disproportionately on recent developments in the United States, I remain committed to the idea that the enterprise we are discussing here needs to be thoroughly global in scope. The opportunity, as I see it, lies precisely in helping emerging forms of political consciousness in the Global North to cross-fertilise with and learn from the significantly more advanced thinking and organising that has been going on in the Global South for many decades now. Since I earlier lambasted the field of International Relations, let me go ahead and pile it on even further. In the average IR textbook, the 1955 Bandung Conference appears—if it does at all—as a spontaneous and curious distraction or aberration in the inevitable unfolding of a bipolar world order in which all international politics become reduced to little more than manifestations of US-Soviet rivalry (perhaps with some local colour and flavour). Missing from this story is any recognition of the extent to which Bandung relied on and represented the continuity of longstanding anti-colonial intellectual and political movements in Africa and Asia, or any appreciation of the fact that 1955 lived on in the form of the Non-Aligned Movement, the Afro-Asian People's Solidarity Organisation (AAPSO), and eventually the Organisation of Solidarity with the Peoples of Asia, Africa, and Latin America (OSPAAL). It is an impulse that endures even today in the work of Tricontinental: Institute for Social Research, a 'movement-driven research institute' led by Vijay Prashad with a presence on three continents and whose work is directly informed by the intellectual legacies of key postcolonial and decolonial thinkers such as Frantz Fanon as well as, politically, the original Tricontinental conference hosted by Cuba in 1966.

So let me be clear that I am not calling for a re-run of WOMP, or a direct sequel; that particular modality of world order scholarship (and the worldview that produced it) is a product of a bygone time. What I would like to see is a renewed commitment to a systematic research programme that is both globally and intellectually inclusive (in the sense of making space for diverse ideological commitments), focused on recognising and revealing the common macro level forces that create or sustain widely varying—in form and expression—localised manifestations of exclusion around the world, and committed to remedying structural injustice by identifying the contours of possible alternative world orders and practical pathways toward achieving them. I'll say it again: this kind of approach is decidedly out of style these days. It smacks of the worst of grand, centrally planned development paradigms during a time when our prevailing tendency is to valorise the scrappy entrepreneur who throws out the blueprint in favour of just solving the problem (hopefully with some nice return on investment to boot). But innovation within an inherently exclusionary system yields little more than new ways to oppress people. There is value in starting with an understanding of how particular world orders inherently promote or constrain specific possibilities (including the rights, status, and welfare of specific groups of people) and then devising alternative architectures that can eliminate or at least minimise these exclusionary effects. The goal here is not to be strictly or comprehensively prescriptive in the sense of regarding any one particular alternative world order as our necessary destination. Rather, I see the exercise of imagining alternative world orders (and the discipline associated with doing so in a systematic fashion) as a crucial step in revealing possible strategies that can then in turn become subject to debate. Much needed resources, in other words, for our fraught and precarious existence.

TEN WORLD (DIS)ORDERERS

Jordi Serra

The world order as we know it is seriously threatened. In the coming years and decades, we will face several (dis)orderers – I know, there is no such word, but that does not stop me from inventing it! – that could, indeed would, upset the status quo in different ways. While individually all of them present a real challenge, some of them can reinforce each other in a kind of feedback loop leading to major shocks and upturns.

Let us examine them one by one.

1. Temperature Rise

Climate change has become a commonplace concept and no longer seems to raise major concerns to many persons. That is why some scholars and activists prefer to call it a climate crisis, especially as the effects of climate change are now being felt more acutely.

Focusing on just one aspect, temperature rise, will let us see the enormity of the unfolding situation. The UN's Intergovernmental Panel on Climate Change has concluded that greenhouse gases are responsible for the global warming we are experiencing. The World Health Organisation warns that the temperature increase is already causing more than 150,000 deaths every year and the figure will double by 2030. But the total death toll is probably higher due to other effects such as the melting of glaciers (that are fundamental to provide freshwater in many places), the increase in droughts, the upturn in diseases currently restricted to warm or tropical regions, substantial crop reduction in many locations, more frequent and more violent storms (especially in coastal areas), a higher frequency of wildfires, the loss of biodiversity, and a general decrease in the quality of life for millions.

We can anticipate which countries will be hit harder, or we can study how many places may be rendered uninhabitable, and thus estimate how many people will be forced to move or to relocate. We will also need to determine if we will be able to produce enough food or if we will have the capacity to fight new, emerging pandemics. In short, the international community and overall humanity is going to be tested – and then we will see if we are up to the challenge.

2. Artificial Intelligence

In 2014, Stephen Hawking told the BBC that 'the development of full artificial intelligence could spell the end of the human race'. As a top scientist, his opinion carried much weight. Yet it must be noted that he said this using an improved software programme that was able to predict most of the words he would use. So yes, artificial intelligence can be risky, but it also carries the promise of great enhancement of human capacities. And this is the key concept here – the human.

We continue defining artificial intelligence as the ability of a computer or a robot to reproduce the human mind's capabilities – skills such as learning from experience, identifying patterns, understanding and responding to common language, solving problems or, the top one, making decisions. Although the kind of AI that is akin to Skynet in the *Terminator* franchise does not exist yet, we do have many specialised AI applications on which we are becoming more and more reliant.

Nevertheless, Hawking's argument stands. Full AI would be capable of out-evolving us and could even consider humanity a pest that needs to be purged from the Earth. Then again, it could also help us to overcome our struggles with gender, ethnicity, or nationality. It could prove what real rationality is and help us to evolve.

So far though, it seems that AI is too human for its own good. Microsoft chatbot Tay had to be shut down after it turned into a bigoted, misogynistic Nazi after less than a day interacting with humans. But transhumanists may be right and the pursuit of AI may help us to reach the singularity – the key moment of merging between the organic and the artificial, which would take humanity to a new stage. Or to the beginning of its demise.

3. Pervasive Surveillance (Internet of Things plus 5G)

We are constantly granting apps access to our personal data. With the use of smartwatches and health gadgets our vital signs can be monitored 24/7. Our cars and home appliances are also giving away information about us. Our lives are compacted in neat data packages so we can be more accurately targeted. In the West, this is occurring mostly for commercial purposes, but China is already showing us what a Big Brother on steroids can know about us.

American scholar Shoshana Zuboff's book *The Age of Surveillance Capitalism* describes how capitalism is using present technology to follow us and our life in scary detail. More and more facets of our daily activity are being recorded and analysed. Our very identity is being transformed into data that can be commodified and marketed. With the imminent arrival of worldwide 5G technology plus the continuous deployment of the Internet of Things (IoT), the potential to track and record every single aspect of our life will reach a new high.

Of course, we like the comfort this connectivity provides, including the ease when writing, researching, scrolling or, of course, shopping. Our phones contain most of the keys to operate and move around the present world – we don't get lost, we are constantly in contact, we are completely mobile, and we can do almost anything from everywhere. But, in the process, we may not feel the numbness this entails or the dependence and the privacy we forsake. Furthermore, the same pics we like to post on our social networks can be instrumental in preventing us from getting a job or a loan. And, right now, this information is mostly in the hands of private companies that are subjected to little or no accountability.

4. Feminist Consciousness

One thing that all old hegemonic systems and orthodoxies share is that they are deeply rooted in a structural patriarchy. We live in a world that systematically marginalises, oppresses, and harasses more than fifty per cent of its population. On average, women earn about thirty per cent less than men for the same job. Not only that, women perform most of the domestic tasks and are often trapped in economic dependence. In numerous places around the word, they need a man's authorisation to get a passport, own a bank account, or even decide where they can live. Sexual harassment, abuse, or assault is minimised, enabled, or even condoned through legislations in many countries. Cultural bias against women has caused a huge but undetermined femicide of baby girls in China, genital mutilation in several African countries, and countless deaths all over the world.

Fortunately, the consciousness that this must change is growing and we may have reached a turning point. Initiatives like #MeToo made many women realise the power they have when acting collectively. More to the point, Covid-19 has shown that some of the countries that have dealt better with the pandemic and its associated crises are governed by women. Their administrations have eloquently shown that it is possible to lead in a more empathic and caring way and still be effective. It is difficult not to conclude that many of the present problems we face are caused by men. Could it be that the constant resort to violence and aggression is a consequence of patriarchy? Could women provide much needed alternatives to a more sustainable, compassionate, and equitable world? In any case, it is only fair to let them give it a try.

5. CRISPR

Do you fancy making your own honey in groovy colours – green, blue, brown, or even technicolour? Would you like your pet mice to be green or fluorescent? Well, your desire can now be fulfilled. Just visit www.the-odin.com and you can order your genetic engineering beginner's kit for US$350 or an advanced one for US$900. You can even order a kit-and-class pack on human tissue engineering for US$650. It would be easy to believe that the Odin site is an exception, but the fact is that more and more sites are offering gene editing services. Origene (www.origene.com), for instance, sells Genome Knockout Kits. Genome Knockout - would you believe!

The more we know about our gene pool the more we realise how our DNA determines different aspects of our present and future wellbeing. And CRISPR – an acronym for clustered regularly interspaced short palindromic repeats – offers an easier (and cheaper) way to cut out and fix gene malfunctions and thus get rid of many 'undesirable' hereditary traits or predispositions to certain diseases. Unfortunately, it also allows for more questionable interventions that could border on eugenics or just to please some parents who would like their children to uphold hegemonic beauty standards. This, as with any new technique that allows us to do something that was impossible before, poses some real hard questions. Do we have the right to prevent children from inheriting traits that would make their life harder? Can we deny the removal of certain genetic conditions wholeheartedly? Would gene engineering techniques lead to eugenics? Or, is CRISPR just the lastest tool for the privileged to remain on top?

6. Pandemics

There is little doubt that SARS-CoV-2 – the virus that causes Covid-19 – is one of the nastier varieties of coronavirus. Its combination of high infectivity with high lethality has made Covid-19 one of the worst pandemics we have suffered. But there are much worse viruses around with even higher lethality ratios, and our current globalised lifestyles generate wide opportunities for them to thrive. As the effects of climate change progress, the possibility of more and worse pandemics increases. Tropical diseases will spread to much bigger areas, the melting of the permafrost will also let ancient pathogens resurface, and the collapse of the biosphere may trigger as-yet-unknown biohazards.

Covid-19 has shown that we lack the global governance tools to fight pandemics effectively. It has exposed the limits of our present nation-state system when dealing with a global epidemic. The thing with global plagues is that if we are not able to address them globally, we will never truly overcome them. The current Covid-19 crisis will leave many countries in a dire condition. If another outburst happens before recovery, it will be far more damaging, leaving us even more exposed to another one. Overall, it boils down to one pressing question – will we be able to put in place the structures to prevent, manage, or fight new global pandemics?

7. China's Hegemony

China is on the rise. For decades it has shown robust growth that has made it the world's main economic power. Not only does it own the biggest share of the world market, it also controls a big share of world's production and supply. Additionally, it is using its growing political influence to secure critical resources like rare-earth metals, and has accumulated a significant percentage of other countries' debts (it currently owns about US$1.1 trillion of US debt). China is also showing an increasing technical and innovation proficiency that has made it a space power on its own. Its military strength is rising too. After years of American dominance, it looks like China's moment has arrived. Being the focal point of the current pandemic could have been a real source of concern, but China has responded with strong and decisively enforced management. As a result, it has been one of the first countries to bounce back to normalcy.

China is becoming more and more conscious of its own power and demands acknowledgment from the rest of the world. President Xi Jinping embodies this new China, with a more muscular and belligerent leadership. China may have a plan for world domination; and it has the patience, resources, and the determination to implement the plan. Just look at the way Beijing has repressed democratic opposition in Hong Kong, interned the Uyghurs in enslavement camps, and its growing political and military pressure on Taiwan. But, it may be that the rest of world needs China more than China needs the rest of the world.

8. Food Scarcity

There are many indicators that we are facing a global food problem. Firstly, according to the US Global Change Research Program's Fourth National Climate Assessment report, 'warming temperatures, severe heat, drought, wildfire, and major storms will increasingly disrupt agricultural productivity, threatening not only farmers' livelihoods but also food security, quality, and price stability'. Secondly, there is the overexploitation of certain resources, such as fish – we have already killed ninety percent of large fish populations (especially tuna or marlins). Thirdly, our current lifestyles, particularly in the West, are unsustainable – as David Attenborough puts it in *A Life on Our Planet*, 'Earth can't support billions of large meat-eaters', because our current consumption of meat requires too much space and too much energy and generates too much waste. Any of these three elements is important enough in itself to risk food production – combined, they build up to a very big challenge.

In the meantime, we may be facing the disappearance of highly significant products like cocoa or coffee due to a perverse market logic. We may even be jeopardizing many other crops by eradicating bees. All in all, we may be left with few options such as resorting to consuming invertebrates to increase our protein intake. The European Union has recently started to consider mealworms as food. Similar measures will surely be taken regarding insects and jellyfish.

9. Democratic Decline

According to the American NGO Freedom House, 2021 is the lowest point in global freedom since 1995. Its last report, *Democracy Under Siege*, indicated that less than twenty percent of the world population lives in a free country enjoying a full democratic regime. However, Freedom House's concern is not just about those states that are clearly authoritarian, but also what it refers to as troubled democracies – for example, the United States and India, and also Spain and Hungary.

Freedom House indicates that there has been a sustained deterioration in democratic quality since 2006. Another report by Swedish institute IDEA, the International Institute for Democracy and Electoral Assistance, indicated a similar concern in 2019 when they stated that 'democracy is under threat and its promise needs revival'. Both reports agree that after decades of sustained democratic expansion we are witnessing how democracies are being eroded and their citizens are growing disenchanted with the democratic promise.

Among the factors that can be listed are: the crisis of representation that political parties are undergoing which it makes it easier for populist figures and movements to gain public attention; the spreading of democratic backsliding with more and more countries willing to reduce the scope of rights and liberties; the shrivelling of civic space worldwide; the upsurge in corruption; and, what is even worse, the spreading perception that corrupt leaders always manage to escape unscathed.

Finally, what may be the most concerning element is democracy's incapacity to react to new forms of digital manipulation and misinformation. It is quite evident that, in many regards, the present democratic design was meant for an analogic world – what the Canadian philosopher Marshall McLuhan called the Gutenberg Galaxy. Liberal democracy was attuned for an industrial context. It was fitted for the rise of nation states, rationalism, mass production, and mass media. But it does not seem to be so adequate for a postnormal world that is far more complex, chaotic, and contradictory, and where facts do not seem to hold any currency.

And Covid-19 has become a justification for even further cutbacks in democratic regimes. Freedom House has denounced how public health has been widely used as an alibi to undermine rights and even the rule of law. For instance, the press has experienced all sorts of restrictions in most countries, and new 'emergency' legislation, meant to fight the pandemic, has often been passed but it remains to be seen if it will be withdrawn once the situation improves.

10. Access to Outworld Resources

In November 2020, NASA discovered a very valuable asteroid, 16 Psyche, between Mars and Jupiter. The interest in 16 Psyche comes from the fact that it is almost entirely made of metal and its estimated value is in the US$10,000 quadrillions. This mind-boggling figure means that, if distributed equally among all Earth's inhabitants, each of us would get more than one billion US dollars.

It is no wonder that there is such a gold rush to access the resources of other planets and asteroids. Several companies are already actively working on how to solve the many technical and legal issues to be able to exploit these resources. The potential gains are so large that even astronomical investments seem reasonable. Right now, the initiative is private, but some countries are also moving this direction – the US passed a bill in 2015 to grant property rights over asteroids and their resources to private companies, and Luxembourg is working to become the regional hub for mining businesses. The current projects to establish bases on the moon by China and the US, plus the Space X initiative to create a settlement on Mars, will also include the potential tapping of available resources. We can speculate that these countries and companies will use the resources to expand their wealth and, ultimately, their power base.

Nonetheless, with a declining biosphere and many environmental challenges coming up, it may be that the focus must shift from gaining money to securing resources that are necessary for the salvation of humanity and the Earth. And yet, it is hard not to wonder what it could mean to seize that valuable asteroid – the end of poverty on Earth or... the mother of all inflations!

These (dis)orderers are very important when considered separately. But we are living in a postnormal world and we must realise that the most likely scenario is that at least some of them will happen *simultaneously* – and that will mean that a new world order, whether we like it or not, will have risen.

CITATIONS

Unholy Deserts of Evil by Abdelwahab El-Affendi

The citation from The European Council on Foreign Relations is from Policy Brief 15 by Asli Aydıntaşbaş and Cinzia Bianco, 'Useful enemies: How the Turkey-UAE rivalry is remaking the Middle East', March 2021; Jacob Mundy quote is from 'The Middle East is violence: on the limits of comparative approaches to the study of armed conflict', *Civil Wars 21*(4), pp.539-568 2019; and John Stuart Mill quote is taken from Beate Jahn, 'Barbarian Thoughts: Imperialism in the Philosophy of John Stuart Mill,' *Review of International Studies,* Vol. 31, No. 3 (Jul., 2005), pp. 599-618, which can be downloaded from: https://www.jstor.org/stable/40072091.

See also: Abdelwahab El-Affendi, 2004. 'Waiting for Armageddon: the "mother of all empires" and its Middle East quagmire' in: Held, D. and Koenig-Archibugi, M. (ed.) *American power in the Twenty-First Century,* Oxford, Polity Press, pp. 252-276. *The Conquest of Muslim Hearts and Minds: Perspectives on US Reform and Public Diplomacy Strategies,* Brookings Institution, 2005; and Salim Hamidani, 'Colonial Legacy in Algerian–French Relations', *Contemporary Arab Affairs* (2020) 13 (1): 69–85.

For the reaction from the Tunisian lawyer, see 'Tunisia lawyer ends hunger strike', *BBC,* 10 December, 2003, http://news.bbc.co.uk/2/hi/africa/3307909.stm; for the UAE ambassador meeting, see 'UAE ambassador meets spiritual leader of ultra-Orthodox Shas party,' *The Times of Israel*, 30 May 2021, at: https://www.timesofisrael.com/liveblog_entry/uae-ambassador-meets-spiritual-leader-of-ultra-orthodox-shas-party/.

Where is the Ummah? By Anwar Ibrahim

The quotes are from: Francis Fukuyama, 'The "End of History" debate', *Dialogue 89*, 1990, pages 8-13; Malek Bennabi, *Islam in History and Society,* translated by Asma Rashid (Islamabad, Islamic Research Institute, 1988), p7; Cemil Aydin, *The Idea of the Muslim World* (Harvard University Press, Cambridge, Massachusetts, 2017), p5, 3; Bertrand Badie, 'The impact of the French Revolution on Muslim societies: evidence and ambiguities', *International Social Science Journal,* 119, 1989, p15; Marshall Hodgson, *The Venture of Islam* (Chicago University Press, Chicago, 1974), volume 1, p346; Shahab Ahmed, *What is Islam?* (Princeton University Press, 2016), p14; and Chandler Barton from his review of *The Idea of the Muslim World* in Maydan: https://themaydan.com/2017/12/book-review-cemi-aydin-idea-muslim-world-global-intellectual-history/

Works mentioned include: Peter F. Drucker, *The New Realities* (Oxford, Heinemann, 1989); Ibn Khaldun, *The Muqaddimah: Introduction to History*, translated by F. Rosenthal (London, Routledge and Kegan Paul, 1967); Frantz Fanon, *Wretched of the Earth*, (Macgibbon and Kee, London, 1965); Ziauddin Sardar, *Science, Technology and Development in the Muslim World* (Croom Helm, London, 1977); Sarah Strouma, *Freethinkers of Medieval Islam* (Brill, Leiden, 2016); Ziauddin Sardar, Jordi Serra and Scott Jordan, *Muslim Societies in Postnormal Times: Trends, Emerging Issues and Scenarios* (International Institute of Islamic Thought, London, 2019).

See also: H. A. R. Gibb & C. F. Beckingham, translaters,. *The Travels of Ibn Battuta,* (Hakluyt Society, London, 1994), Hasan Moinuddin, *The Charter of The Islamic Conference and Legal Framework of Economic Cooperation Amongst Its Membership States* (Clarendon Press, Oxford, 1987); Abdullah al Ahsan, *OIC: The Organisation of the Islamic Conference* (International Institute of Islamic Thought, Herndon, VA, 1988); and Bernardo Kastrup, *The Idea of the World* (Iff Books, Winchester, 2019).

The Edict of Race by Yuri Prasad

The quotes are from the following sources: Leo Africanus and Dutch trader, Charlie Kimber, 'Aid, governance and exploitation', *International Socialism*, issue 107 2005, p64; David Hume cited by Peter Fryer, *Staying Power* (Pluto, London, 1984, p152); Angela Saini, *Superior: the Return of Race Science* (4th Estate, London, 2019, 60-61); W E B Du Bois, *Black*

Reconstruction in America 1860-1880 (Free Press, New York, 1965, p700-701); Satnum Verdee, Racism, *Class and Racialized Outsider* (Red Globe Press, London, 2014, p36); Arun Kundnani, *The Muslims Are Coming* (Verso, London, 2014, p10-11); Samuel Huntington, Samuel, *Who Are We? The Challenges to America's Identity* (Simon and Schuster, New York, 2004, p62); and Francis Wade, 'Paul Gilroy, Whiteness just Ain't Worth What it Used to Be', *The Nation* (28 October, 2020), available at: thenation.com/article/culture/paul-gilroy-interview/

Other works motioned: Theodore Allan, *Invention of the Whit Race* (Verso, London, 2012, two volumes); and Shashi Tharoor, 'East India Company: the original corporate raiders', *New Statesman* (19 September 2019).
See also: Robin Blackburn, *The Making of New World Slavery* (Verso, London, 1997); Sumit Sarkar, *Modern India 1885-1947* (Macmillan, London, 1983); Esme Choonara, 'Racism: individual, institutional and structural', *International Socialism*, issue 168 2021; Hasan Mahamdallie, 'Islamophobia: the othering of Europe's Muslims', *International Socialism*, issue 146 2015; and Utsa Patnaik and Prabhat Patnaik, 'Imperial Britain's draining of India's Wealth', *Monthly Review*, volume 72, issue 9 2021.

For the Rudyard Kipling poem in full see kiplingsociety.co.uk/poems_burden.htm; and for a distinctly defensive take on Macron's outburst, see politico.eu/article/macron-g20-angry-reaction-to-emmanuel-macrons-remark-that-africa-has-a-civilizational-problem/

Culture Wars by Samia Rahman

Baroness Warsi's comments on the Batley Grammar School blasphemy controversy were expressed on the BBC Radio 4 Today programme on 26 March 2021 and her twitter feed @SayeedaWarsi. The outcome of the inquiry into the incident is reported at https://inews.co.uk/news/batley-grammar-teacher-suspensions-lifted-review-finds-prophet-mohamed-lesson-not-intended-offend-1021377

To read more about the Prussian government led by Otto Van Bismarck and its conflict with the Catholic church see: Ronald J Ross, *The Failure of*

Bismarck's Kutltukampf, (Catholic University of Press America, 2000). On Culture Wars see: James Davison Hunter, *Culture Wars: The Struggle to Define America* (Basic Books, New York, 1992) and Joseph Darda, *How White Men Won the Culture Wars* (University of California Press, 2021) and Emma Dabiri, *What White People Can Do Next* (Penguin, 2021), and the King's College London report 'Culture Wars in the UK: how the public understand the debate', May 2021: https://www.kcl.ac.uk/policy-institute/assets/culture-wars-in-the-uk-how-the-public-understand-the-debate.pdf

David Graeber, *Debt: The First 5000 Years* (Melville House Publishing, 2014) and *Bullshit Jobs* (Penguin, 2019) provide background to the fragmentation of the world. Rahul Rao's blog post, 'The Disorder of Things', is good on the statues: https://thedisorderofthings.com/2016/04/02/on-statues/ See his 'Newsnight' interview on 21 August 2017 https://www.bbc.co.uk/news/av/world-41005758 as well Gary Younge's argument for why all statues should come down published in the *Guardian*: https://www.theguardian.com/artanddesign/2021/jun/01gary-younge-why-every-single-statue-should-come-down-rhodes-colston

To read more about Islamo-leftism visit https://www.theguardian.com/commentisfree/2021/mar/12/academics-french-republic-macron-islamo-leftism and https://www.media-diversity.org/islamo-leftism-an-analysis-of-the-strawman-rhetoric-feeding-frances-culture-wars/ Adam Curtis documentary, 'Can't Get You Out of My Head' (2021) is available on BBC iPlayer.

An Economy Fit for Purpose by Colin Tudge

The John Maynard Keynes quotation is from Archie Mackenzie, *Faith in Diplomacy* (Caux Books, 2002, p 200; Joan Robinson quotes is taken from Linda Yueh's *The Great Economists* (Penguin Books, 2019), Pope Gregory I quote can be found in A.S. Attack, *John Clare: Voice of Freedom* (Shepheard-Walwyn, 2010), p. 84; and Kate Raworth comments are her *Doughnut Economics* (Random House, Business Books, 2017).

See also: Adam Smith, *The Wealth of Nations* and *The Theory of Moral Sentiments* (Penguin Classics, 2000 and 2010); and Aneurin Bevan, *In Place of Fear* (MacGibbon and Kee, London, 1952).

Manifestos of the End by Christopher B Jones

The manifestos discussed in this article include: Paul Kingsnorth and Dougald Hine *Uncivilization: The Dark Mountain Manifesto*, The Dark Mountain Project, 2019, available at: dark-mountian.net; Chellis Glendinning, Glendinning, C. (1990). 'Notes towards a Neo-Luddite manifesto', The Anarchist Library, 1990: http://www.jesusradicals. com/wp-content/uploads/luddite-manifesto.pdf; Dona Haraway, 'A Cyborg Manifesto: Science, Technology, and Socialist-Feminism in the Late 20th Century', J Weiss et al, editors, *The International Handbook of Virtual Learning Environments*, Springer, Dordrecht, 2006; Simon Young, *Designer Evolution: A Transhumanist Manifesto*, Prometheus Books, 2006; Gregory Little, 'A Manifesto for Avatars' *Intertext* 3 (2) 1999; Robert Pepperell, 'The Posthuman Manifesto', *Kritikos,* Vol.2 Feb. 2005: http:// intertheory.org/pepperell.htm; and Ted Kaczynski, *The Unabomber Manifesto: Industrial Society and Its Futures*, originally published in *The Washington* Post, 19 September 1995, it has several independently published editions.

See also: Paul Kingsnorth and Dougald Hine, editorial, 'It's the end of the world as we know it (and we feel fine)', *Dark Mountain*. Issue 1, Summer 2010, 1-4; Bill Joy, 'Why The Future Doesn't Need Us', *Wired* April 2000: https://www.wired.com/2000/04/joy-2/; Ray Kurzweil, *The Singularity Is Near: When Humans Transcend Biology*, Viking, New York, 2005; d Meadow et al, *Limits to Growth. The 30-year Update*, Chelsea Green Publishing, New York, 2004; Timothy Morton, *Hyperobjects: Philosophy and Ecology after the End of the World*, University of Minnesota Press, 2013; Naomi Oreskes and Erik Conway, *The Collapse of Western Civilization*, Columbia University Press, 2014; David Wallace-Wells, *The Uninhabitable Earth*, Penguin, London, 2019; and Roberto Vacca, *The Coming Dark Age*, Doubleday, New York, 1973.

Postnormal Adventures by Jerry Ravetz

My classic study, *Scientific Knowledge and its Social Problems*, was published by Oxford University Press (1971), the quotation is from p9. The seminal paper on postnormal science is Jerry Ravetz and Silvio Funtowicz, 'Science for the Post-Normal Age', *Futures*, 25/7 735-755 1993. On contradictions, see Jerry Ravetz, 'Postnormal Science and the maturing of the structural contradictions of modern European science', *Futures* 43, 142–148 201. And on non-violent science, see Jerry Ravetz, 'Towards a non-violent discourse in science' in: B. Klein Goldewijk and G. Frerks, editors, *New Challenges to Human Security: Empowering Alternative Discourses* (Academic Publishers, Wageningen, 2006)

The postnormal times papers, including Ziauddin Sardar's seminal 'Welcome to Postnormal Times' (*Futures* 42 435-444 2010), have been collected in *The Postnormal Times Reader* (IIIT, London, 2017).

On the geographical shift in science, see M Yuasa, 'Center of Scientific Activity: its Shifts from the 16th to the 20th century', *Japanese Journal of the History of Science*, 1, 57-75 1962.

On 'nature trick', see S MacIntyre, 'Keith's Science Trick, Mike's Nature Trick and Phil's Combo', https://climateaudit.org/2011/03/29/keiths-science-trick-mikes-nature-trick-and-phils-combo/ for analysis, and Skeptical Scientist (n.d.) 'Clearing up misconceptions regarding "hide the decline"'. https://skepticalscience.com/Mikes-Nature-trick-hide-the-decline-advanced.htmm for defence.

On 'confounding variables' and 'feedback loop', see: Steve Rayner and Daniel Sarewitz, 'Policy Making in the Post Truth World', *Breakthrough Journal*, 13, pp. 15-44 2021.

On corrupted statistical techniques, see: D Bishop, 'Rein in the four horsemen of irreproducibility', *Nature* 568 p.435 (2019) and M Baker, 'Statisticians issue warning over misuse of P values', *Nature* 531 p. 151 (2016). And on original Covid-19 modelling in UK, see the interview with Neil Ferguson, 'No. 10's infection guru recruits game developers to build coronavirus pandemic model', *The Sunday Times* 3 June 2020.

See also: See also: Peter Gluckman, 'Policy: The art of science advice to government' *Nature* 507,163–165, 2014; M B Crawford, 'How science has been corrupted' at: https://unherd.com/2021/05/how-science-has-been-corrupted/? =thepostindexfrmemail

The Mercator clock can be found at: https://www.mcc-berlin.net/en/research/co2-budget.html.

Emerging Nigeria by Ahmad Adedimeji Amobi

Chinua Achebe's *Things Fall Apart* and *No Longer At Ease* are available as Penguin classics (2006 & 2010); Wole Soyinka's *The Chronicles form the Land of the Happiest People on Earth* has just been published by Bloomsbury; and Pius Adesanmi, *Naija No Dey Carry Last: Thoughts on a Nation in Progress* is published by CreateSpace Independent Publishing Platform (2015).

On Nigerian music, see: https://amp.www.complex.com/music/how-lagos-nigeria-became-an-international-music-hotspot; and OPEC's *A special date for Nigeria* (2006) can be downloaded at: https://www.opec.org/opec_web/en/press_room/848.htm

'Greater Serbia' 2.0 by Jasmin Mujanovic

Djordje Stefanović quote is from his article, 'Seeing the Albanians through Serbian eyes: The inventors of the tradition of intolerance and their critics, 1804-1939, *European History Quarterly* 35(3): 465-492 2005, pp. 469-70. For the so-called land swap proposal see: https://www.euronews.com/2021/04/19/balkans-rocked-as-leaked-memo-explores-redrawing-bosnia-s-borders-along-ethnic-lines; for the recent 'non-paper' scandal, see: https://www.euronews.com/2021/04/19/balkans-rocked-as-leaked-memo-explores-redrawing-bosnia-s-borders-along-ethnic-lines. For the link of Serbian Orthodox Church's link to the nationalist establishment, see: https://balkaninsight.com/2021/06/03/

serbias-vucic-wants-to-control-the-montenegrin-govt-it-may-
backfire/?utm_source=twitter&utm_medium=social-share&utm_
campaign=organic

President of the Rich by James Brooks

Macron's Paris consensus interview is available as a transcript and edited
video on the website of Le Grand Continent at https://bit.ly/3vk3srX. A
translation in English is available at https://bit.ly/3cBbRkh. A video of
Macron's February 2017 London rally is available at https://bit.
ly/3gfbgqA. The analysis of Macron's bourgeois bloc is from 'The Last
Neoliberal: Macron and the Origins of France's Political Crisis', Bruno
Amable, Stefano Palombarini, translated by David Broder (Verso, 2021)
The joint statement from unions on the Paris-Saclay merger is available as
a PDF at https://bit.ly/3iG9FM7.

Amnesty International quotes from press release 'France: Unjust counter-
terror measures used to "persecute not prosecute"' 22 November 2018,
https://bit.ly/2URpeXk; 'Man with the gun' quote from David Graeber
'The Utopia of Rules: On Technology, Stupidity, and the Secret Joys of
Bureaucracy' (Melville House, 2015); Macron's G20 quote from 'En
lâchant le gros mot de 'civilisationnel', M. Macron a ravivé une vieille
blessure', Abdourahman Waberi, Le Monde, 14 July 2017 - https://bit.
ly/2TirKoV (paywalled). French Ministry for Colonial Affairs quote and
others from 'Philanthropic Imperialism', Stephen Smith, London Review of
Books, 22 April 2021, https://bit.ly/3iCdp1m (paywalled)
This essay was written in loving memory of Robert Painter Brooks
(1946–2021).

The World Tree by Naomi Foyle

The Violence Paradox (BBC 4, 2021) is still available on BBC iPlayer. Jurgen
Habermas, William Stanley Jevons, Philip Roscoe and Wendy Brown are
all quoted by Joan Walton in 'The Entanglement of Scientism,
Neoliberalism and Materialism' published in Paradigm Explorer 135 (The
Science and Medical Network, 2021). In The Science of Storytelling

(London: Harper Collins 2019) Will Storr applies to literature the
reductionist science propounded by Richard Dawkins, whose terminology
for the brain is cited and criticised by Mary Midgley in *Science and Poetry*
(London: Routledge, 2006), and whose atheist manifesto *The God Delusion*
(London: Black Swan, 2006) is challenged by Rupert Sheldrake in *The
Science Delusion* (London: Hodder & Stoughton, 2012). The Scientific and
Medical Network can be found (and joined) at www.scientificandmedical.
net. SMN members can access past webinars, including 'Miracles in an
Age of Disbelief: Theory and Practice' given by Prof Michael Gosse on
May 12th 2021 and 'Polyvagal Theory and the Soul's Journey' by Dr
William Bloom, given on Weds Jun 9th 2021, unfortunately just past the
deadline for this essay. The full and layman's reports of The Galileo
Commission can be freely downloaded at www.galileocommission.org.
Ziauddin Sardar's remarks on the tree metaphor in classical Islam occur at
the start of Chapter 8 of *How Do You Know* (London: Pluto Press, 2006).
'The Tree Symbol in Islam' by Noble Ross Reat was published by *Studies
in Comparative Religion*, Vol. 9, No. 3. (Summer, 1975); the full text
complete with theological references can be found at: www.
studiesincomparativereligion.com/Public/articles/The_Tree_Symbol_
in_Islam-by_Noble_Ross_Reat.aspx.

Apart from Reat's citations of Islamic texts, Surah 22 is quoted from *The
Meaning of the Glorious Qur'an*: (Birmingham, Islamic Dawah Centre
International, 2004), translated by Marmaduke Pickthall and Surah 53 is
quoted from *The Message of the Qur'an* (London: The Book Foundation,
2003/2012) translated and explained by Muhammad Asad. The Mahmoud
Darwish poem 'If only the young were trees', was published in *A River Dies
of Thirst (Diaries)* (London: Saqi Books, 2009), translated by Catherine
Cobham. Further information on ancient olive trees in Palestine and the
destruction of the 'directions tree' on the land of the Djab Wurrung can
be found, respectively, at www.middleeasteye.net/discover/tree-trust-
meet-man-guarding-palestines-oldest-olive-tree and www.bbc.co.uk/
news/world-australia-54700074.

The discussion of the myth of the Huluppu-tree is drawn from *Inanna:
Queen of Heaven and Earth: Her Stories and Hymns from Sumer* (NYC: Harper

and Row, 1983), translated by Diane Wolkstein, with commentaries by Diane Wolkstein and Samuel Noah Kramer. *The Poetic Edda* (New York: The American-Scandinavian Foundation, 1923), translated by Henry Adams Bellows, can be read online at the non-profit library Internet Archive: www.archive.org. The benefits of cross-laminated timber are explored in 'Wood for Good', an episode of the BBC podcast *39 Ways to Save the Planet*, available on BBC Sounds. Roger Leakey is quoted from his article 'Trees are More than the Lungs of the World', published at internationaltreefoundation.org/trees-more-than-lungs-world/. The growth of tree-hugging is explored at www.wellandgood.com/benefits-of-tree-hugging/. Zeshan Akhter's article 'Wild in the Forest' can be found in *Critical Muslim 19: Nature* (London: Hurst, 2016). The 'doughnut' graphic of doughnut economics can be viewed at doughnuteconomics.org/about-doughnut-economics. 'Are Trees Sentient Beings? Certainly, Says German Forester' (Nov 16, 2016), an interview by Richard Schiffman with Peter Wohlleben, was published in *YaleEnvironment360* by the Yale School of the Environment at e360.yale.edu/features/are_trees_sentient_peter_wohlleben. Finally, Wikipedia was, as ever, a Tree of Knowledge; pages consulted include The Tree of Life, The World Tree, Norse Mythology, Seiðr [Norse Magic], Yggdrasil, and the Crowns of Silla, while further examples of World Trees in the essay came from *An Illustrated Encyclopaedia of Traditional Symbols* (London: Thames and Hudson, 1979) by J.C. Cooper and 'The World Tree and its Function in Myth' by the gnostic writer Aethyrius, published at www.transcendenceworks.com/blog/world-tree/.

The Order of Covid by Kanchana Mahadevan

Pandita Ramabai quote is from 'About the Government Provisions during the plague epidemic' in *Pandita Ramabai: Life and Landmark Writings*, edited by Meera Kosambi (Routledge, London, 2016); *A Life Misspent* by Suryakant Tripathi Nirala is published by HarperCollins India (Delhi, 2018); and Rajinder Singh Bedi's 1938 short story 'Quarantine' has been republished in *Indian Literature* September-October 2020.

On Maurice Merleau Ponty notion of touch see the chapter 'The Intertwining-The Chiasm' in his *The Visible and the Invisible* (Northwestern University Press, Evanston, 1964). On 'Indian Cholera' by Henrik Wergeland, see Joachim Schiedermair, 'The Masses and the Elite: The Conception of Social Equality in 1840s Scandinavian Literature' 2012 *Romantik,* 1(1) 125-138 (2012). Albert Camus' *The Plague* is available as Penguin Modern Classic (2002). *Wild: A Journey from Lost to Found* by Cheryl Strayed is published by Atlantic Books (New York, 2015)

See also: Nathan Nunn and Nancy Qian, 'The Columbian Exchange: A History of Disease, Food, and Ideas' *Journal of Economic Perspectives* 24 (2): 163-188 2010.

The List: Ten World (Dis)Orderers by Jordi Serra

Shoshana Zuboff's *The Age of Surveillance Capitalism* is published by Profile Books (London 2019). The interview with Stephen Hawking is available at: https://www.bbc.com/news/technology-30290540. The case of the Nazi robot is here: https://www.cbsnews.com/news/microsoft-shuts-down-ai-chatbot-after-it-turned-into-racist-nazi/. Information on China's debt ownership can be found on Investopedia: https://www.investopedia.com/articles/investing/080615/china-owns-us-debt-how-much.asp. The quote on food scarcity from the US Global Change Research Program's Fourth National Climate Assessment can be found at: https://yaleclimateconnections.org/2019/09/a-brief-guide-to-the-impacts-of-climate-change-on-food-production. The Freedom House report can be accessed here: https://freedomhouse.org/report/freedom-world/2021/democracy-under-siege. The news on the asteroid 16 Psyche can be found here: https://observer.com/2020/10/nasa-discover-asteroid-pysche-metal-10-quadrillion/. For colourful honey, see: https://www.nationalgeographic.com/animals/article/121011-blue-honey-honeybees-animals-science

CONTRIBUTORS

Halimah Adisa is a Nigerian poet and writer ● **Ahmad Adedimeji Amobi**, a student of English at the University of Ilorin, Nigeria, was longlisted for the maiden Punocracy Prize for Satire ● **Iason Athanasiadis**, a multimedia journalist, is the current holder of a Balkan Investigative Reporting Network fellowship for Journalistic Excellence ● **Salah Badis** is a writer and translator from Algeria ● **James Brooks** is a science journalist and writer ● **Andrew Brown**, former leader writer at the *Guardian*, is a freelance journalist ● **Abdelwahab El-Affendi** is Provost and Acting President of Doha Institute for Graduate Studies, Doha Qatar ● **Naomi Foyle** is a well-known science fiction writer ● **Anwar Ibrahim**, Malaysian politician, is President of Peoples Justice Party and Leader of Opposition ● **Christopher B Jones** is Senior Fellow of the Centre for Postnormal Policy and Futures Studies ● **Scott Jordan** is Executive Assistant Director of the Centre for Postnormal Policy and Futures Studies ● **Kanchana Mahadevan**, Professor at the Department of Philosophy, University of Mumbai, is the author of *Between Femininity and Feminism: Colonial and Postcolonial Perspectives on Care* ● **Iftikhar H Malik** is Professor of History at Bath Spa University, England ● **Peter Mandaville** is Professor of Government and Politics in the School of Policy and Government at George Mason University, Virginia, USA ● **Jasmin Mujanovic**, a political scientist, is the author of *Hunger & Fury: The Crisis of Democracy in the Balkans* ● **Sari Omer** is a Sudanese photojournalist ● **Yuri Prasad** is the author of *A Rebel's Guide to Martin Luther King* and other books ● **Jerry Ravetz** is a world renowned philosopher of science ● **Jordi Serra** is Deputy Director of the Centre for Postnormal Policy and Futures Studies ● **Shanon Shah** is the Director of Faith for the Climate, an England-based charity that brings together different faith groups working on climate justice ● **Colin Tudge**, a co-founder of the Real Farming Trust and the College for Real Farming and Food Culture, is the author of *The Great Re-Think*.